THE
MOUTH
THAT
ROARED

MY SIX OUTSPOKEN
DECADES IN BASEBALL

Dallas Green
and Alan Maimon

TRIUMPH
BOOKS

Library of Congress Cataloging-in-Publication Data

Green, Dallas, 1934–
  The mouth that roared : my six outspoken decades in baseball / Dallas Green and Alan Maimon.
    p. cm.
  ISBN 978-1-60078-805-5
1. Green, Dallas, 1934– 2. Baseball players—United States—Biography. 3. Baseball managers—United States—Biography. I. Maimon, Alan. II. Title.
  GV865.G668A3 2013
  796.357092—dc23
  [B]

                                                              2012045132

This book is available in quantity at special discounts for your group or organization. For further information, contact:
    Triumph Books LLC
    814 North Franklin
    Chicago, Illinois 60610
    (312) 337-0747
    www.triumphbooks.com

Printed in U.S.A.
ISBN: 978-1-60078-805-5
Design by Patricia Frey
Page production by Amy Carter
Photos courtesy of the author unless otherwise indicated

For my family and my baseball family

FOREWORD

I CAN STILL HEAR his thundering voice, all these years later. The sonic booms still explode inside my head. The words still come roaring at me, as loudly, as emphatically, as unforgettably as they did on the night that Dallas Green and I came to be linked in Philadelphia baseball lore forever.

Linked by three words I'll never live down—and neither will he: "(Bleep) you, Jayson."

The date was August 12, 1981. I was a young Phillies beat writer for the *Philadelphia Inquirer*. Dallas was already a living legend, the only man in the history of his franchise to manage the Phillies to a World Series championship. I'd been covering him for one year, 11 months, and 12 days. Not one of those days was what you'd call boring. Not one. And that was all the manager's doing. All of it.

I'd come to learn, in those 23½ months, that you never knew what Dallas might say or do—especially say—on any given night at the ballpark. He was the smartest man in the room. He was also the loudest voice in the room. Any room. He was larger than life. He was louder than life. And when he had a message to deliver—which was pretty much every minute of every day—he had a way of getting his point across.

And when those messages came spilling out of him, you didn't just need a pen, a pad, and a tape recorder to take them all in. You needed a Richter scale.

But in all the time I'd covered Dallas Green, I don't ever remember finding him in such a constantly agitated state as I did in the first couple of weeks of August 1981. The baseball strike had just ended. The season was getting ready to rev up again. And no one was more aggravated than the manager of the defending champs that baseball had decided to split its season in two: if you were in first place when the strike hit in June, as the Phillies were, you had already clinched your playoff spot. So, there were Dallas and his team, with two months and 52 games to play, but, essentially, nothing to play for.

Let's just say his unhappiness, over what he so affectionately called that "split (bleeping) season," came up once or twice. Or 12 times. Or 50. You could feel something building inside him. And it wasn't good. But then, on that fateful night of August 12, Mount Dallas-uvius erupted.

The season had resumed two days earlier. The manager was hopeful his pitchers would keep his team focused and competitive while the position players eased back into playing shape. But three games later, his pitching staff had coughed up 23 runs. And as the press corps tip-toed into his office following a gruesome 11–3 whomping by the St. Louis Cardinals, the tension hung over the room like a smog bank.

That's when a young, dopey writer from the *Inquirer* decided to try to lower the stress thermometer with an ill-fated stab at a light-hearted question.

"Does this mean the pitchers aren't ahead of the hitters anymore?" I asked, hoping the manager would at least get a mild chuckle out of even a meager attempt at humor.

Four seconds later, it was clear he wasn't in the mood to attend my little Comedy Cabaret.

"(Bleep) you, Jayson," he snapped.

There wasn't another question asked for three minutes. Uh, no need for that—because it turned out Dallas Green had a few thoughts he needed to share. At a decibel level normally reserved for space shuttle launches. Livened up by the use of, by my count, 42 colorful words you'll never hear on, say, *Sesame Street*.

No need to recap them all. If you've heard cursing before, you can imagine what much of it sounded like. But a couple of passages in this stirring monologue were so powerful, I'd be remiss not to share them with you.

On the theories (which, to be honest, were probably initiated by him) that his troops had no particular motivation to play these games to win, the manager roared:

> *And no, we're not trying to lose the (bleeping) game. I'll answer that (bleep-bleeper) before you (bleeping) guys start on it. I'm (bleeping) sick and tired of some of the (bleeping) comments I see in this (bleeping) press. You (bleep-bleepers) think we're in this (bleeping) game for 25 (bleeping) years [and] don't have a nickel's worth of (bleeping) pride? The (bleep) we don't have it.*

Woo. Good one. And then there was this, one of the greatest sentences ever uttered by any manager in the history of postgame oration:

> *I want (bleeping) stopped all the (bleeping) (bull-bleep) about how (bleeping) (horse-bleep) this (bleeping) split (bleeping) season*

is. I can't do a (bleeping) thing about that, either. You (bleep-bleepers) write what the (bleep) you want to write. But I'm sick and (bleeping) tired of reading about how the (bleeping) ballplayers are going to quit on you. The (bleeping) ballplayers won't quit on you unless you (bleeping) guys keep hammering it in our (bleeping) heads all the time.

Wow. Awesome. But as this soliloquy came pouring out of him, I began to notice something: while I may have been the lucky guy to kick off these festivities, this clearly wasn't aimed at me. Not in the big picture, anyway. No, this one was for his players.

Outside the door to his office, they sat at their lockers, hanging on every word. And trust me. They could hear him. At the volume level this speech was delivered, they could have heard him from the 700 level, way out in the center-field upper deck. But just to make sure they were paying attention, Dallas actually took a stroll out of his office in mid-rant, stomped into the clubhouse, looked around, and stomped back to his desk to finish his pithy remarks.

And then, once he'd vented, it was over. Period.

"Aw, it ain't your fault, either," he said, finally, decibels sinking with every word. "(Bleep) it. All right, let's get down to some serious talking. What the (bleep) we got?"

And that was that. It was vintage Dallas. When his temper flared, everyone in his area code knew it. But when it was over, when he'd said what he had to say, he was a man with the remarkable ability to flip the off switch and move on. No fuss. No muss. No grudges. Not just that day. Every day. I was off his list of least-favorite media guys within minutes. We've been friends ever since. For three decades. A few weeks later, he even presented me with a T-shirt (actually, he threw it across the room at me). On it were the words: "(BLEEP) YOU, JAYSON." I still have that shirt. (Don't tell my wife.)

But I don't need a faded T-shirt to remind me of that momentous occasion—Bleep You, Jayson Night. When I think back on it, I recall much more than those three magic words or the many lively bleep-words that followed. I think more about the man who spoke those words, and the powerful impact he had on me and everyone who crossed his path.

It would be so easy to remember Dallas Green for his vocal cords. But if you've been measuring this man with a volume button all these years, you've been making a big mistake. There's so much more to this fellow than just a big voice. And there always has been.

Would Phillies history have been the same without him? Without the strong-willed leader who drove the 1980 Phillies all the way to the parade floats? Ask yourself that. I think you know the answer.

Would Cubs history have been the same without him? Without the tough, stubborn, relentless team president who understood that, unless the Cubs had the courage to erect light towers, the magic of Wrigley Field could never endure? I think you know that answer, too.

I've always believed that in this world, there are certain people who are built for certain moments. And that was Dallas Green. The perfect fit for his signature moments in time.

The battles he needed to fight weren't for the weak or the mild-mannered. They required a strong man with strong opinions, a towering presence, and a command of every room he entered. And that, too, was Dallas Green.

If he had to accuse a bunch of Phillies who had won three division titles in a row of quitting, of not looking in the mirror, of not caring whether their team won or lost, then that's what he had to do.

If he had to threaten to shut down Wrigley and move the Cubs to Schaumburg, Illinois, or even (shudder) to Comiskey Park, then that's what he had to do.

If he had to stand up to George Steinbrenner's second-guessing in the Bronx by referring to the Boss as "Manager George," then that's what he had to do—to salvage his pride, if not his job.

If he had to deliver a message to his superiors on the Mets by announcing it was time for Dwight Gooden "to go elsewhere" after the ace had failed his fourth drug test, then that's what he had to do.

These were stands that very few men I've ever met in baseball were capable of taking. But they were made to order for Dallas Green. Always shrewd enough to understand the meaning of the moment. Never afraid of the consequences of saying or doing what that moment required.

And the true measure of his life's work is that now, all these years later, so many of the people who felt his wrath back then are the first to tell you how much better off they are for having known him, for having their lives and careers shaped by his powerful presence.

And I'm one of them. On an August evening in 1981, I lit a fuse in Dallas Green that neither of us will ever forget. But three decades later, it's the man who has left a lasting impact on me, not the three magic words that came out of his mouth that one night in August.

—Jayson Stark

ANYONE WHO PLAYED, WORKED, or rooted for the Philadelphia Phillies during their first 95 years of existence knew heartache intimately well. As a 45-year-old man who played, worked, *and* rooted for the team at different points in my life, I guess I could count myself among the most afflicted.

As a teenager in Delaware, I pulled hard for the Phillies in the 1950 World Series against the New York Yankees. But the Whiz Kids got swept in four games.

I pitched for the 1964 Phillies team that seemed destined for an October rematch with the Yankees. But we let the National League pennant slip through our fingers in the final weeks of the season.

And I worked in the Phillies front office when the team won three consecutive division titles from 1976 to 1978. But we got eliminated each year in the National League Championship Series.

In between those near misses was a lot of futility. The Phillies carried a burden of never having won a World Series. And the weight was crushing.

That brings us to 1979, the year we all expected the weight to be lifted.

In my role as director of the minor leagues for the Phillies, I took satisfaction in seeing the emergence of players who came up through our system, guys like third baseman Mike Schmidt, shortstop Larry Bowa, left fielder Greg Luzinski, and catcher Bob Boone.

Paul Owens, our general manager, as well as my longtime friend and mentor, was the chief architect of the team. The Pope, as he was known, had supplemented our homegrown talent with smart trades and free agent signings. Ruly Carpenter, the team's principal owner, helped out by making funds available for us to lure Pete Rose away from the Cincinnati Reds before the 1979 season. Bill Giles, the team's vice president of business operations, sealed the deal by getting Taft Broadcasting to chip in a few bucks for the cause. Steve Carlton, a couple of years removed from a Cy Young Award, anchored a strong pitching staff.

The team had the look of a winner. But simply amassing more wins than losses wasn't the goal. Coming off three straight playoff disappointments, we looked at 1979 as World Series or bust.

The only bit of uncertainty going into the season involved the man who would be filling out the lineup card. Danny Ozark had managed the Phillies since 1973 and was a good baseball man. But Pope, chief scout Hugh Alexander, and I questioned whether he had the toughness to get a talented team to realize its full potential. Seated next to Danny in the dugout the past several seasons was Bobby Wine, a former teammate of mine and a man whom Pope liked a lot.

Our inner circle debated the question at length before ultimately deciding to give Danny another year to fulfill our high but realistic expectations of winning a championship.

The year that everything was supposed to fall into place turned out to be the year not a helluva lot went right. We lost some players to injuries, but even after the team got healthy, it played uninspired baseball. In late August, we were in fifth place in the National League East. All season long, Danny's rallying cry was, "Wait until we get our guys back, and then we'll be okay." Well, that wasn't the case.

The problem seemed evident. The players weren't responding to Danny anymore.

• • •

Our inner circle had a ritual. A few hours before every home game, we'd get together to have a drink or two and talk shop. On August 29, 1979, the dominant topic of the day was whether Danny should stay on as manager. Hughie was on a scouting trip to Kansas City, so that left Pope and I to hash out the situation.

The conversation continued during that night's game against the Reds. As the booze flowed and we watched the Phillies stumble to the end of a homestand in which we lost eight of nine games, the matter took on a new urgency. We tossed around names of guys we thought might help get us back on track. Bobby Wine, a skilled game strategist, was at the top of the list.

After the game, we remained in Pope's office. Other colleagues filed in and out of the room as we sought a resolution to our dilemma.

Amid all the comings and goings of team personnel, my name entered the mix around midnight.

There was precedent for a Phillies executive coming down to manage the team on an interim basis. Pope, in his first year as general manager, did it for the second half of the 1972 season. He had no intention of keeping the job beyond that point but viewed field managing as a good way to evaluate his talent up close.

I was content with my front office job. It was generally accepted that I was in line to take over as general manager when Pope decided to retire.

I hemmed and hawed and indicated that I had no interest in taking over for Danny. Nor did I believe I was qualified. I had managed two seasons in the low minor leagues in the late 1960s, but that was the extent of my experience.

Pope ignored my protests. At about 1:00 in the morning Central time, he phoned Hughie's hotel room in Kansas City to get his input on the idea.

"Hughie, do you think Dallas can manage this team?" he asked.

The conversation lasted all of 30 seconds. After Pope hung up the phone, he repeated what Hughie just told him: "He says you can absolutely manage this team. You worked with a lot of our players in the minors. You know how to handle them. And the rest of the guys know you well enough to know they'll have no choice but to play hard for you."

Now Pope was certain I was the right man for the job. When the meeting broke up at about 3:00 AM, I told Pope I'd go home, talk it over with my wife, Sylvia, and get back to him in a few hours.

A long night got a little longer. Sylvia, too, was convinced I should manage the team. Hesitant still, I found myself enumerating the reasons why taking the job on an interim basis might not be such a bad idea.

"It'll only be for a month," I told her. "And it'll give us a chance to see who wants to play this game the right way and stay in Philadelphia."

Sylvia, never one to hold back an opinion, agreed that arrangement made sense. With her blessing, I picked up the phone a few minutes before 5:00 AM.

"Pope, I'm your man," I told my boss. "I'll do it, and I wanna do it, and I think I can do it as well as anybody on an interim basis."

I was scheduled to fly to Oklahoma City the following day to visit our Triple-A club. Pope told me to go ahead and make the trip. That would give him time to talk to Ruly and make the switch official. The next day I boarded a plane from Philadelphia to Oklahoma City. I'm not sure I ever left the airport in Oklahoma City before catching a flight to Atlanta, where the Phillies were opening a three-game weekend series against the Braves.

And that's where the next phase of my baseball career began. After a decade in the Phillies front office, I was returning to a major league dugout for the first time since my playing career ended in 1967.

For the veteran players who knew my temperament and style, this did not come as welcome news.

• • •

From a young age, I wanted to be the best. In school, I wanted to earn all As. On the field or court, I wanted to be the star player. In my neighborhood, I wanted to cut the grass better than the kid down the street.

If I accepted a job or task, I committed myself to doing it with pride, even if at first I was reluctant to do it at all. After I retired as a player and Pope asked me to manage Low-A ball in Huron, South Dakota, I told him no thanks. Having just finished a 13-year professional playing career, I didn't envision packing my bags again and heading for South Dakota. I thought I was ready to go into the front office right away. But Pope insisted, so I went to Huron and tried to be the best goddamn manager in the Pioneer League.

In 1979, I found myself in a similar situation. I didn't seek to become the Phillies manager, but once Pope talked me into it, I resolved to put every ounce of my being into seeing that the team played up to its ability.

The problem with Danny Ozark was that he let his players do whatever they wanted. That laissez-faire style of managing had worked, to a point. He took a young team and led it to three straight division titles, a pretty noteworthy accomplishment, after all. But it rankled us how the 1978 and 1979 Phillies had lost focus and discipline. Pope believed I could restore those qualities to the team.

Danny wanted to be friends with his players. I didn't care if they liked me or not. My opening speech to the team in Atlanta made that clear.

"Guys, we all know what Danny has done for us in the past, but I wouldn't be standing here if you were playing the game the way you're supposed to be playing it," I said. "Danny got fired because of you. I'm not here to do anything other than what you say you want to do, which is to win a championship. I've been in Philadelphia for much of my baseball career, and I want nothing more than for the Phillies to be successful. I want *you* to be successful. But I'm not going to sit back and wait for you to wake up. I'm going to push you, and I'm going to needle you, and I'm going to bang you when I have to. We're going to pay close attention this month to see who wants to continue playing in Philadelphia next year."

That was a cleaned-up version of my opening salvo. My straight talk took some players aback. In their eyes, I compared unfavorably to Danny. "There were a lot of tears in the clubhouse," Larry Bowa told reporters on the day of Ozark's firing. "He was a players' manager who always stuck up for you."

Bowa felt the team had lost a buddy, one who averaged 97 wins from 1976 to 1978, and gained a bully, one with no experience managing in the majors.

• • •

Whereas Danny never criticized his players in the press, I had no intention of holding back in that regard. I refused to lie to reporters. If a player made a mistake, I didn't believe it was my obligation to protect him. At the same time, if a player did something well, I was the first to pat him on the back. I remained standing almost the entire game, shouting words of encouragement whenever they were necessary. I hoped the players would feed off my energy.

In my first weeks on the job, I sent a lot of messages through the newspapers, more out of necessity than design. Like Danny, who didn't have a real knack for words, a lot of players on the '79 team avoided journalists at all costs. They were notorious for running into the shower or the trainer's room when the sportswriters came looking for quotes. When the writers couldn't track down a certain player, they came looking for me. I told the team, "If you don't want to hear me run my mouth in the press, stand up like men and do some talking yourselves."

Mike Schmidt, who played his entire 18-year career with the Phillies, never fully warmed up to Philadelphia writers or fans. In his final season in the big leagues in 1989, he expressed his feelings toward these groups with the type of quote he had withheld much of his career: "It just seems like if you're a writer there, or a fan there, you have to look for the negative. Maybe it's in the air or how they're raised. Maybe they have too many hoagies or too much cream cheese or too much W.C. Fields."

Of course, Schmitty made that statement to the *Los Angeles Times*, and not one of the Philadelphia papers.

I had a different take. The writers covering the team in the late 1970s and early 1980s were tough and well-respected pros. They knew the game of baseball. And I saw no reason to hide from them.

• • •

No doubt the final month of the 1979 season felt like shock treatment to Bowa, Schmidt, and the rest of Danny's advocates.

I immediately enacted some unpopular rules. Card playing was restricted and kids were banished from the clubhouse. I could hear the bitching and moaning about arbitrary edicts and the new manager trying to flex his muscles of authority. In their opinion, I needed to lighten up. In my opinion, they were a bunch of underachievers who needed a kick in their collective ass. By minimizing potential distractions at the ballpark, I hoped they'd focus more on the game.

Change was hard. And I represented change. Being a Philadelphia Phillie was no longer going to be a cushy job. I demanded effort, concentration, and accountability.

The first time my mouth roared as Phillies manager came during a September 20 game against the Pittsburgh Pirates at Veterans Stadium. In the sixth inning, Keith Moreland hit a drive to left field that umpire Eric Gregg ruled a three-run home run. As Keith rounded the bases for the first time in his major league career, Pirates manager Chuck Tanner protested that the ball had curved foul. Chuck could complain all he wanted, but back in those days, the call on the field stood. Or at least that was how it was supposed to work. Instead, Gregg sought a second opinion from home-plate umpire Doug Harvey. When Harvey reversed the call, I barreled out onto the field. After hurling every curse word in the book at Harvey, I went back to the dugout and hurled baseballs out on the field. Not surprisingly, I got ejected.

This was the first time my team saw my truly volatile side. When I was a major league pitcher, I didn't give an inch to opposing batters. Now that I was managing, I wasn't going to give an inch to umpires or anyone else who crossed me. And that included my own players.

I could scream and yell with the best of them, but the team didn't see too much of that side of me at first. The jabs I took came mostly in the form of matter-of-fact statements about what I perceived as the team's lack of effort or its failure to play the game the right way.

I guess I got their attention. We showed signs of life in those final weeks, going 19–11 in September to finish the '79 season with a winning record. We ended up in fourth place, 14 games behind the Pirates, who went on to win the World Series.

Our strong September pleased me. Our unhealthy clubhouse dynamics did not. Some of the veterans had formed cliques and shut themselves off from the rest of the team. Danny had no problem with the cliques. But I've always been of the opinion that it takes 25 guys united in purpose to go out and win games. A team splintered into groups isn't united.

• • •

The final month of the '79 season gave me a good look at some younger players on the team, including Moreland, Lonnie Smith, Dickie Noles, and Kevin Saucier. I felt these guys weren't far off from contributing at the big league level. If I stayed on as manager, they would get more chances to prove themselves. I believed in awarding playing time based on performance, not years of service.

During the final series of the '79 season, Pope and I discussed whether to remove the interim tag from my job title. I was still the director of our minor league system, a job I loved, so I wouldn't have been too bent out of shape if the Phillies had decided to bring in someone else to manage. There were reports that Whitey Herzog, who had recently been fired as manager of the Kansas City Royals, would take the Phillies job if it was offered. Other articles suggested Pete Rose might become player-manager. And Bobby Wine's name still remained in play.

I didn't consider myself the manager of the future. But Pope and I realized 1980 *was* the future as far as the Phillies were concerned. The core of the team was getting older. By the start of the '80 season, only two everyday players, Luzinski and Manny Trillo, would be under 30. The window on winning a championship was closing. And if it didn't happen in '80, Pope was going to have to make significant changes.

A new manager would need time to get acclimated. During my brief stint in the dugout, the players had gotten a taste of what I was all about. More importantly, they knew I was a "company man" who had the strong backing of Pope and Ruly Carpenter.

A few weeks after the '79 season ended, Pope announced I'd be returning for a full season in 1980. I told reporters that my first order of business was to set up an off-season exercise program for the team. I didn't buy the idea that guys could play their way into shape during the season. I wanted everyone to report to spring training in good

physical condition and ready to work on some of the baseball fundamentals I felt had been neglected in recent years.

The players had returned home for the winter, but I imagine some
of them let out a loud groan when they heard I was coming back. My
time in the dugout was supposed to be temporary.

Now they were stuck with me a while longer. Not only that, but
I was going to make them sweat during the off-season!

• • •

I've always believed a manager is only as good as the coaches around
him. With that in mind, I made tweaks to my staff. I brought in Lee
Elia as third-base coach, Ruben Amaro Sr. as first-base coach, and
Mike Ryan as bullpen coach. Herm Starrette, Billy DeMars, and Wine
stayed on as pitching coach, hitting instructor, and bench coach, respectively. I felt these guys could help implement my program.

My program was a tough sell, however.

During spring training in Clearwater, Florida, I posted signs in
the clubhouse that said, "We, not I," another way of saying, "Check
your egos at the door and play team baseball." That message didn't
sit well with the cliques, which thought of me as some kind of High
School Harry. *We're seasoned vets*, they thought. *How dare this guy try
his crap motivational ploys on us.*

My tactics really got under Bowa's skin. Though he didn't like
talking to reporters, he did like to talk. That's why a local radio station gave him his own call-in show. His favorite topic became me and
how full of horseshit I was.

Luzinski was another guy inclined toward disliking me. We had a
long history. I managed him during his first year of professional baseball in South Dakota, and he remembered how much I yelled and how
hard I pushed players. In 1979, he didn't play like the All-Star he had
been the previous four seasons. And by midseason, he heard a lot of
boos at Veterans Stadium. He admitted that the fans in Philadelphia

got inside his head. He ended up hitting over .300 on the road but under .200 at home.

To his credit, Bull got in shape before the '80 season. When he showed up to camp, he was 25 pounds lighter than he'd been the previous October. Physically, he looked ready to play. He talked about the importance of going into the season in the proper frame of mind. I think he feared a few insults from me might set him back mentally.

It irritated the hell out of me at prior spring trainings that a lot of veterans seemed more interested in hitting the links than hitting baseballs. I'm sure a lot of tee times were missed as we worked on hit-and-run plays, advancing runners, and scoring guys from third base with less than two outs.

In certain situations, I was willing to bend my rules. For example, while all the other pitchers on the team ran their butts off in Clearwater, I let Steve Carlton do his own program. Lefty came to camp in tremendous shape every year and worked out rigorously once he got there. His guru was strength coach Gus Hoeffling. During the off-season, I told Gus to run me through Steve's regimen, which included a lot of agility and stretching exercises. It worked for me. I came to camp more flexible than I had been in years.

Rose and Lefty bought into my program right away. Others, like Tug McGraw and Bake McBride, were on the fence. Then there were Bowa, Luzinski, Schmidt, Boone, and Garry Maddox, who saw me as a threat.

Whether we won, lost, or just ripped each other to shreds, 1980 was going to be a memorable season.

• • •

Call me a loudmouth or honest to a fault. Or call me a jackass, as I'm sure a few baseball people have. I like to speak my mind. Always have. I look at it this way: if you're asked a question and don't give an honest answer, you're not doing what you're paid to do. And I don't like to lie. Discretion has never been my strong suit, and I credit that for my greatest successes. I also blame it for my greatest failures.

I've worked for teams in the most passionate sports towns in America—Philadelphia, Chicago, and New York (for both the Yankees and the Mets). That's a chronological list, not one that ranks the cities in order from most passionate to least passionate, or vice versa.

A long time ago, I was a pitcher for 13 professional seasons, five of them in the majors. I played nearly my entire big league career for a manager who didn't believe in communicating with players. In my opinion, his inability or unwillingness to connect with his team kept him from being one of the all-time greats. We're all shaped by our experiences, and playing for Gene Mauch certainly helped shape me. When I managed, I had an open-door policy. Any player who came into my office got an honest evaluation of where he stood.

Throughout my career, I've been accused of not protecting my players by freely and publicly discussing their on-the-field mistakes. I always found that accusation ridiculous. Here's why: if 40,000 fans in a stadium saw a fielder make an error, and another million or so watched it on TV, how could I be expected to say the player fielded the ball cleanly? If a player struck out three times, how could I have argued he had a decent day at the plate? The alternative would have been to say nothing at all. But that's never been my style.

Other than occasionally calling someone an "asshole," I was never into name-calling. I didn't see any point in getting personal. I also saw no value in holding grudges. If someone took my criticism personally and decided to hate me forever, well, that was his problem. In all my years, I never beat up on anyone I didn't think deserved it. Again, I've always sought to tell the truth. In some cases, my version of the truth might have been open to debate. But that's what makes life—and baseball—interesting.

After all my years in baseball, I still adhere to the same philosophy: play the game hard, play the game right, and play up to your potential. Any player who follows these instructions gets along with me pretty well.

Over the course of my career, a lot of people have asked me about my loud voice. I do seem to talk (and scream) louder than most. My mom, Mayannah Green, often said I cried and screamed louder than any youngster in the neighborhood. She claimed it was colic—I think it was just practice for the future. Throughout school, I maintained a good, loud voice. But it really became an instrument all its own during my time in professional baseball.

Time and again, I asked players to "look in the mirror" and to judge whether they were getting the most out of their abilities. When I look in the mirror, I see six decades of triumphs, defeats, and heartbreak in the game I love. And while there are certain things I wish I had handled differently, I see no real regrets.

2

BEFORE I BECAME AN OGRE, I was a middling ballplayer just trying to keep my head above water.

In 1964, I was almost 30 years old and going into my fifth year
in the big leagues.

Too young to be considered a journeyman and too banged up to
be touted as a player with a bright future, I wished I could have looked
in the mirror and seen a more seasoned version of the 21-year-old
flamethrower who had blazed his way through the minors.

But that wasn't what reflected back at me. I still looked like a pretty
good ballplayer, but my lame pitching arm told a different story. Every
day, I wondered if I still had what it took to be a major league pitcher.

I set a goal for myself in 1964. Through hard work, I would stay
in the majors and find a way to contribute to my team, the Phillies.

I didn't know what my role on the team would be. Phillies manager
Gene Mauch, "The Little General," wasn't big on assigning roles. If he
handed you the ball, he expected you to get hitters out. That was your
role. In my first four seasons with the team, I pitched in short relief,
long relief, and started some games. Thanks to the team's improved
pitching rotation in 1964, I realized without Gene telling me that I
was destined for the back end of the bullpen.

Sure enough, I became a mop-up guy. But there's always a place
in baseball for the mop-up guy.

Some days I was able to keep us in ballgames. I made quality pitches and got outs when I needed them. I started the season with a nine-inning scoreless streak and notched a win in the process.

When I was bad, however, I had a helluva time retiring anyone. A May night in Pittsburgh when I gave up six runs in just 1⅓ innings provided evidence of that.

I accepted the fact that I'd rarely get the ball in pressure-filled situations. We had an experienced sinkerball pitcher named Jack Baldschun who closed most of our games. And if Jack didn't come in to earn the save, Ed Roebuck, who the Phillies purchased from the Washington Senators early in the season, usually got the job done.

I tried to hang in and battle, because from a team standpoint, we were looking awfully strong. Jim Bunning, who we picked up in a trade with Detroit the previous December, threw a perfect game at Shea Stadium on Father's Day. At the top of our pitching rotation, Bunning and Chris Short gave us a reliable chance of winning every time they took the mound. And Dick Allen and Johnny Callison had emerged as two of the best young hitters in the game. We lacked the experience of other teams in the league and didn't have an established star along the lines of Willie Mays or Henry Aaron. But a Phillies team that had lost 23 straight games just a few seasons earlier had started to look like it could compete with anybody. We went 9–2 in April, 16–13 in May, and 18–12 in June and found ourselves at the top of the National League standings at the All-Star break.

Gene stressed the importance of playing smart baseball. By bunting and scoring runners from third base with less than two outs, we won games that otherwise might have been lost. Gene had plenty of faults, but focusing on fundamentals was one of his positive qualities. Otherwise, he was a tyrant who made the whole team jumpy when he was around. He had his favorites, like Callison and some of the veterans, but the rest of us felt barely acknowledged, except for when

Gene barked at us for doing something wrong. I didn't feel it was an atmosphere conducive to long-term success, but we were doing well, so I didn't question it too much. Later, when I became a manager myself, I barked a lot, too. I tried to pound into my players that they needed to play the game the right way, with focus and energy, and alert to game situations. They weren't going to be able to simply out-talent opponents anymore.

• • •

We entered play on July 25 leading the National League by two games over the second-place San Francisco Giants. A game that day at Connie Mack Stadium became very memorable for me, but not for the right reasons. We trailed the St. Louis Cardinals 6–2 when I came in for mop-up duty in the eighth inning. I yielded a pair of unearned runs in the top of the eighth and another couple of runs in the ninth. Down 10–2 going into our last at-bat, we strung together four singles and four walks to cut the lead to 10–8, all before making our first out of the inning. We put another run on the board, but the comeback fell one run short. I wasn't the reason we lost, but my shaky performance helped the Cardinals get the insurance runs they needed to hang on to win.

That outing came exactly one week after the Reds bombed me for eight runs in 4⅓ innings, a miserable performance that featured the first and only grand slam of Pete Rose's career. And he still loves to remind me of it.

Gene's scowl made it obvious he didn't like what he'd seen from me of late. After the heartbreaking loss to the Cardinals, he gave me the bad news. About a week shy of my 30th birthday, the Phillies were sending me down to pitch for the Triple-A Arkansas Travelers. I would swap places with right-handed pitcher Gary Kroll, who appeared in two games with the Phillies before getting traded to the New York Mets.

I signed with the Phillies in 1955, and it took me five years to get to the majors. Once I made it, I stayed there—until I got called into Gene's office in July 1964.

It hurt like hell to leave my teammates at such a critical point in the season. It stung even more to have to pick up the phone and tell my dad I had been demoted. It wasn't that he was a huge baseball fan or even a vocal supporter of mine. At 64 years of age, he was a recovering alcoholic who had recently been diagnosed with lung cancer.

I shared a name, George Dallas Green, but not much else with my father. His drinking had brought a lot of financial and emotional hardship on our family. We didn't play catch when I was a kid, and he didn't push me into sports—or anything else, for that matter. When he wasn't working at the garage he operated in Wilmington, Delaware, he'd sit down in the cellar of our house drinking hard wine and smoking cigarettes like a fiend. It'd just be him, a small heater, and a couple of overhead light bulbs. He never laid a finger on me, my mom, or my sisters. He was a very quiet drunk.

When I reached the majors in 1960, a switch inside of him seemed to click. His son had "made it," and I guess he started to regret missing out on my journey to that point. He started drinking less and then stopped altogether. He never came to see me play, but I could sense he was proud. I felt he had gotten his life back on track. And that's when the cancer whacked him. My mom and sisters took care of him as his body became increasingly weak.

My dad didn't say much when I told him I was going back to the minors. He didn't need to. He knew we'd both been defeated.

• • •

I had to keep my emotions inside for a while. On the night of my demotion, Sylvia and I had dinner guests at our house in Newport, Delaware. I put on a happy face during the meal. After our guests left, I told Sylvia what happened.

I was really ticked off by the demotion. Born and raised in the Philadelphia area, my allegiance to the Phillies couldn't have been stronger. And now, when it appeared we might win the pennant for the first time since 1950, I was nothing to them.

The team made World Series tickets available to players in July. I bought several and distributed them to friends and family. As badly as I wanted to see the Phillies in the Fall Classic, it crushed the hell out of me that I might be using one of the tickets myself.

The summer of 1964 forced me to take another hard look at myself.

Five years after hurting my pitching arm as a prospect at Triple-A Buffalo, I knew I'd never be the same pitcher again. I had learned to block out the pain, but I couldn't fix the underlying problem—my arm couldn't do the things it once could. There were no sports medicine doctors back then, so I never really learned the full extent of the damage.

Prior to the injury, I was considered the hardest thrower in the Phillies organization. But after my right arm went out on me, I had to completely revamp my pitching style. Before then, I would just rear back and try to overpower hitters. After the injury, I tried to outsmart hitters by changing speeds and turning the ball over. I guess you could say I really learned how to pitch after the injury. But it turned out I wasn't good enough to get successful results on a consistent basis.

I had gone from living at home with my wife and children to holing up in a dingy motel in Little Rock, Arkansas. The only way to get back to Philadelphia was to show Mauch and general manager John Quinn (Mr. Quinn to his players) that I still had enough left in my arm to help the team win the pennant. In the Pacific Coast League, I transitioned from major league mop-up guy to minor league starter. And I put together a couple of really good outings.

From a thousand miles away in Arkansas, I kept tabs on my dad's worsening health. I used his situation as added motivation to return to the Phillies.

While I was in the minors, the Phillies separated themselves from the rest of the pack in the National League. The team's inspired play started getting a lot of attention. Callison graced the cover of *Sports Illustrated* in August. In an accompanying story, Jack Olsen wrote, "The Phutile Phillies of years gone by have become the Phantom Phillies of 1964, a bunch of invisible men who do not seem to understand that a team without stars should not be a pennant contender." Olsen praised Mauch, whom he described as "a gritty, gutsy little thinker who brought the team from the ninth circle of hell to pennant contention."

Thanks to Gene, I had traveled in the opposite direction.

A few weeks after arriving in Arkansas, I was out raising Cain with teammates Lee Elia and Pat Corrales when Arkansas manager Frank Lucchesi tracked me down to give me the news I'd been dreading. My dad had lost his battle with cancer. I returned home to Delaware for the funeral before resuming a season that was looking worse all the time.

To this day, I believe my demotion killed my father. It took me a long time to come to terms with his death.

Amid my anger and sorrow, I decided to finish out the season and then retire from the game.

Through early September, the Reds, Cardinals, and Giants could only give chase. Back then, there was no wild-card berth. The winner of each 10-team league advanced directly to the World Series. In the Phillies' case, that would have meant a matchup with the Yankees.

The sizable lead we built just got me more pissed off. Why wasn't I there to be a part of it? Why couldn't my arm do the things I wanted it to do? And would I be the ultimate invisible man on a team filled with invisible men?

• • •

There's a time for pouting. You get it out of your system, and then you go out and play, or you quit. I didn't see it this way at the time, but looking back, I know 1964 imparted lessons I carried with me for decades to come. Baseball can kick you in the gut and double you over. And sometimes you have to dig down to find what you need to pull yourself back up.

I pitched well at Arkansas, going 4–1 with a 2.62 ERA in my two months there. The Travelers won the PCL's East Division with a 95–61 record and met up with San Diego for the league championship. I pitched a shutout in the opener of the series, which we went on to lose in seven games.

The next day I rejoined the Phillies, who led the National League by 6½ games with only 12 games left in the season. The team was coming off a tough 1–0 loss to Cincinnati at Connie Mack Stadium. The only run in the game came on a steal of home in the sixth inning by Reds infielder Chico Ruiz, who made the daring move with Cincinnati's best hitter, Frank Robinson, at the plate. I don't think anybody thought much of it at the time, but that play ended up lingering in the hearts and minds of Phillies fans for many years.

I sat and watched from the bullpen as we lost five more games in a row to the Reds and Milwaukee Braves. Suddenly the Phillies clubhouse felt like a different place. You could feel a tension and tightness that comes from forgetting how to win games at the worst possible time.

Before the losing streak started, Gene decided to try and wrap up the pennant by pitching his two aces on short rest. Injuries to two other guys in the rotation, Dennis Bennett and Ray Culp, helped explain why Gene sent Bunning and Short out to the mound every three days. The strategy didn't work, however. Jim and Chris went 1–5 during the two-week experiment.

As the losses mounted, Gene retreated into a shell. Earlier in the season, he yelled and screamed and threw stuff around the clubhouse. He even goaded opposing players from the bench. Now he was silent. We all waited for him to step up and say something to shake us out of our funk, but it never happened. He let us stew in it. It was unbelievable.

When asked by reporters about the team's September swoon, Gene expressed defiance: "For a long time, everybody has said we're lucky. Now they're saying we're tense. Before it's over, they'll take a bite on those words."

• • •

On September 27, I finally got into a game. The Braves had knocked Bunning around pretty hard, and I entered in the top of the fourth inning. The Phillies trailed 4–3, and the Braves had two men on base and nobody out. By the time I retired the side, it was 8–3. The damage might have been much worse had Hank Aaron not grounded into a double play. I returned for a second inning of work and gave up four more runs. Milwaukee went on to win the game 14–8.

The loss dropped us into second place for the first time since July 16. With a week left in the season, we never saw first place again. The losing streak eventually grew to 10. If not for two meaningless wins at the end of the season, we would have finished in third place. The Cardinals won the pennant and went on to beat the Yankees in the World Series.

Hindsight is always 20-20. The most frequently cited reason for the Phillies' collapse was Gene's overreliance on Bunning and Short at the end of the season. What most people neglect to mention is that he also mismanaged the bullpen. And I don't say that because I thought I should have played a greater role down the stretch. Baldschun had been our closer all year. But Gene got mad at him and stopped using him in tight situations. He also didn't go to Roebuck often enough. We lost a lot of games in the late innings because Jack and Eddie weren't in there. John Boozer, Bobby Locke, and, yes, Dallas Green, all of whom pitched well at Arkansas in 1964, came up short at one time or another for the Phillies in September.

My experience that year gave me strong feelings about what it takes to be a major league closer. Obviously talent is part of it. But preparation and head and heart are also vital. Jack and Eddie had the mental and physical attributes required to do the job. The rest of us might have *thought* we were capable of pitching in those situations, but we weren't. You can think of yourself in whatever light you want, but when you're out on the mound late in a game facing Willie Mays with the bases loaded, you show who you really are.

The events of 1964 were traumatic for the team, its fans, and the city of Philadelphia. Entire books have been written about the catastrophic end to what looked like a dream season.

The whole thing hit me particularly hard. We lost the pennant, I lost my dad, and all I saw in the mirror was a pitcher with a gimpy right arm.

I still have those tickets for the 1964 World Series, by the way.

3

CERTAIN GAMES IN MY PLAYING career stand out in my memory. I remember the shutout I tossed against the Los Angeles Dodgers in my rookie season, a big save I got against the Chicago Cubs in 1963, and the rough outings that led to my demotion to the minors in 1964.

Also near the top of that list is a high school basketball game that took place in a gymnasium in Newport, Delaware, in the winter of 1952.

On that night, Bernard "Bunny" Blaney and the Newark High School Yellowjackets came to our school and got humbled. Blaney, the top high school scorer in the state of Delaware, scored 12 points, half his per-game average that year. I scored 22 for Henry C. Conrad High School. And we won the game 52–38.

At the time, I couldn't imagine a better feeling or more satisfying win. On the heels of our victory, my teammates and I couldn't resist having a little fun at Bunny's expense. So, we drafted him a letter:

Dear Mr. Blaney,
Any time you feel like being held to a minimum in scoring, please
get in contact with the point-average wrecking crew of Conrad
H.S. Any request that we receive from you will be complied to
immediately and done with great pleasure. When you stop crying
over last Friday night's disappointment, you can come back to

*Conrad and pick up your girl because you forgot her. I guess the
reason for your low point production wasn't the fact that you were
deathly sick. Ha ha. The real cause was probably because your two
left feet were getting in the way.*

Sincerely,
The Conrad Wreckers of 1952

For a 17-year-old kid growing up in Delaware, the win over
Newark High represented the height of athletic accomplishment.
Newark was big-time, and Bunny, who went on to play football at
Duke, was the top dog in the state. All these years later, I still remember the defensive scheme we used to shut him down that night. While
four of our players, including me, hung back in a loose zone, our fifth
and speediest guy shadowed Bunny all night. And it worked like a
charm.

Newport, Delaware, located 40 miles down the road from
Philadelphia, was the center of the basketball universe that night, as
far as I was concerned.

Sixty years after our upset of Newark High, my old high school
pals and I still get together to reminisce about that victory and other
good times we had at Conrad.

Like most people, I look back on my teenage years with a great
deal of fondness. I knew adulthood and the responsibilities that
come with it were right around the corner, but I was too preoccupied
with sports and other diversions to think very much about my post-
graduation plans. The future didn't concern me too much.

I came of age between wars. As a kid in suburban Wilmington, I
remember the gas rations brought about by World War II. But by the
time I reached high school, our boys were coming home from Europe
and the Pacific. With the Korean War still a few years away, the late
1940s were a great time to be young. It helped that Delaware enjoyed

a lot of post-war prosperity. Chrysler and General Motors built factories there, and the population of the state boomed. I remember it as an upbeat time.

My parents shielded me from any bad news, whether generated at home or in the larger world. We didn't discuss the war or politics, and my dad never talked about business. I'm sure he and my mom, who kept the books at the garage he owned, had it out a time or two over finances, but I never heard any yelling or screaming about it. Despite mounting money problems, we somehow found a way to move into a bigger house as I was starting high school. And that's where I lived until I left home for good.

. . .

My young life revolved around sports. I lettered in football, basketball, and baseball every year of high school. And in my senior year, just for kicks, I went out for the track team. I threw javelin, did the high jump, and even made one ill-fated attempt at pole vaulting.

Of all the sports, basketball held the biggest place in my heart. Having reached my maximum height of 6'5" during high school, I had enough size to exert my will near the basket. My scrawny frame earned me the nickname "Spider," but I still relished the physicality of posting up and boxing out opponents in the lane. In my senior year, only Bunny and two other high school players in Delaware scored more points than I did. My play that year earned me a spot on the All-State Scholastic Quintet.

I loved whatever sport I happened to be playing at the time, but I guess you could say basketball was my main sport. If you mentioned my name around Delaware back then, most people would have said, "Oh yeah, Dallas Green, the basketball player."

I recognized, however, that I lacked the athleticism needed to play the game professionally. I was okay with that. I knew basketball would remain a part of my life regardless of how long I played on a team. Even after I became a professional baseball player, I made time to play hoops two or three times a week in some very good semipro leagues around the Delaware Valley.

In baseball, I was never the best player on my school team. Part of that had to do with the quality of our squad, which went undefeated my junior year. The left-handed ace of our pitching rotation that year, a senior named Paul Tebbutt, signed a contract with the Cleveland Indians. Another left-handed pitcher, Bob Garvey, signed with the Cardinals.

Another factor was the partial break in my right arm that prevented me from playing up to my ability and cost me a chance to compete in a national amateur baseball tournament in the summer of 1954.

I contributed to the unblemished season by pitching 14 innings and playing right field the rest of the time. To this day, Tebbutt likes to remind me that I saved one of his two no-hitters that year by throwing out a guy at first base from right field.

By the time I graduated high school, I felt I had become a pretty seasoned baseball player. During summer vacation, I played on an American Legion team. And when I turned 18, I played for a semipro team that competed against squads with players in their twenties and thirties. We'd barnstorm around the state, traveling to towns like Farmingdale and Harrington. The level of competition in that league was higher than anything I saw until I reached the minor leagues.

• • •

Nobody in my family cared much for sports. Neither of my parents was athletic. I inherited my size from my paternal grandfather. So did my older sister, Thelma, who grew to be nearly 6'0".

My father's life, at least until his drinking got the better of him, centered on working. As I said, he owned a garage in Wilmington where he fixed and stored cars. That's where I learned to drive—during the summer of my 13th birthday. I'd go onto the lot and move cars around until they were all squeezed in as close as possible. A lot of his customers worked at the nearby DuPont chemical plant. Because the apartment building they lived in lacked parking, they left their cars with us. Every morning, we'd pick a few of them up and drive them to work. At 5:00 PM, either my dad or I would ride down and pick them up.

When he wasn't shuttling workers to and from the DuPont building, my dad fixed up cars. I'd sit and watch in amazement as he completely disassembled and reassembled vehicles without missing a bolt. I always admired him for that, partly because it was a talent I never developed.

Other than summers at the garage, my dad and I didn't spend much time together. Our only shared activity was hunting. On a pretty regular basis, he, my grandfather, and I would go railbird shooting down at the Delaware Marsh. My dad would pole the boat through the marsh, and my grandfather and I would sit and wait for the birds to pop up. I came to be a fairly good shot on those outings and maintained an interest in hunting for the rest of my life.

In fairness to him, I didn't exactly seek out my dad for companionship. The truth of the matter was I wasn't around that much. If I missed dinner, my parents knew I was out playing ball. My mom would put a platter in the refrigerator for me to eat when I got home. Every now and then, I'd catch hell about not being home for a special dinner, but for the most part, my parents let me do my thing. They recognized that I could take care of myself, including in the classroom. I took college prep courses and usually made the honor roll.

To earn a little pocket money, I mowed lawns in the neighborhood. My only other break from sports came on Saturdays, when I headed to the local movie theater to catch a Western or war movie. The theater was a mile from my house. To stay in shape, I ran there and back. Sitting in the dark theater, I watched in awe as John Wayne or another leading man of the day took on the bad guys.

My mom, Mayannah Green, was a saint. She kept the family together. My sister Thelma, who passed away at the age of 89 in 2012, was 11 years my senior. My younger sister, Carole, is four years my junior. Despite the financial difficulties that arose as my father's drinking problem worsened, my mom kept the household running. Whatever we needed, we usually got. She was a church-going gal, and I grew up going to Bible school and Sunday services. After I signed a professional baseball contract, I remember her saying, "Dad's not keeping the bills right. We're struggling." That was news to me.

After he lost his garage, my dad ended up with a paper route. To compensate for my family's lost income, my mom waited tables at Newark Country Club and New Castle Army Air Base. She never cried poor, and she made sure my sisters and I were never lacking for food or anything else.

• • •

Two of my high school coaches helped mentor me. My football coach, John Chanowski, encouraged me to stay on the team even though I wasn't a naturally gifted football player. "Don't quit," he told me. "It'll help you with your other sports." He was right. Frank Loucks, my basketball coach, took me aside after my junior year and told me he would work with me to make the all-state team my final season. He did, and I made all-state.

When I became a senior, several major league scouts took notice of me. The Phillies, Philadelphia A's, Giants, Boston Red Sox, and Pirates all came to see me play. I attended a three-day try-out camp with the Pirates in Elkton, Maryland, the summer I graduated high school. I still have the invitation from Pirates scout Rex Bowen that reads, "Boys are asked to pay their own expenses to the school, but if they are ever signed to a contract, all of their expenses will be refunded."

In my senior yearbook, I listed a straightforward future ambition: "To go to college and make myself a career in the sports world." While others in my class of 148 students hoped to "raise a herd of Hereford cattle" or become a "first-class plumber," I knew my future was in sports. I was voted the most popular male student in my graduating class. So, yeah, I guess you could say my high school years were pretty special.

I wasn't disappointed that I didn't get offered a professional baseball contract out of high school, because Bob Carpenter, a Delaware businessman who preceded his son, Ruly, as owner of the Phillies, offered me a pretty inviting alternative.

Mr. Carpenter ran the Friends Foundation, which for all intents and purposes was the University of Delaware's scholarship program back then. There were no baseball scholarships at the time, but Mr. Carpenter knew my ability on the hardwood and got me a basketball scholarship. The idea was for me to play basketball for the Blue Hens in the winter and baseball in the spring. As far as I was concerned, it was an ideal situation.

Mr. Carpenter's generosity made me feel even more positive toward the Phillies. Growing up in Delaware, they became my favorite major league team. I never attended a game at Shibe Park, or Connie Mack Stadium as it was later renamed, but I listened to games on the radio. As a pitcher, I looked up to Robin Roberts and Curt Simmons, the aces of the 1950 Whiz Kids team that reached the World Series when I was in high school.

By my junior year of college, I was co-captain of the Delaware basketball team and made the All-Middle Atlantic Conference team. I knew I wouldn't go any further than the college level, but I enjoyed the opportunity to play a few more years of organized basketball. It was exciting to play against a lot of the Philadelphia schools and a few East Coast powerhouses.

• • •

The university was very much a football school at the time. Baseball was treated like a red-headed stepchild. Unfortunately, my baseball coach at Delaware turned out not to possess much acumen. He was a professor who got the coaching job because nobody else wanted it.

Mr. Carpenter was a big fan of all the university's sports teams and even traveled to some of our away baseball games. He was in the stands for a game I pitched my junior year at West Chester University, which had a couple of players the Braves were looking to sign.

I took a one-run lead into the bottom of the ninth inning. We were one out away from wrapping up the win when a West Chester player hit a bomb to center field. The ball would have cleared almost any fence in existence, but luckily for me, this field didn't have any fence at all. Still, it looked like a certain inside-the-park home run. I turned around and watched the ball sail over the open field. I also watched as our center fielder, Jimmy Zaiser, started closing ground on it. Jimmy stuck up his glove and speared the ball about 450 feet from home plate to preserve the win. After the game, Mr. Carpenter slapped me on the back and told me he had just witnessed the best performance he'd ever seen from a college pitcher.

Thanks in part to that amazing play by Jimmy, I went 6–0 with a 0.88 ERA my junior year.

The same scouts who looked at me in high school periodically checked in with me during my college career. But the Phillies had an obvious edge over the rest of the pack. Not only were they the closest thing I had to a hometown team, but their owner had paid my way to college. If the Phillies offered me a contract after my junior year, I was going to sign it. And in the spring of 1955, at the age of 20, I did just that. My signing bonus was $4,000.

Harold "Tubby" Raymond, an assistant football coach for Delaware and a friend of the Carpenter family, gave me a ride that day to Mr.

Carpenter's Philadelphia office. Raymond went on to coach baseball at UD for eight seasons and was head football coach at the university for 36 seasons.

I split my first year of professional baseball between Mattoon, Illinois, and Reidsville, North Carolina. I got off to a bumpy start at Class-B Reidsville, going 1–1 with a 10.06 ERA. That earned me a quick demotion to Class-D Mattoon. I fared better there. On my 21st birthday, I fanned 15 hitters in a game against the Hannibal Citizens. To that point, I had struck out 40 hitters in 23⅓ innings of work. Over my entire time with Mattoon, I went 4–3 with a 3.44 ERA.

My ambition was to make a career for myself in the sports world. I knew I had to make the most of this opportunity, and it felt great to get the journey started.

4

IN THE FALL OF 1955, back home after my first year of professional baseball, I cruised over to my old high school in a new yellow-and-black Mercury I had just bought with my signing bonus. I felt like some kind of conquering hero as I drove around the grounds of Conrad High.

I was making a loop around campus when a petite brunette on the field hockey team caught my eye. As the petite brunette would later tell it, she and her friend saw me, too. "Look at that car!" her friend exclaimed as I drove by. "Look at the guy driving that car!" my future wife responded.

I didn't stop to introduce myself to Sylvia Taylor but later I did some asking around about her. In a small town like Newport, Delaware, you didn't need to work too hard to find out about someone. I learned that Sylvia attended Conrad, where she was a varsity field hockey, basketball, and softball player, as well as a drum majorette. As luck would have it, her cousin worked with my sister Thelma at the DuPont Company in Wilmington. I asked Thelma if she and her co-worker could fix me up with Sylvia, and a few days later, Thelma said Sylvia would be expecting a call from me.

I phoned Sylvia and invited her to go out to the movies with me that weekend. She agreed. When I picked her up for the date, she asked what movie we were going to see. She probably wanted to catch

Rebel Without a Cause, Picnic, or *Guys and Dolls,* all of which were box-office hits in 1955.

The car had cost a lot of money, and I was running a little low on cash, so I had to dash Sylvia's hopes of sitting in a movie theater balcony and watching James Dean, William Holden, or Marlon Brando.

"Actually, I thought we could go and watch home movies with my friends," I told her.

I'm lucky she didn't get out of the car and run back inside her house. She stayed, and we ended up having a great time. She got along well with Hoddy and Sandy, my married friends who hosted the movie night. At some point during the evening, Sylvia told the room full of 21-year-olds that she was a 15-year-old sophomore. That came as a surprise. Sylvia carried herself like a college girl, however, so our difference in ages didn't really bother me. We arranged to go out on a second date, and pretty soon, we were going steady.

Sylvia's parents may have had a different take on our respective ages. They were wary of me. One night that fall, I didn't bring her home until 2:00 AM. The moment Sylvia opened the front door, her father, a big man, came hurtling down the stairs. "If you can't get my daughter home at a more decent hour, then you'll have to find another girl!" he barked at me.

I assured him it wouldn't happen again.

Fortunately, Sylvia's father liked baseball. To make up for bringing their daughter home late some nights, I got into the habit of bringing Mr. and Mrs. Taylor hoagies and a half-gallon of ice cream every time I came over to pick her up.

When I left for spring training, I had to put my burgeoning relationship with Sylvia on hold. It was difficult at the time, but I think the separation served a purpose. For one thing, she needed to focus on finishing high school. Her mother, the first person in her family to graduate from college, worried that our romance would distract

Sylvia from her studies. To keep the relationship alive, we wrote tons of letters back and forth while I was off playing ball.

• • •

In February 1956, the Phillies became the second major league team to open a "rookie school" in Florida (the Red Sox were the other). The idea was to give the organization's top prospects a chance to work out in Clearwater with Phillies manager Mayo Smith before the start of regular spring training. I was one of 39 players invited to take part in the program.

It was at the rookie school that I hit it off with Paul Owens, a 32-year-old player-manager for the Phillies' Class-D affiliate in Olean, New York. Paul loved the game and still played it pretty well, but for reasons not entirely clear to me, had long since abandoned hopes of pursuing a major league career.

After a year at Rider College in the early 1940s, Paul enlisted in the Army and went off to Europe to fight in World War II. He returned home to finish his degree at St. Bonaventure University, where he played first base on the school baseball team. Then, at the age of 27, he finally took a crack at professional baseball. He signed a contract with a then-unaffiliated Class-D team in Olean, which wasn't far from his hometown of Salamanca. He hit .407 to lead the PONY League. The St. Louis Cardinals took notice of his performance and signed him to play at Class-B Winston-Salem the following year. He went out and hit .338, but then Paul suddenly gave up professional baseball to take a government job in Salamanca.

When I met him, he was giving the game another go, with an eye toward getting into baseball management. Back with Olean in 1955, he hit .387. A couple of years later, he surpassed the .400-mark for the second time in his career.

In Clearwater, Paul picked up on the fact that I was a hard worker. At the end of rookie school, Mayo Smith selected four minor leaguers to stick around to throw batting practice to the major leaguers. I'm pretty sure Paul had something to do with me being one of those four. It was an honor. A batting practice pitcher is supposed to throw low-velocity fastballs right down the heart of the plate, but out on the mound in Clearwater, my adrenalin kicked in, and I found myself trying to throw the ball past the likes of All-Stars Richie Ashburn and Del Ennis.

Over the next several years, Paul and I ran into each other every spring in Clearwater. He was a natural when it came to teaching and relating to young players. He loved to grab a bat and ball and work with the guys from the minor leagues. In that regard, he separated himself from a lot of his peers and superiors. Most managers and coaches at the time were aloof. Rather than instructing young players, they allowed us to sink or swim. With a major league season to prepare for, they didn't have time to waste on kids.

Several years later, Paul became "Pope" to everyone who knew him. Soon after Paul VI was elected to the papacy in 1963, Phillies clubhouse manager Ted Zipeto remarked how much our friend resembled the new pope. Ted dropped to his knees and kissed a ring on Paul's finger. "Pope Paul, you're my boss!" he joked. A nickname was born. Over the years, the resemblance between the two men only grew.

On that subject, my high school nickname, "Spider," fell by the wayside after I entered the Phillies organization. By my second or third year in the minors, my body had really filled out. I was now "Big D."

• • •

In my second year of pro ball in Salt Lake City, I struck up a friendship with fellow pitchers Jerry Kettle and Tom Cronin. Each of us was 6'5", which gave the sports editor of the local newspaper a good photo opportunity for a story about the size of our pitching staff. He had us stand next to Salt Lake manager Frank Lucchesi, who stood about a foot shorter than the three of us.

I missed Sylvia a lot. When Kettle and Cronin found out she loved horses, an animal I'd rarely been around, they decided to help out this girl they'd never met by giving her boyfriend riding lessons.

We drove out to a ranch at the base of the Rocky Mountains, where we rented some horses and headed out for an afternoon on the riding trail. At least that was the idea. My teammates quickly got their horses to gallop along, but mine refused to budge. I nudged the horse a little bit and let out a "giddy up," hoping the animal would get its act together. The horse finally started moving—in circles.

I called out for help, and the guys returned to lend me a hand. Armed with a few tips, I figured out how to make the horse walk straight. Trotting, cantering, and galloping would have to wait for another day.

To this day, Kettle remembers the incident well. He says I looked like someone out of a movie—not a John Wayne movie but a comedy Western. I guess I'm lucky I didn't return from the outing with a new nickname like "Hopalong."

Over the years, I've heard time and again that I remind people of John Wayne, my favorite actor of all time. My tough-guy persona and commanding presence prompt the comparisons. The difference between us is Duke rode his horse off into the sunset, while I rode mine in circles.

Fortunately, my pitching that summer was better than my horseback riding.

In a June game against Billings, I earned a complete-game victory and helped my own cause by hitting a grand slam. For the year, I went 17–12 with a league-leading 226 strikeouts. That performance earned me Pioneer League Rookie of the Year, a strangely named award considering not many guys spent more than a year in the league before moving up—or down—the minor league ladder.

My pitching mechanics were still a work in progress. I had a real big leg kick at the time that helped me throw with a lot of velocity but not much control. I walked way too many batters in Salt Lake City, 187 in 239 innings. I led the league in that category, too.

• • •

I was all set for my third year of pro ball when I got a telegram that changed my plans.

Back in the 1950s, there was only one kind of draft, and it didn't involve major league teams selecting the best amateur players in the country. It was Uncle Sam calling you to service. In 1957, four years after the end of the Korean War, I got that call after Congress reinstated the draft to keep America prepared for any potential conflicts.

Instead of traveling from spring training in Florida to North Carolina, my next scheduled stop in the minors, I took a bus to an Army office in Philadelphia.

I couldn't really process what was happening. My name had started to pop up in newspaper stories in Philadelphia about the top prospects in the Phillies minor league system. Just a few days earlier, I had been throwing batting practice to major league stars. Now my baseball career was about to go on hiatus.

In Philadelphia, I sat in a room full of future soldiers. The Army officials told us we'd undergo physicals that day, and assuming we passed, we'd then be shipped off to Fort Benning, Georgia, for two years.

The player I most admired as a kid, Ted Williams, sacrificed some of the best years of his career to serve his country in World War II. Unlike Williams, however, I was at the start of my career. There were no guarantees that a job would be waiting for me after two years in the Army. The other difference was that ballplayers called to active duty in the early 1940s were actually fighting for their country. I'd be sitting at an Army base waiting for a conflict to happen.

I returned home to Delaware to await the results of my physical and attend a going-away party thrown by family and friends. I tried my best to hide my disappointment. I said my good-byes and told everyone I'd see them soon. It didn't escape me that I'd be away from baseball *and* Sylvia for two years.

The next day I got a telegram from the Army that informed me of the results of my physical. I had a hernia. Because of that, I got slapped with the 4-F tag. I was physically unfit for duty, thankfully.

I never asked if Phillies owner Bob Carpenter had anything to do with that diagnosis. A few months later, I had surgery to fix the problem.

I unpacked my bags and we had another party in Delaware to celebrate my reprieve. Instead of heading off to Fort Benning, I headed to High Point, North Carolina. My friends were tired of partying and glad to see me go.

• • •

In some ways, it was a different era in baseball.

Fresh off his perfect game in the 1956 World Series, which I attended with friends, Don Larsen of the Yankees was looking for a pay raise. The amount he and the team agreed upon? $20,000.

And on April 22, 1957, the Phillies became the last National League team to integrate when John Irvin Kennedy entered a game as a pinch runner. He got into just five games that season, his only big league appearances, coming to bat twice.

In other ways, the game was much the same as it is today, especially in the minor leagues, where I was among thousands of players plugging away in the hopes of getting a shot at the big time.

In the Carolina League, I took a step in that direction by walking far fewer batters than the year before, a major step forward in my development as a pitcher.

But sometimes, admittedly, I missed the strike zone on purpose.

In those days, pitching inside was part of the game, a way to keep hitters from getting too comfortable at the plate. I was a dedicated practitioner of the brushback pitch. That pissed off some hitters, who for some strange reason didn't like seeing a 95 mile-per-hour fastball coming toward their chins. But whether they liked it or not, I didn't back off.

In a June 1957 game against Winston-Salem, I threw a couple of inside fastballs to Gene Oliver, a burly catcher who later enjoyed a long major league career that included a season with me in Philadelphia. After the second high-and-tight pitch, Oliver shot me a scowl and raised his index finger in the air. He wasn't signaling that he was No. 1. He was saying that if I came in on him one more time, he was going to have something to say about it.

My teammates, including Kettle, who followed me from Salt Lake City, knew exactly where the next pitch was going. I reared back and uncorked a fastball designed to knock Oliver on his ass. Down he went. After getting up, he came out to have a word with me, as promised. I didn't wait for him to get out to the mound. I took two steps forward and landed a haymaker to Oliver's face. He got in a few punches as both teams spilled out onto the field. Kettle came out with a batting helmet on. What followed wasn't your average baseball brawl, in which players grab each other and mill around. This one was a real donnybrook, with haymakers and wrestling and probably some eye-gouging. When the dust cleared, our manager, Frank Lucchesi, ended up in possession of the umpire's home-plate brush. I'm still not sure how that happened.

A few days later, I got a telegram from the president of the Carolina League that read, "You have subjected yourself to the automatic Carolina League fine of $5 for accepting Winston-Salem player Oliver's challenge to fight. For actually participating in a fight, you are hereby fined another $5, making the total fine $10."

Believe it or not, that was a good amount of money at the time for a minor league baseball player. Who did they think I was? Don Larsen?

Later in my career, I was involved in another brushback incident. Future Dodger John Roseboro thought I was throwing at him, so he bunted a ball up the first-base line. As I bent over to field the ball, he bowled me over. He was playing good hard baseball, and so was I. Many years later, as a catcher for the Dodgers, Roseboro took exception to inside pitches being thrown by Juan Marichal of the Giants. With Marichal at the plate later in the game, Roseboro made sure his return throws to Sandy Koufax came as close to Marichal's head as possible. In what became an infamous episode, Marichal retaliated by hitting Roseboro over the head with his bat.

• • •

Still young and single, I had some fun times in High Point, the sleepy southern town I called home for the summer. It was mostly of the good, clean variety. Almost half the team lived side by side on a nice residential street in High Point. Kettle, Eddie Keegan, and Freddie Van Dusen lived in one house, and I lived with Dick Harris and a couple of other guys next door.

To pass the time between games and practices, we formed a commando group that went on secret late-night missions. On one hot night/morning, while drinking some beers, we decided to go for a swim at the local country club. We weren't members of the club, and even if we had been, I doubt we would have been permitted to take a dip in the pool at 2:00 AM.

We drove over to the country club but the gate to the pool was bolted shut. We could have aborted our mission at that point, but that wouldn't have made us very effective commandos.

A tall metal fence surrounded the pool. We had consumed too many beers to do any serious fence climbing, but Kettle had an idea.

"Boys, we're going *under* the fence," he announced.

"We're tunneling in?" Harris asked.

"Nope, the fence is going up," Kettle replied.

Kettle got a jack out of the car, hooked it up to the fence, and proceeded to hoist it out of the ground. One by one, we slid underneath the uprooted metal.

After splashing around in the water for a while, Harris noticed the headlights of our car were still on. At an otherwise pitch-dark country club, the lights cut a bright path through the night, providing a road map for a security guard who would have loved to catch some pool-hoppers.

We decided to get the hell out of there. My teammates slid back under the fence and jumped in the car. I was at the top of a ladder leading to a diving board when they all took off. Without thinking, I jumped about 20 feet down to the ground and landed awkwardly on my ankle. Man down! My teammates came back to retrieve me, pulling me across the pool area and back under the fence.

The next day at the ballpark, my ankle hurt like hell. The other commandos tried to cover for me by helping me get dressed and out onto the field. Fortunately, I wasn't pitching that day. After a while, Lucchesi and trainer Pete Cera noticed me hobbling around. I told them I sprained my ankle going after a ground ball.

In addition to making uninvited visits to country clubs, I won 12 games at High Point, second-most on the team. At the end of the season, the Phillies promoted me all the way to Triple-A Miami, which put me just one step from the major leagues.

• • •

When I signed with the Phillies after my junior year at the University of Delaware, I was still several credits shy of graduating. During my off-seasons, I took classes at Temple University and UD in an attempt to earn my degree in business administration. I liked the idea of having an education to fall back on in case my baseball career didn't pan out. But more than that, I just wanted to finish what I started.

While I was playing at High Point, Sylvia graduated from Conrad High School. She enrolled at UD that fall. In January 1958, a few days after Sylvia's 18th birthday, we got married and then honeymooned in the Poconos. After that, she moved in with me at my mom's house. More than 50 years later, we're still together.

In the first years of our marriage, Sylvia went wherever I did, continuing her studies in whatever minor league city we happened to be in. We agreed to put off starting a family until she completed her education. This pleased her parents, who had been concerned that marrying young would interfere with her getting a college degree.

Sylvia completed her first two semesters in Delaware and then hit the road to join me in Miami for the 1958 season.

You hear a lot about the rough life of a minor leaguer: low pay, long bus rides, backwater towns, that kind of stuff. I experienced all of the above in Mattoon, Reidsville, High Point, and to a lesser extent, Salt Lake City.

My Triple-A experience in Miami didn't exactly follow that script, however. I spent the tail end of the 1957 season and all of 1958 playing there. Long before the Florida Marlins relocated a few miles south and became the Miami Marlins, multiple minor league clubs used that name, including a Phillies farm team that played in the International League between 1956 and 1960.

For newlyweds, Miami was an exciting place to spend a few months. We lived in a motel on the 79th Street Causeway, a lively part of town back in the late 1950s. Sylvia says if she ever writes a book, it will tell of the colorful characters we met at the motel's communal swimming pool.

Our neighbors included a gun runner who made regular trips to Cuba to sell his wares; a contractor who earned and squandered millions of dollars in the construction business, all in the span of that single summer; a downtrodden widower who lost his wife in a hurricane; two lesbians; and a busty stripper whose husband may or may not have been her pimp. The gal who ran the motel was a former B-movie actress whose head shots adorned the property. In addition to telling stories of near-stardom in Hollywood, she'd fix mai tais for everyone at the pool.

When Sylvia wasn't hanging around the pool, she was in class. She took 16 credit hours during the summer session at the University of Miami. One of the qualities Sylvia and I share is taking pride in the tasks we set out to do. With an eye toward becoming a schoolteacher, Sylvia took a full load of education classes and got three As and a B. She was so conscientious about her studies that she passed on accompanying me to Cuba when the Marlins played the Havana Sugar Kings. The next year, Fidel Castro seized power in the country.

Sylvia has a passion for travel. Just recently, she returned from a two-week solo trip to Thailand and Myanmar. To this day, she regrets not visiting Havana before it was closed off to Americans. What's worse is that the University of Delaware, which approved her to take classes in Miami, would only transfer her grades back as Cs.

• • •

My Miami team consisted mostly of older players hoping for a last go-around in the majors. Baseball had taken its toll on them and their families. I recall a time at the Miami airport when the wife of one of my veteran teammates showed up at the boarding area clutching a handful of papers. Apparently she had stumbled upon a batch of letters he had written to another woman.

"You son of a bitch!" she screamed at him before ripping up the letters and tossing them in the air.

The next set of papers he saw were divorce documents.

I witnessed the seamier side of minor league life in Miami, but I also saw extraordinary grace.

The oldest player by far on the Miami team was Satchel Paige, who turned 52 midway through the 1958 season. He was a right-handed pitcher who dominated the Negro Leagues for 18 seasons but didn't have an opportunity to pitch in the majors until his early forties. Satch went 10–10 with a 2.95 ERA for Miami in 1958. It was the second season in a row that he tallied 10 wins and a sub-3.00 ERA. I was amazed by what he could still do at such an advanced age. He was thin and wiry and didn't move around really fast, but he had unbelievable command of his pitches. I'm proud to say I got to play with Satch during his last season in the Phillies organization. Remarkably, he remained active a while longer. At 59 years of age, while pitching for the Kansas City A's, he threw three scoreless innings against the Boston Red Sox.

• • •

I had a decent season in Miami but did nothing to set myself apart from the other guys hoping to get called up to the majors. I was one of five pitchers to start at least 15 games that season but the only one to finish the season with an ERA above 3.00. After four years in the minors, I still wasn't ready for the big leagues.

My return trip to Havana in 1959 came as a member of the Buffalo Bisons, who replaced the Miami Marlins as the Phillies' Triple-A affiliate.

Sylvia's studies again kept her from the trip of a lifetime. She was back finishing up a semester at the University of Delaware. By 1959, Cuba had become a volatile place, and International League officials ordered us to stay in our hotel to avoid trouble. Later that summer, gunshots rang out during a game between the Sugar Kings and the Rochester Red Wings. A Rochester coach and player were grazed by bullets, prompting the game and the rest of the series to be called off.

I got on a roll in Buffalo, pitching one complete game after another. For the first time in my professional career, I had control of the strike zone. By dramatically cutting down on walks, I didn't have to constantly pitch with runners on base. As a result, my ERA dropped significantly.

With the Phillies stumbling toward a last-place finish in the National League, it served to reason that they'd again look to the minors for pitching help. I had no doubt that Buffalo manager Kerby Farrell was keeping them apprised of my performance.

• • •

After going the distance for a fifth consecutive start, I experienced extreme pain in my right arm. I didn't think too much of it, because I figured even strong arms like mine get sore from time to time, especially after so many complete games. All of those starts took place while Lake Erie was still frozen over, and pitching in the bitter cold couldn't have helped the situation. During the third complete game, I felt tightness in my arm around the seventh inning. I rubbed hot ointment on it in the dugout and went out and finished the game. I was on a roll and didn't want to admit I was hurting. I stayed sore throughout the next two outings. I hoped a few days of rest would cure the problem. But by my next start, on Mother's Day, the pain was so acute that I had to take myself out of the game in the third inning. By that point, I could barely reach home plate with my pitches.

Sylvia was in the midst of a six-week summer course at the University of Buffalo when I returned to Philly to get my arm checked out. She was a good sport about staying in upstate New York without me.

In Philadelphia, I met with Phillies trainer Frank Wiechec to talk over the situation. I was relieved to hear Frank say he thought I had nothing more than a strain. All I needed was additional rest, he said.

Those starts for Buffalo convinced me I was a big-league-caliber pitcher. As I missed games waiting for my arm to heal, I couldn't help but worry. I saw the way shoulder and elbow injuries had turned Robin Roberts of the Phillies from a consistent 20-game winner into a sub-.500 pitcher. Robbie's natural ability and knowledge of how to pitch allowed him to remain a productive major leaguer. I, meanwhile, had yet to pitch an inning in the big leagues. If my arm didn't get better, I wouldn't have the same savvy and experience to fall back on.

On Frank's orders, I abstained from all physical activity during the winter of 1959. When I reported to spring training the following February, my condition hadn't improved. My arm still hurt and my fastball still lacked pop.

As long as I played, I never found out the exact nature of the injury. The only surgery I ever underwent came at the ripe old age of 77, when I could no longer lift my right arm.

In Buffalo, I simply tried to cope with the pain and adapt to pitching with it. In 11 starts in 1960, I pitched four complete games. With less velocity on my pitches, I relied on hitting my spots. To my coaches, it appeared I had successfully adapted to my new set of circumstances.

Those months in Buffalo included one last visit to Havana, the final trip of any International League team. As we departed Cuba after the three-game series, we saw plumes of smoke rising from American-owned oil tanks. Not long after that, the Havana Sugar Kings became the Jersey City Jerseys.

And bad arm and all, I became a member of the Philadelphia Phillies.

5

THE 1960 PHILLIES WERE NEVER going to be confused with the 1927 Yankees—or even the 1959 Phillies. Nobody understood that better than manager Eddie Sawyer. Fired two years after leading the Phillies to a National League pennant in 1950 and then rehired in 1958, only to see his team lose and lose some more, he had evidently given up hope. Following an Opening Day loss to the Reds in 1960, he announced his resignation. Before walking out the door, he muttered something about being 49 years old and wanting to live to see 50. His plan worked. Sawyer died in 1997 at the age of 87.

To the surprise of many, the Phillies went outside the organization to replace Sawyer, bringing in Gene Mauch, who had been managing the Red Sox's Triple-A affiliate in Minneapolis.

Mauch, a former journeyman infielder who played for six major league teams, had no experience as a major league manager. With his hiring, he became the youngest skipper in the game. The 1960 season marked the beginning of his 26-year managerial career with four different teams.

When I got called up to the Phillies in mid-June, the team was already 16 games out of first place. In light of the team's woes, general manager John Quinn figured he'd give some younger players a shot. To make room for me, the team demoted veteran right-handed pitcher Ruben Gomez. I narrowly missed out on becoming the first Delaware native ever to play for the Phillies. About a year earlier, pitcher Chris Short, who hailed from Milford, had earned that distinction.

With the Phillies bound for another losing season, I got a chance to prove myself as a starting pitcher.

In the first inning of my major league debut in San Francisco, I faced Willie Mays—and walked him, the second of three walks I yielded that inning. My wildness led to two Giants runs. By the time I struck out Mays in the fourth inning, we trailed 5–0. I took the loss that day.

Five days later, I started against the Cubs and gave up three runs in 6⅔ innings. I left with the game tied and got a no-decision in a 4–3 Phillies win.

I had yet to embarrass myself. I had also yet to dazzle anyone.

On June 28, 1960, I went to the mound at Connie Mack Stadium for my third major league start against the defending World Series champion Los Angeles Dodgers. As in my previous two outings, my goal was to keep us in the game and avoid an early hook from my manager. But after two walks and an error loaded the bases in the first inning, it looked like Gene might be getting some exercise. But a fly out by John Roseboro ended the threat.

It was smooth sailing from there—until the ninth inning. We led 2–0, and I had surrendered just two hits. But I gave up a hit and a walk with only one out.

Though I had thrown more than 130 pitches, Gene stuck with me. I got Roseboro to fly out and Charlie Neal to ground out to end the game. With that, I became the first Phillies rookie in more than two years to throw a shutout.

"Yes, sir, he pitched a nice game," Dodgers manager Walter Alston told reporters in the visitors' clubhouse. "He deserved to win. Only three or four foul balls were hit good."

That game boosted my confidence. On a good day, when I hit my spots, I could hold my own in the big leagues. On a bad day, when I couldn't locate my pitches, it was like I was throwing batting practice.

For the remainder of the season, I split my time between starting and relieving. I finished the year with a 3–6 record and a 4.06 ERA on a Phillies team that finished in the National League cellar.

My arm felt fine as long as I did resistance exercises and long tosses that helped improve my range of motion and arm strength. But that regimen didn't help me rediscover my good stuff. It was frustrating knowing my right arm would never be the same as it was in the minor leagues.

I had reached the majors, and my next challenge was to stay there. I knew my sore arm would make that a daily struggle. Would I be in the big leagues for one year? Five years? Ten? I had no idea. I wish I could say I was simply enjoying the moment, but in reality I walked around with the anxiety that comes with knowing you're a borderline major leaguer.

• • •

Gene came up with the brilliant idea of rooming me on the road with Turk Farrell. Turk was a decent pitcher, but his true love was the nightlife and all that came with it. Turk, Jim "Bear" Owens, and Jack "Bird" Meyer were known as The Dalton Gang. Compared to Turk and his buddies, I was a real goody-two-shoes.

After a game in Chicago, Turk approached me in the Wrigley Field clubhouse with an urgent request.

"Dallas, I'm in trouble, and you gotta help me out," he said. "I've got a stewardess flying in tonight, and I promised to take her to dinner. But I found this other gal I want to stay with for a while."

"What do you need me to do?"

"When the stewardess gets to the hotel, I need you to have dinner with her. I'll be back as soon as I can."

Late that evening, there was a knock on our hotel room door. I opened it to find a 6'0" blonde staring back at me. I hadn't done much to prepare for her visit, other than to throw on some clothes. Normally I slept in the nude, so for me, I had already gone above and beyond the call of duty.

I ordered room service for the gal and told her Turk would be back shortly. He was meeting with our manager, I explained. She and I chitchatted for a while about Turk, her life in the skies, and my rookie year with the Phillies. Soon after finishing our meal, Turk bounced in and took her off my hands.

The next day, he gave me a box from one of the Chicago department stores.

"Here, roomie, I got a present for you," he said.

I opened it to find a pair of silk pajamas.

"If you're going to entertain my broads, I want you looking good," Turk said, walking away.

Turk was a real piece of work. One time, our team plane got caught in a hellacious thunderstorm and was jerking up and down like a yo-yo. We were all pretty scared, especially Turk.

"Oh, dear God, if you get us down safely, I'll quit drinking and fooling around!" he blurted out.

The plane landed without incident. After the close call, I figured Turk would keep his word for at least a little while. No chance.

"Okay, guys, let's go get a drink and find some broads," he said as he grabbed his bags.

• • •

Through her travels with me in the minor leagues, Sylvia knew a lot about the life of a ballplayer. When I returned from road trips, she got a real kick out of my Turk stories. Off the field, the early 1960s were a special time for Sylvia and me. When I got called up to the Phillies, we moved out of my mom's house in Newport and bought a small brick house in Eastburn Acres, another suburb of Wilmington. Not long after that, Sylvia learned she was pregnant with our first child.

Like thousands of other workers from the Wilmington area, I commuted by rail to Philadelphia. On days the Phillies had a home game, I'd board a train bound for North Philadelphia station. From there, I'd make the 15-minute walk from Broad and Glenwood to Connie Mack Stadium. After games, I'd catch the train back home. That was sometimes an adventure, because the last train from North Philadelphia left at 10:30 PM. With most night games running until about 10:00, I had to hustle to get to the station on time. That meant no showering or lingering around the clubhouse. If I missed the last train from North Philly, I'd have to spend $10 on a cab ride to 30th Street Station.

I looked forward to the times when friends from Wilmington came to games—that meant I had a lift home. Sometimes Sylvia would come along with them. By all accounts, she fit right in with the other Philadelphia fans. Whenever Gene made a decision she didn't like, she let him have it. Most of the time, the decision involved removing me from a game. On one occasion, he had a light-hitting infielder named Bobby Malkmus pinch-hit for me. When Sylvia saw Malkmus walking into the on-deck circle, she loudly blurted out, "Oh no, not Malkmus!" Her exclamation prompted the woman in front of her to turn around. The woman was Malkmus' wife, who had probably heard worse considering her husband had a lifetime batting average of .215.

With so few people in the stands, voices tended to carry at Connie Mack Stadium.

At the start of the 1961 season, Gene promised his team would "win more games than anybody expects." He was wrong.

The Phillies went 22–55 at home en route to a 107-loss season. During a stretch in July and August, we dropped 23 straight games. On August 20, we mercifully got a win in the second game of a doubleheader in Milwaukee. Frank Sullivan, a pitcher who liked to say he was in the twilight of a mediocre career, came up with a plan for dealing with the hundreds of Phillies fans waiting for us at the airport upon our return from Milwaukee. "Okay, guys, we gotta spread out," he instructed. "That way, the rocks won't hit us all at once."

Despite the historic losing streak, Phillies owner Bob Carpenter and general manager John Quinn insisted Gene's job was safe. For his part, Gene seemed shell-shocked by all the losing. "I've tried everything," he told reporters after our 21st loss in a row. "If there's anything else, I'm willing to try that, too."

My 1961 season couldn't have started off better. After breaking camp with the Phillies for the first time in my career, I went the distance in my first start against San Francisco, blanking the Giants on five hits. Hall of Famers Willie Mays and Willie McCovey went a combined 0-for-8 against me.

It went downhill from there.

Later that season, Mays and the Giants got the better of me. In the first inning of game in late June, Willie whacked what I thought was a nasty curveball into the lower deck at Connie Mack Stadium. Gene wasn't pleased. "Green, you big donkey, what the hell are you throwing him curveballs for?" he yelled. "Throw him a fastball!"

When I faced Mays again in the top of the third, I started him off with two fastballs, both for strikes. My instincts told me to keep Willie on his toes by throwing a breaking ball in the dirt. But mindful of Gene's instructions, I came back at him with an inside fastball. He hit it over the roof of Connie Mack. As Willie rounded the bases, I gave my manager a piece of my mind.

"I hope you're satisfied, Gene!" I yelled into the dugout. "He hit yours a lot further than he hit mine!"

Following several rough outings, Gene relegated me to bullpen duty. After the season, the Phillies put me on a list of unprotected players available to the expansion New York Mets or Houston Colt .45s. Those teams passed on me, however, so I returned to Philadelphia.

The Phillies shocked a lot of people in 1962, finishing a game over .500, an amazing turnaround from the season before. I chipped in with six wins, including a complete-game victory over Houston. We went a combined 31–5 against the two expansion teams.

In accepting *The Sporting News* Manager of the Year Award, Gene said, "I don't want to be just another big league manager. I want to be the best in the business."

He never made it.

• • •

More than individual games, what I cherish most from my days in the major leagues are the relationships I forged. In 1963, I got to continue my friendship with Richie Ashburn, who returned to the Phillies as a broadcaster after finishing up his playing career with the Cubs and Mets.

Richie was one of the most honest and decent guys I ever came across in baseball. Sylvia and I first got to know him during spring training in the late 1950s. In an atmosphere where veterans and farm-hands didn't mix too much, Richie took me under his wing and treated me like an equal. That kind of gesture from a future Hall of Famer meant the world to me.

When I became manager of the Phillies decades later, Richie, Harry Kalas, Andy Musser, Chris Wheeler, and the rest of the broadcast team flew on the team plane with us. Their narration of 1980 is preserved on every highlight reel of that special season.

On camera, Richie gave a family-friendly performance. But behind the scenes, he wasn't shy about using salty language to question my in-game strategy. On the rare occasion I had runners on first and third with less than two outs and the pitcher up to bat, I'd call for a bunt to advance the runner on first. It was a conservative strategy intended to prevent the pitcher from hitting into a double play. Richie hated that move with a passion, because he saw it as giving up an out. "Goddamnit, Dallas, you can't do that!" he yelled one time right before the cameras started rolling on a pregame interview. "Let the pitcher swing the bat!" Not that Richie was opposed to bunting. An outstanding bunter himself, he'd sometimes work with our players on how to best lay one down.

When Richie returned to Philadelphia in '63, he joined a group of us who played pick-up basketball games during spring training and the off-season. I had nowhere near the baseball ability of Richie, Curt Simmons, Chris Short, Johnny Callison, and some of the other Phillies who took part in the games. But on the basketball court, where I had many proud moments in high school and college, I could claim a certain degree of superiority. Only Robin Roberts, who captained the Michigan State basketball team for two seasons, had bragging rights over me.

Robbie was the self-appointed team leader. Before every game, he'd say, "Alright, big boy, get the ball, throw it to me, and I'll put it in the basket."

The strategy usually worked. We took on all comers and usually came away with a win.

One time, Bobby Wine arranged for us to scrimmage against Visitation of the Blessed Virgin Mary, a church parish in North Philadelphia. Father Larkin, the parish priest, planned to raise funds by selling tickets to the exhibition.

It sounded like a worthy cause, so we accepted the invitation without even asking who exactly we'd be playing. We figured it'd be a high school team or a group of priests, but it turned out to be teachers who worked with troubled kids at a school affiliated with the church. These weren't kindly old schoolteachers. I noticed in warm-ups that quite a few of them could dunk the ball.

A pretty large crowd filed into the gymnasium to watch the parish team take on a squad that included a couple of future baseball Hall of Famers. Father Larkin had a front-row seat for the action.

From the opening tip, we took it to our opponents—at least on the scoreboard. But the teachers didn't seem to care about the score. They were too busy knocking us around.

I was getting banged around pretty hard in the lane. After a particularly flagrant foul, Richie looked over at Father Larkin and yelled, "Goddamn, your guys are the dirtiest sons of bitches I've ever played against!"

At halftime, we regrouped. Dating back to high school, I could play the game as rough as anybody. I got a little physical with the teachers in the second half.

I don't remember the final score, but I know that if someone had pledged a dollar for every foul committed that night, the parish would have made out very well.

It was exactly the type of situation Quinn wanted to avoid when he tried to ban us from playing these games out of fear one of us would get hurt. Maje McDonnell, a member of the Phillies coaching staff who also liked to shoot hoops, helped convince Quinn to let us keep playing.

• • •

In 1963, Gene got closer to his lofty goal of being the best manager in the business by guiding the Phillies to a record of 87–75.

My future with the team hinged largely on Gene's opinion of me. I was never going to be the ace of his pitching staff, so I went out and did the little things Gene admired. In 1963, I bunted when asked and didn't commit an error. I also put together my best year on the mound, going 7–5 with a 3.23 ERA in 14 starts and 26 relief appearances. Above all, I worked hard and learned every facet of the game.

It was hard to know, however, if any of this impressed a manager who had a reputation for loathing pitchers and younger players. I was a pitcher, and at least for a while longer, still a younger player.

Ruben Amaro Sr., my Phillies teammate from 1960 to 1964, describes Gene this way: "Gene Mauch wasn't an easy manager. He was a very ornery man who was angry at the world. He was even angrier that the teams he managed in the early 1960s were too young to compete with the rest of the league. But he also had trouble handling a team once it started winning." In the words of *Philadelphia Daily News* columnist Stan Hochman, Gene was "a woeful people person."

Gene considered himself a manager and a strategist, but not a teacher. He demanded that players be fully formed major leaguers the day they joined his team. This attitude was difficult to understand considering he was 34 years old when the Phillies hired him and not that far removed from his own days as a rookie.

His in-game strategy reflected his disdain for young players. For a while, Gene platooned Ruben and Bobby Wine at shortstop. He'd fill out a lineup card with one or the other's name on it, but if he changed his mind once the game started, he'd have no qualms about pinch-hitting for the starter *in the first inning*. If you're going to bench a guy, then bench him. But that way of handling players left us all walking on eggshells.

Gene didn't care if he made you look like an ass, either. In a game against the Cubs, rather than coming to the mound to take me out, he stayed on the bench and signaled his displeasure with my outing by putting two fingers in his mouth and letting out a piercing whistle. I left the ball on the mound and walked off the field. Yep, Gene was a lousy people person, all right. That act was as unprofessional as it gets.

Gene hated to lose, which must have made the 1960 and 1961 seasons agonizing for him. Then again, he might have realized the futility of getting worked up about a lost cause. Once we started winning more often, he seemed to take every defeat personally.

And he threw some legendary fits.

After a tough loss at Houston in September 1963, a game that ended on a hit by rookie Joe Morgan, Gene raced into the clubhouse and with a couple of violent sweeps of his arm cleared a buffet table loaded with ribs, chickens, and salads. By the time the team came off the field, he had retreated to the shower. We looked around at the mess and wondered if a Houston fan had sabotaged our postgame meal. Some of the food was still dripping off lockers, indicating that whoever committed the crime was still in the area. A teammate with a future in detective work put two and two together.

"I think Gene did this," he said.

A few minutes later, we heard the click-clack of Gene's plastic shower shoes on the hard clubhouse floor. We all stood in silence as he entered the dressing area. All of us had our street clothes on, except for Wes Covington and Tony Gonzalez, whose wardrobe had taken the brunt of the flying food.

Gene looked at their stained clothes and growled, "Buy yourselves a couple of suits and give me the bill."

After Gene walked back to the shower area, Gonzalez picked a rib up out of Covington's shoe. "Hey, roomie," he asked Covington. "Do you think this is still good?"

• • •

Back in those days, a college boy like me was assumed to have the intelligence and communication skills necessary to advocate for his teammates' needs. That's how I, by default, became the Phillies' player representative. The Major League Baseball Players Association formed in 1954, but until Marvin Miller came on the scene 12 years later, it didn't really have much clout.

Player rep was a thankless job in the early 1960s. The most frequent complaint I fielded dealt with the facilities at Connie Mack
Stadium. Our clubhouse had a radio, but no TV. We had stools, but
no chairs. And perhaps worst of all, our training room was located in
a room above the clubhouse, meaning an injured player had to walk
up a flight of stairs to get treatment. Quinn brushed aside all of these
gripes.

On the road, there was a rule stating we had to wait for our beat
writers to finish their game stories before returning to the team hotel.
Gene also took his sweet time getting on the bus after games. That
meant sitting around for two hours before leaving the stadium.

My teammates felt this was unacceptable. They agreed the bus
should depart for the hotel exactly one hour after the end of the game.
I mentioned this demand to Quinn, but all I got back was a grunt.

Back in Houston for another game, we decided to unilaterally put
the policy in effect. The entire team sat on the bus, but several writers,
our traveling secretary, and Gene were nowhere in sight.

"Hey, Big D, we got two minutes," someone yelled from the back
of the bus.

A few more minutes passed. Some writers scurried onto the bus,
but still no Gene.

Figuring there was safety in numbers and surely a cab somewhere
on the premises of the ballpark, I gave the bus driver the green light
to leave.

The bus started rolling away, but the driver missed the entrance
to the freeway and had to circle around to where we started. And
there were Gene and our traveling secretary. The doors swung open,
and they got on.

I think I saw steam coming out of Gene's ears.

"This goddamn bus doesn't leave until I tell it to leave!" he fumed.

It got real quiet. Then a couple of teammates finally broke the silence.

"But Dallas said to go."

Ah, the life of a player rep in the early 1960s.

When Jim Bunning came to the Phillies from the Tigers after the 1963 season, our complaints got taken more seriously. As a veteran who had established himself as one of the better pitchers in the game, Jim wasn't a guy Quinn could send down to the minors or trade. In other words, he wasn't like the rest of us. Even Robin Roberts had fallen out of favor with the Phillies, who sold him to the Yankees after the 1961 season.

Quinn and Phillies ownership established another rule that forbade us from leaving tickets for friends or family when we played the Dodgers or Giants. Both teams still had large East Coast fan bases and Quinn hoped games against Los Angeles and San Francisco would sell out. A sign on a mirror in the clubhouse spelled out the rule: "No tickets/No passes for Dodgers/Giants."

My teammates already were unhappy about their families being given nose-bleed seats. But no seats at all? That crossed the line. When Bunning heard about the rule, he went upstairs to Quinn's office and had a word with him. After a few minutes, Jim came back down, walked over to the mirror, and ripped up the sign.

A few years later, Bunning and Roberts were instrumental in bringing Miller over to the players association. With that, a new era of baseball began.

• • •

John Quinn was one of the toughest general managers you'd ever run across. He was old-school and hard on everyone, from his players to his subordinates. At home, he was probably hard on his family. He came to work every single day dressed to the nines in a coat and tie, and he stayed that way the entire day. The son of a baseball owner and general manager, he felt you couldn't run a team professionally if you didn't dress professionally.

Mr. Quinn, as players addressed him, was also a heavy drinker. And when he drank, he became erratic. He was sharp as a tack earlier in his career, but as the years went by, he developed an off-putting demeanor.

I experienced that side of him after the 1963 season, which turned out to be my best season in the big leagues. When Quinn sent me my contract for the following year, I was surprised to see I hadn't earned a raise. I wrote him a note explaining why I felt my performance warranted an extra $500.

At 29, I wasn't getting any younger, and I felt I needed to stick up for myself. A few days passed before his secretary called me at home and said he wanted to meet with me.

On the appointed day, I went up to Philadelphia to make my case for a raise. Quinn greeted me with, "Hey, Dallas, how are you? How's the family? Good, good, good!" It was classic Quinn small talk. He loved to ask and answer his own questions. The players joked that someone could say, "Well, Mr. Quinn, my wife's dying of cancer, and my kids got eaten by a bear," and he would still respond, "Good, good, good!"

I knew he didn't like to waste time, so I got right to the point. "I had a nice season, Mr. Quinn, and I think I've earned a raise," I said.

I waited for an answer but got none. He didn't say anything. He just sat at his huge desk staring out the window. I didn't say anything, either. It remained silent for a long while. Occasionally, he would refocus his attention on something other than what was going on outside his window. But he never looked at me.

"Well, it was nice meeting with you, Mr. Quinn," I finally said, fleeing his office.

Without a contract, I couldn't participate in spring training activities. There was a picture of me in one of the Philadelphia papers peering through a chain-link fence at my teammates taking batting practice. In the photo, you can see Quinn standing a few feet away from me.

A few days into camp, Phillies owner Bob Carpenter called me and said, "Sign the damn thing, Dallas. You don't want this to go on any longer."

We ended up working out a deal that allowed everyone to save their pride. Per its terms, I would get an extra $500 at the end of the season if we drew a certain number of fans to Connie Mack Stadium in 1964. It was an unrealistic figure that we had no way of reaching. We drew a record-setting number of fans in 1964, but not enough for me to collect the bonus.

That meeting remains my most vivid memory of Quinn. I guess I was lucky. Some of my teammates saw his uglier side. Ruben Amaro Sr. still talks about Quinn's habit of calling him late at night and berating him.

Quinn wasn't all bad. The Jack Tar Hotel in Clearwater, our spring training home, refused to rent rooms to our African American players, forcing them to stay in apartments and eat their meals in a segregated part of town. As the team's player representative, I went to Quinn in 1963 and asked if we could switch hotels to protest the Jack Tar's discriminatory policy. To his credit, he agreed to my request and made arrangements to move to a motel over the causeway, near Tampa.

The story didn't have a happy ending, however. We moved the whole team to the other motel, which was owned by George Steinbrenner. On our first goddamn day there, Ruben went down to eat at the motel restaurant—and they wouldn't serve him. We said, "Screw this," and went back to the Jack Tar.

• • •

The mouth that roared wasn't doing so much roaring in those days, at least not in the newspapers. Behind the scenes, however, I enjoyed frank conversations with teammates about Gene, our team, and the game in general. The Philadelphia teams of the early 1960s had genuine camaraderie. Our common bond was that Gene had managed to put the fear of God in all of us. Even Johnny Callison, who made three All-Star appearances with the Phillies, was scared to death about getting sent back to the minors.

"Christ, Johnny, you're playing every day," I told him. "I haven't been on the mound in eight days. If I screw up, I might not get back out there for another month."

I can only remember one time that a conversation with a teammate turned into an argument. It happened when a bunch of us were yakking and Art Mahaffey, who pitched for the Phillies from 1960 to 1965, confessed to me he didn't necessarily want other pitchers on the staff to do well.

"If you're pitching, I don't root for you, because you never know who might end up taking your job," he said.

Art was four years younger than I was and enjoying considerable success the majors. In a game against the Cubs in 1961, he struck out 17 batters, a Phillies team record that still stood at the end of the 2012 season.

I had a hard time understanding his way of thinking. Then again, he was the same guy who demanded to know why Quinn had promoted me instead of him from the minors in 1960.

"Jesus Christ, Art," I said. "We're a team. You have to root for your team. When you go out there, I'm rooting like hell for you. I hope you strike everyone out. If you look good, we all look good."

Art didn't buy it. He firmly believed that the success of others, even if they were teammates, could only hurt him.

In all honesty, he didn't have anything to worry about from me. I was the 24th or 25th man on the roster every season.

I'd like to be able to say that my major league career was marked by sheer enjoyment. But I don't think I ever really stopped to reflect on how lucky I was to have made it to the game's highest level. Instead I was locked in a constant battle with myself.

As my teammate Bobby Wine says, "We were at the mercy of the manager and general manager. Nobody dared buck the system. If you did, your butt was off to Triple-A."

In a way, my experience toughened me in the long run. I trusted my baseball abilities and instincts, even if my body wouldn't allow me to perform at an elite level. The adversity I faced as a player helped prepare me well for the future. At the time, I didn't view it that way, however.

6

My 1963 Topps baseball card featured this bit of information about me: "Once plagued by wildness, Dallas can now consistently get the ball where he wants it."

Unfortunately, just as often I put the ball exactly where hitters wanted it. And after a couple of subpar outings in 1964, I was back in the minors.

I badly wanted to be in Philadelphia that August helping the Phillies sew up a pennant, but instead I was a member of the Triple-A Arkansas Travelers.

This wasn't supposed to be how the 1964 season played out. I had grinded out a major league existence long enough to experience one of those magical years where everything falls into place for a team. But a few lousy games did me in. And all I could do upon my return to the Phillies in September was watch as the team blew a chance to go to the World Series.

That season, coupled with the death of my father, sapped my drive to stay in the game. I was angry that my damaged right arm couldn't make the pitches it used to. And I was furious at the Phillies for considering me minor league talent and dumping me just when it looked like we were going to win a pennant.

• • •

During the off-season, I returned home to Delaware and contemplated a life after baseball. I met with a businessman in Chadds Ford, Pennsylvania, whose company serviced all the big farms in that area. As a local kid made good, I had helped him drum up business by joining him on sales presentations. We got to know each other pretty well, but Sylvia was suspicious of the guy. She thought he was more interested in me helping him improve his social life than his business. "Of course he likes having you with him at bars," she said. "It helps him meet girls." I ultimately turned down his offer to come work for him full-time. It was a wise choice. About a year later, he lost his business.

A couple of buddies at the DuPont Company in nearby Wilmington helped me get interviews there. And a former ballplayer friend of mine, Harry Anderson, who worked for a machine company in Elkton, Maryland, that manufactured heavy machinery, arranged for me to meet with the owner of the company.

"Dallas, you've got all these years in baseball, and the game's been a part of you forever," Harry's boss told me. "If you come here, you might end up running the company, but you're going to start low."

Sylvia shared that point of view. She had seen the ups and downs of my playing career, because she had been by my side every step of the way. She knew the '64 season had taken a toll on me and encouraged me to wait a while longer before deciding to write off baseball.

Coming to terms with my father's death helped straighten out my thought process. He and I were never close, and for much of my adult life I resented him for allowing alcohol to take over his life. His drinking caused him to lose the family business, but it also caused him to look in the mirror and confront what he saw. He loved fixing cars, but because of his addiction, he couldn't do that for a living anymore.

He also saw he had been neglecting his family. He began to take an interest in my career, but not in an overt way or because he hoped my salary could help support the family. It was because he was proud of me. It crushed him to see me sent to the minors in 1964. And I held that against the Phillies, particularly after he passed away.

In hindsight, I realized the Phillies weren't to blame. I hadn't pitched well enough to assure myself a spot on the roster all season. Everybody has to earn his keep, and I hadn't. That experience gave me insight that I later used when I became a major league manager and general manager.

• • •

The Phillies wanted to give me an opportunity to play in the majors, if not for them, then for a team willing to pay a few bucks for me.

At the end of spring training in 1965, they sold me to the Washington Senators on a 30-day trial basis. If the Senators liked my performance, they could pony up $20,000 to keep me. If they weren't satisfied with their purchase, they could return me to Philadelphia.

It bothered me that the Phillies didn't want me anymore, but I decided I would no longer take baseball personnel matters personally.

I did okay with the Senators, starting a couple of games and relieving in others. According to the terms of my sale, Washington wouldn't have had to pay the Phillies a nickel if I accepted a demotion to one of their minor league teams. So, they tried to demote me. That's how cheap the Senators were at that time.

If I was going to finish my career in the minor leagues, I wanted it to be with friends and allies in the Philadelphia organization. So, I returned to the Phillies and reported back to Arkansas to finish out the 1965 season.

My wife, Sylvia, and our two young children, Dana and John, had just arrived in Little Rock to move into an apartment that would be our home until the Phillies decided to recall me. *If* the Phillies decided to recall me, that is.

When I got to the apartment complex, Sylvia met me outside our unit with a frown on her face. "We're leaving," she informed me. "It's filthy."

So, we went back to the motel where I'd been staying until the apartment got cleaned up.

It sure wasn't the big leagues. I remember getting stuck on an airport runway in Little Rock after an all-night flight from the Pacific Northwest. The Spokane Indians, managed by future Phillies skipper Danny Ozark, sat on the Trans World Airlines flight with us. On our way east, we had dropped off the Denver or Salt Lake City team. Or maybe it was both. That's how long the flight felt. The Pacific Coast League must have gotten a heck of a deal on the booking of the TWA Constellation, a huge plane with three tail wings best known for making military transports during World War II.

I guess some signals got crossed, because when we landed at 5:00 AM, no one was at the airport to roll a stairwell up to the plane. It was already 90 degrees in Little Rock, and the plane didn't have air conditioning. All I wanted was for somebody to open the goddamn doors!

We waited and waited. Finally, my teammate John Boozer, a country boy from South Carolina who liked spitting tobacco juice in the air and catching it in his mouth, had an idea.

"If they're not coming for us, we're just going to have to go to them," he said.

Booze convinced the flight crew to open the cabin door and release an escape rope. One by one, we shimmied down the rope onto the tarmac.

• • •

The Phillies came back to earth in 1965. A season after coming agonizingly close to a pennant, they finished sixth in the National League. They wouldn't sniff the playoffs again until the 1970s.

I can't help but think Gene Mauch's style hurt the Phillies in the long run. He managed the team to winning records from 1962 to 1967, but his lack of people skills undermined the team's chances of getting to the next level.

Gene's inherent mistrust of younger players was one of his most significant flaws. In 1965, the Phillies had a 22-year-old pitcher who had performed well in the minors and in his first outings in the majors. But Gene simply didn't like Ferguson Jenkins, so he had general manager John Quinn trade him to the Cubs for two pitchers in their midthirties. "It's the best deal we could have made," Gene told the newspapers at the time. "I think it complemented our staff exactly the way we wanted." The pitchers acquired by Philadelphia stuck around the majors another couple of years. Fergie reeled off six straight 20-win seasons with the Cubs during a Hall of Fame career.

In June 1968, with the Phillies at .500, Gene got fired. He went on to manage the Expos, the Twins, and the California Angels. Though he got close a few times, he never managed in a World Series.

I'll be the first to admit that Gene possessed extraordinary baseball knowledge. And I'd like to think some of it rubbed off on me. He was a firm believer in the value of fundamentals and playing the game the right way, offensively and defensively. He expected his teams to build big innings by hitting in the clutch and running the bases well. I embraced this philosophy when I later became a manager. For all his faults, which included the belief that all of his players were dummies, Gene influenced me a lot.

• • •

As one of the few major or minor leaguers who remained in the Philadelphia area during the off-season, I became a regular on the banquet circuit, representing the Phillies at all manner of engagements in the Delaware Valley. Every late fall and winter for several years, I appeared and spoke at about 75 events, earning $25 a pop. In the process, I handed out more goddamn Little League trophies than you could shake a stick at. Occasionally, I walked away with some hardware myself. As a sign of appreciation for my attendance, some of the groups would present me with a plaque.

There were no GPSs back then, so I spent a lot of time getting lost on the back roads of many towns and suburbs in Pennsylvania, New Jersey, and Delaware. That made me nervous as hell, because I knew the banquets couldn't start without me.

Eventually, I got my routine down pat. My go-to opening line was, "I know your banquet committee requested a 20-game winner. Well, here I am. Unfortunately, it took me five years to get there." That always got a yak. So did my Gene Mauch stories.

I also stated an opinion that probably didn't sit too well with some of the coaches in the room.

"I hear a lot of people say it doesn't matter if you win or lose; it's how you play the game," I began. "I disagree. When you hire a lawyer, do you care how he presents the case? No—the only important thing is whether he wins or loses. Would you be happy with a heart surgeon who tried his best but didn't perform a procedure correctly? Of course not. Winning matters in terms of your growth as an athlete. Winning is important in life."

After my speech, every kid stepped forward to accept a trophy for participation.

Sylvia joined me at one of the events, which honored a local fire department. Appropriately, I guess, the event took place at the fire house. I was about to give my speech when the goddamn siren went off! We had to take a break until the fire engine was loaded up and on its way. That was Sylvia's last banquet.

Every now and then, I'm approached by men in their fifties who say they heard me speak at a Little League banquet in Downingtown,

Ardmore, or some other locality. That was a long time ago. My rousing oratory must have made quite an impression on them.

• • •

The Phillies moved their Triple-A affiliate to San Diego for 1966, and that's where I played that year until the Phillies sold me again, this time in the middle of the season, to the Mets. After four major league relief appearances with New York, the Mets returned me to the Phillies, who immediately put me back in Triple-A. I led San Diego with 14 wins that season, leaving no doubt I was still a very capable minor league pitcher.

Having turned 32 during my brief stay with the Mets, my playing days were winding down. But I knew I wanted to stay in baseball in some capacity. After the 1966 season, I talked over my options with Phillies farm director Paul Owens and Ruly Carpenter, who was gradually taking over the day-to-day operations of the organization from his father.

We agreed I still had plenty left in my arm to pitch in the minors, so it was decided I'd spend the 1967 season as a player-coach in Reading, Pennsylvania, the location of the Phillies' new Double-A affiliate. Pope, who himself had been a player-manager in Philadelphia's farm system, felt the Reading gig would prepare me well for a future job in the front office. In preparation for the assignment, I went through spring training in Clearwater as Reading's pitching coach and continued in that capacity during the season, in addition to pitching every fourth day.

The season in Reading turned out to be a lot of fun. Playing in a fifth different town for manager Frank Lucchesi, I posed a sub-2.00 ERA for the first time in 13 seasons of professional ball. I also got a taste of working with young players, including 21-year-old shortstop Larry Bowa.

At least one pitcher on the squad hardly needed any tutelage from me. Released by the Cubs earlier in the season, future Hall of Famer Robin Roberts was attempting a comeback with the Phillies. At the age of 40, he was back in the minors for the first time in 19 years.

Here was a guy with 286 major league wins playing in shabby stadiums with dingy, cramped clubhouses and lousy pitching mounds. But the man who is today memorialized with a bronze statue outside of Citizens Bank Park in Philadelphia was determined to work his way back to the majors. He pitched well in his time at Reading, going 5–3 with a 2.48 ERA and striking out 65 batters against just seven walks.

Robbie and I had been friends for a long time, and our time in Reading brought us even closer together. My association with him is one I'll always treasure. He was a wonderful guy with a sharp baseball mind. I loved talking pitching with him.

In mid-June, a spot on the Phillies' major league roster opened up after pitcher Chris Short got hurt running in the outfield before a game. Robbie was battling a leg injury at the time. A few days later he ended his comeback attempt.

Much to my surprise, I got the call to Philadelphia to replace Short.

At that time, players needed five full years in the majors to qualify for a pension. I was 108 days shy of that, so Bob Carpenter saw to it that I got recalled to the big league club. It was a very nice gesture on his part. The chance to pitch one last time for the Phillies and get my pension provided me with closure. And it eliminated any lingering resentment I felt toward the organization for demoting me to the minors in 1964.

The Reading pitchers were in capable hands in my absence. Lucchesi was a veteran manager who knew how to handle players.

It was just like old times in Philadelphia. In two of my first four outings, I got absolutely bombed. In the other two, I pitched well.

• • •

After the 1967 season, I retired from the game with my sights set on joining the Phillies front office. But Pope had other plans for me.

"Dallas, you're not coming in immediately," he informed me. "I know you want to join us right away, but you're going to manage our Class-A team in South Dakota."

I had seen small-town America during minor league stops in Mattoon, Illinois, and Reidsville, North Carolina. And with my playing career over, I looked forward to settling down with my growing family. A job in South Dakota managing short-season Class-A ball, even for just a few months, didn't appeal to me.

Fortunately, my relationship with Pope allowed for brutal honesty.

"There's no way in hell I'm doing that," I told him. "I feel like I'm ready to come into the front office right now."

"Nope, Dallas, you might feel like you're ready, but you won't really be ready until you know what it's like to handle 25 guys all by yourself, two or three thousand miles from the home office."

Damn that Pope and his superior logic!

I accepted the assignment.

I was supposed to be paid $7,000 to manage the South Dakota team. That was $10,000 less than I earned in my final season in the majors. I had to mount another protest: "Christ, Pope, I have three kids and one on the way! I can't live on that."

Pope pulled some strings and got me a few extra thousand dollars.

At spring training in 1968, still just 33, I took my place alongside all the older coaches who had been in the Phillies organization for years. I felt accepted right away by Lucchesi, Andy Seminick, Bob Wellman, and Al Widmar. They were all solid baseball guys who made me feel part of the family.

I knew Pope intended to send one of his guys to Huron to check on things. That was fine with me—as long as that person wasn't Lou Kahn. Lou was Pope's right-hand man, a real old-school baseball guy whose duties included evaluating the organization's personnel. He was also a real pain in the ass, in my opinion. Over the course of my playing career, I had crossed paths with him several times. He drank a lot and would often come to the ballpark a little shaky. He'd sit on an aluminum chair and bark orders, instructions, and complaints, all while spitting out tobacco juice which ended up all over his shirt and jacket.

I took Pope aside to make an important request: "Whatever you do, please don't send Lou Kahn out to me in Huron. I think he's an embarrassment to the organization, and I don't want someone like that looking over my shoulder."

Before I left for South Dakota, I got the nicest send-off I ever could have imagined from the Reading Phillies, who held a "Dallas Green Night" before a game at Municipal Stadium. Though I only played part of one season for the team, I built some solid friendships there. A lot of my friends from throughout the Delaware Valley made the trip out to Reading for the event.

• • •

In mid-June, Sylvia and I packed up our station wagon with sleeping bags and pillows and drove in shifts from our Delaware home to South Dakota. On our way across the country, we heard on the radio that Bobby Kennedy had been assassinated at a California hotel. Sylvia, who was more politically active than I was, took the news hard. I viewed it with disgust. Just two months after Martin Luther King Jr. had been killed, another nut with a gun had shaken the country with an act of violence.

When we got to Huron, the first people there to greet us were Lou Kahn and his wife, Esther. I made nice with Lou, but as soon as I got inside our rented home, I called Pope and screamed at him for five straight minutes. Then he screamed back at me, "He's staying! He's part of the organization, and he's staying!"

As was usually the case, Pope knew what he was doing.

I didn't let Lou get in my way as I settled in and surveyed the players I had to work with for the upcoming Northern League season. I didn't think too much about how I would handle the team. I figured my style as manager would naturally flow from my experiences as a player. I considered myself a hard worker and a fierce competitor, and I would work to make sure the teenagers under my command showed similar commitment and fire.

From the get-go, the team played lousy, losing game after game. That drove me crazy, and I took my frustration out on my players. I started holding workouts twice a day, once in the morning and once again before an evening game.

My No. 1 rule was every manager's No. 1 rule: get to the ballpark on time.

The day one of my pitchers showed up late for practice, I told him to start running and to keep running until I told him to stop. While he was doing laps, the rest of the team took batting and fielding practice. Then everybody hit the showers. I was under the spray when I remembered the kid was still out there running.

I stressed to my players that they were professionals now and competing against guys with similar backgrounds and abilities. "You're no better than anybody else until you prove it," I'd say. "The only way you're going to do that is to outwork them."

Other than not winning games, I thought I was doing a pretty effective job running the team.

A couple of experiences in Huron really stand out in my mind. One happened on a summer evening when I was with the team on a road trip. Being from the East Coast, Sylvia and I knew very little about tornadoes. At around 7:00 PM that night, Sylvia and the kids were upstairs in our house when all the lights started dimming. It was an otherwise sunny day, so Sylvia didn't know what to make of it. A few minutes later a tornado ripped a path through Huron. Somehow, it didn't cause much damage, though it did knock out a light standard at the ballpark.

Oddly enough, the other incident also involved damage to Huron's Memorial Ball Park. We had a kid named Allen Bowers, an outfielder who was the fastest player on the team. In one of our games, an opposing player lifted a fly ball to right field that Bowers went after with great gusto. He sprinted toward the outfield fence, and as the ball left the park, he ran right *through* the fence. The moment was preserved by an almost cartoonish wooden outline of his body.

• • •

In Huron, I first met Manny Trillo, an amateur free agent from Venezuela. He was 17 years old, skinny as a rail, and didn't speak a word of English. After taking one look at him, I decided to make my first personnel decision as manager. Manny had been a catcher back in Latin America, but there was no way I was going to put this fragile-looking teenager behind the plate. I tried him out at shortstop and third base that season. Later he found a home at second base.

I had to keep tabs on 38 different players in Huron, but I found time to give Manny a little extra attention. He was one of the few Latin kids on the team. The Phillies didn't see an influx of Spanish-speaking players until Pope and I hired Ruben Amaro Sr. as a scout in 1973. I could only imagine how difficult it was for Manny at that time. In the lower minor leagues, you make peanuts. Some of the players had pocket money from their parents or past summer jobs. I slipped Manny a few bucks here and there, because I knew he had nothing.

I always admired the Latin players who came to this country with only the shirts on their backs and a dream of making the major leagues. During my first year playing in the minors, I befriended Orlando Cepeda, then 17 and playing for a team in Kokomo, Indiana. I pitched against him one night, and when I saw him off to himself after the game, I invited him out to dinner. I don't think Orlando ever forgot that. Manny didn't forget our time together, either. He didn't hit much that season in Huron and went to the Oakland A's in the Rule 5 draft two years later. Thankfully, Pope reacquired him a few years after that, and I got another chance to manage him.

Manny and Greg Luzinski took strikingly different paths to Huron. Before he became known as Bull, Greg was a kid from Chicago chosen by the Phillies in the first round of the 1968 draft. He was a natural hitter who slugged about half our team's home runs that season. He and Manny were the same height, but Bull outweighed Manny by nearly 100 pounds. I thought he was a little heavy, so I worked his ass off with running and drills. If he hadn't been 17 years old and trying to impress the organization, I'm sure Bull would have told me off. Instead, he was willing to do whatever was asked of him. That wouldn't be the case later in his career, as I found out all too well when I became the manager in Philadelphia.

A few weeks before our last game, Sylvia, in the eighth month of pregnancy, flew back to Philadelphia. Around that time, Pope and Phillies general manager John Quinn came out to South Dakota to announce the organization was moving its Class-A team out of Huron. So there I was, alone in South Dakota, managing a lousy baseball team in a town the Phillies were about to abandon. The invitations to dinners and other functions suddenly stopped coming. That's the fickleness of minor league baseball. The town elders could forgive me for not winning games, but they didn't want to have anything to do with a lame duck manager. The greatest help to me during those days was Lou Kahn. We talked a lot of baseball. Now that I was a manager, I came to see him as a valuable resource. He and Esther ended up becoming good friends of mine.

We went 26–43 and finished next to last in the Northern League. By winning our last game of the season, we moved past the Aberdeen Pheasants and out of last place. Our whole team was proud of that.

You never know how careers are going to turn out. At Huron, my best pitcher was Denny Lortscher, who accounted for eight of our 26 wins. My best hitter by far was John Magnuson, whose average was 50 points higher than anybody on the team who got more than a couple of at-bats. Neither guy made it past Class-A ball. Luzinski and Trillo were two of only four players from that Huron team who ended up making the majors.

• • •

When Pope and I met after the season, I hoped to hear my apprenticeship as a minor league manager was over. No such luck. Pope still didn't think I was ready for the front office. He told me he wanted me to manage a year of rookie ball in Pulaski, Virginia.

I wished I could say, "For chrissakes, Pope, I just led a team to a championship! What more do you want from me?" But in reality, I had managed a team that barely avoided last place.

When I got down to Pulaski in the summer of 1969, I couldn't believe what a mess our stadium was. The grass at Calfee Park was long and the infield was rocky. I called Pope right away, and he dispatched one of the Phillies' best grounds crew guys down to Virginia. Between the two of us, we redid the entire field and rebuilt the pitcher's mound.

Crisis averted, I went into the season determined to improve on my dismal record in Huron. We had some quality ballplayers on the Pulaski team. One of them was Mike Anderson, our first-round pick in 1969. He crushed the ball that season, giving me every reason to think he'd develop into a wonderful major leaguer. Because of his athletic ability, some of us thought he had more promise than Luzinski. By the time Anderson was 22, he had been penciled in as the Phillies' starting right fielder. But during spring training in 1973, he got beaned in the head by Clay Carroll of the Reds. He suffered a severe concussion and that probably curbed his potential as a player. Baseball can be a cruel sport sometimes.

Pulaski was a different kind of place. And by that, I mean it was a redneck Southern town. There's no other way to put it. Sylvia was working on a research paper the summer we spent down there. The topic was President Abraham Lincoln's suspension of the writ of habeas corpus in 1861. She had become an expert on the Civil War and was pretty enthralled with Lincoln and his presidency. Well, one night we were at a cocktail party at the home of the owner of the Pulaski club, and Sylvia happened to mention her thesis to him.

"You're writing about that sumbitch!" he said, almost spitting out his drink.

This was a time when race relations in the South remained tense.

We had a black base-running coach named Spence Henry. One night he was in the stands watching a game when a black player came to the plate. A guy behind Spence shouted, "Throw him a watermelon!" Spence turned around and scowled at the man. He then surveyed the rest of the stands and saw dozens of white faces glaring back at him. Sensing he might be in trouble, Spence turned back around and before the next pitch shouted, "Throw him a watermelon!"

I was glad I wasn't spending more than a few months in Pulaski. And I know Sylvia was, too. But it ended up being time well spent. We won the Appalachian League championship, which made me very proud.

Back in Philadelphia, I had another confab with Pope and Ruly.

"Dallas, you know how we do things now," Pope said. "I want to focus on scouting, and I'm going to let you run the minor leagues the way you see fit."

And with that, I became the Phillies' assistant director of minor leagues and scouting.

7

In the Phillies front office, I gained a completely different perspective of the game. As a player, I had no control over anything other than my own performance. I went out and tried to pitch well enough to earn a contract and keep myself in the majors. I was constantly being judged. Now, I was one of the judges.

A few days after I started my new job, the Phillies pulled off a trade with the Cardinals that created a stir in the baseball world.

Following a 99-loss season in 1969, the Phillies cut ties with disgruntled first baseman Richie Allen, who had carried the team offensively for years. The biggest name we got in return was outfielder Curt Flood.

I was sorry to see Richie go. In addition to respecting his athletic ability, I genuinely liked the man. It disappointed me that he couldn't control the devils in him that led him to drink and act out. Nobody could hit a ball farther than Richie, who possessed tremendous raw talent and baseball instincts. If he had been in a better frame of mind during his career, I have no doubt he would have become a first-ballot Hall of Famer. But the racism he experienced at Triple-A Little Rock in 1963 took a toll on him. So did some of the treatment he received from Gene Mauch.

Over the course of his seven seasons with the team, Richie developed a turbulent relationship with the Phillies and the city of Philadelphia. He was regularly subjected to verbal abuse and occasionally hit by flying objects at the ballpark. Then there was his well-publicized fistfight with teammate Frank Thomas, who swung a bat at Richie during the dust-up. Richie once commented, "I can play anywhere: first, third, left field…anywhere but Philadelphia."

The time had come to grant his wish. Richie took the next flight to St. Louis.

But Flood never arrived in Philadelphia.

It upset Flood that the Cardinals traded him. It disgusted him that he had been dealt to a team with such a long history of losing. As a Cardinal, he saw the futility of the Phillies firsthand. In 1969, the expansion Montreal Expos, managed by Gene Mauch, lost 110 games but still managed to beat the Phillies 11 out of 18 times. That was atrocious.

There was another dimension to Flood's refusal to join the Phillies. He, like Allen, was black, and Flood questioned whether Philadelphia treated its black ballplayers well. It's true that some of the attacks on Allen in Philadelphia had a racial component. It's also true the Phillies were the last National League team to integrate. But I think Flood crossed the line with his insinuation that Philadelphia fans were racist. I would have wholeheartedly endorsed his sentiment that our fans were an angry and hostile bunch during this period, but that was because the Phillies were a lousy baseball team. Every town has its racists, and unfortunately some of them go to ballgames. But in my opinion, most Philadelphia fans booed black and white players with equal enthusiasm.

Flood appealed the trade to Major League Baseball commissioner Bowie Kuhn. With the backing of the players union and its leader, the late Marvin Miller, he asked Kuhn to void the deal and declare him a free agent. He argued that he should have a say in where he played and not be bought and sold against his will.

Kuhn denied the request, so Flood took the fight to federal court. He lost his lawsuit, but the players union was galvanized by his efforts. Before long, Miller negotiated a change to the reserve clause that allowed players to become free agents.

Rather than report to the Phillies, Flood sat out the entire 1970 season. As compensation, the Cardinals sent us two minor leaguers, including Willie Montanez, who went on to have a few nice seasons for us. Knowing Flood would continue to boycott us, we traded him to the Washington Senators after the 1970 season.

Flood took his unwillingness to play for the Phillies and turned it into a larger cause. The controversy provided an early glimpse of the players union's growing clout. I never imagined the case would have such a ripple effect.

Less than a decade earlier, I was the Phillies' player representative and a believer in the importance of fair pay, pensions, and better working conditions. But now that I worked in the front office, I found myself toeing the party line. That wasn't usually my style, but I saw no point in opposing general manager John Quinn, who hated the union. On top of that, I needed time to sort out how I really felt about these shifting dynamics in baseball.

• • •

My first season in the Phillies executive offices was the last season for Connie Mack Stadium. The North Philadelphia ballpark, which was built in 1909, had seen a lot of baseball as the longtime home of the Phillies and the old Philadelphia A's. But the park had become a relic. Following the lead of owners in Houston, Pittsburgh, Atlanta, and Cincinnati, the Carpenters arranged to move the team into a modern facility in a less congested area of town.

I had a lot of affection for Connie Mack Stadium. I grew up listening to Phillies games on the radio, keeping score as I rooted for the home team. I had the thrill of playing parts of six seasons in the place. It's where the Phillies played in the World Series in 1950, where the team experienced a historic collapse in 1964, and where millions of baseball fans had spent summer afternoons and evenings.

On the last day at Connie Mack, we played the Montreal Expos in a game to decide which team would wind up in the National League East cellar. Only a couple thousand fans showed up for the first two games of the series, but our largest crowd in several years flocked to see the stadium's swan song.

As the game wore on, the crowd turned its attention to souvenir hunting. Pope, Quinn, and I watched from our box as fans started ripping seats out of the concrete. The extra-inning game provided them with a little extra time to plunder. When we scored a run in the 10th to win, the fans took to the field. A lucky few got bases as souvenirs. The others made due with handfuls of sod. I stayed and watched the proceedings, which included men walking out of the stadium carrying seats and urinals.

As everything that was and wasn't bolted down left the stadium, I sat there and cried.

The next season we moved into brand-spanking-new Veterans Stadium, a huge facility that also became home to the Philadelphia Eagles. The opening of the Vet gave Bill Giles, our vice president of business operations, his chance to shine. Bill was a real marketing genius. For a long time, baseball in Philadelphia hadn't generated a lot of excitement. But capitalizing on the new stadium, Bill looked for ways to get casual fans to come to games.

That was an effective short-term strategy. But we all knew that winning was the key to hooking fans on our product.

• • •

A new stadium and new pinstripe uniforms could not make the Phillies a winning team. Curt Flood didn't want to play in Philadelphia, and neither did a lot of other star players. To compensate for our inability to lure this type of talent from other organizations, we set out to cultivate it from within.

Pope became the scouting director just a month before the first amateur draft in 1965. Within a few years, Pope's way of doing business had already taken hold. It centered on hard work, thoroughness, and a passion for the game. Pope demanded his scouts hit the road and produce detailed reports on every player we thought might wind up on our draft board. He taught me the importance of reading every word of every report generated by our scouts. And he spent countless hours quizzing our staff on every conceivable aspect of a player's mental and physical make-up.

Pope had all the qualities of a successful general manager, and it appeared only a matter of time before he got the job. In June 1972, with the Phillies in the throes of another dreary season, Pope replaced Quinn, who left behind a mixed legacy. He had helped turn an awful team into a winning one in the early 1960s, but after that, the Phillies slipped a lot. At least Quinn got to go out on a high note. In his last trade as general manager, he swapped pitchers with the Cardinals. In exchange for Rick Wise, we got Steve Carlton.

We were at a draft meeting in New York when Pope got the call to return to Philadelphia. His promotion meant the Phillies needed a new director of minor leagues and scouting. Though I had been his assistant for only two and a half years, he had no qualms about appointing me to the post. Together, he believed, we could build a winner.

Just a few weeks after naming Pope as general manager, Bob Carpenter fired manager Frank Lucchesi. Frank had managed 14 years in the Phillies' minor league system before finally getting a shot in the big leagues. But his brief tenure in Philadelphia didn't produce winning results. We all felt terrible for Frank. He was exactly the kind of guy we wanted working for us, a good baseball man who was fiercely loyal to the organization. But it just wasn't working out with him as manager. Frank cried when Carpenter told him he was being let go. But he shook it off soon enough and stayed in the organization as a front office adviser.

Pope got the manager's job on an interim basis. At that point in the season, the team was 26–50 and well on its way to another last-place finish. Bob Carpenter asked Pope to spend the remainder of the season evaluating every player on the team to determine who should stay and who should go.

I would find myself in a similar position seven years later.

• • •

Baseball matters occupied all my time at work. And back at home, the game was the cause of a major family incident.

I was at spring training in 1972 when Sylvia called and told me about the drama unfolding in our hometown in Delaware. She said our nine-year-old daughter, Kim, might be facing "nine men in black robes" pretty soon. I didn't have time for riddles, so I asked her what she was talking about. She said she was referring to the United States Supreme Court.

It all started when Kim and two of her friends went down to Little League baseball tryouts in Eastburn Acres, only to be told that girls weren't allowed to play in the league. The girls were upset about being turned away. Kim took it especially hard. She had been a bat-girl in the league the year before, biding her time until she felt she was ready to play on a team.

Sylvia was upset, too. She knew how much Kim enjoyed baseball and had no doubt she could compete with boys her age. If they had given her a chance to participate in tryouts, everyone would have seen that.

Sylvia conducted a little research and found that a New Jersey judge had ruled a few months earlier that Little League teams there had to accept girls. But other states didn't have the same requirement.

Sylvia could have just let it go and found another sport for Kim to participate in. But that wasn't what Kim wanted. She had always played baseball with her older brother, John, and didn't understand why she couldn't play on an organized team.

It turned out that one of Kim's elementary school teachers was very active in the National Organization for Women. She approached Sylvia about pursuing the matter through the courts. The feeling within NOW was that a recently passed federal law called Title IX made it illegal to ban girls from education programs. And I guess they hoped Little League could be considered an education program.

Sylvia was never one to get involved in causes, but this situation was different, because the cause involved her daughter's happiness. She publicly voiced her support for an ACLU lawsuit against the league.

The national media jumped all over the story. Kim appeared on *The Mike Douglas Show* and hit some baseballs in the studio. When reporters asked me about the situation, I said I supported my daughter's right to play. But I added that I felt girls would eventually decide baseball wasn't the game for them.

The lawsuit hit a road block, but the publicity surrounding the issue ultimately motivated Little League to allow girls to play. That decision came too late for Kim and her friends, because that year's team had already been chosen. So, Sylvia and some other parents put together an all-girls team. They won their first eight games and finished with a record of 8–4.

Kim never gave up her love of baseball but she eventually gravitated toward field hockey, the sport that got her a scholarship to San Jose State University.

On the topic of women in baseball, I think back to Pam Postema, who set out a couple of decades ago to become Major League Baseball's first female umpire. All of us in the game knew she probably wasn't going to make it, but not because of her physical attributes or knowledge of the rules of the game. It can get rough on a base-ball field. And it can get personal. Any umpire needs a very strong psyche to put up with all the berating from players, managers, and fans. It's not something most people would want to subject them-selves to. More so than her male counterparts, a woman in that posi-tion needs unbelievable poise and discipline to withstand the barrage of insults that come her way.

Pam worked her way up through the ranks, which impressed me a lot. The life of a minor league umpire is terrible, considering all the travel and the low pay. She got to work a couple of major league exhi-bition games, but that's where it ended for her.

Years later, another young lady close to my heart, my granddaugh-ter Christina-Taylor, followed in Kim's footsteps by playing Little League baseball in Arizona. I admire the Christina-Taylor Greens, Kim Greens, and Pam Postemas of the world who took chances and served as role models for other girls and women.

8

SOME PROMISING YOUNG PLAYERS in our system gave the Phillies hope for the future.

One of them was Mike Schmidt, who made his major league debut at the end of the 1972 season. A year earlier, Paul Owens used our second-round pick on Schmitty, a shortstop whose history of knee problems at Ohio University scared off other teams. In addition to hitting 26 home runs and knocking in 91 runs at Triple-A Eugene, Schmitty also learned to play third base masterfully.

During Pope's tenure as minor league coordinator, we also drafted Greg Luzinski and Bob Boone.

In 1972, my first year in control of our draft board, we took Larry Christenson, a high school pitcher from Marysville, Washington, with the third overall pick. L.C. quickly reached the majors and stayed there for more than a decade.

The following year, I took a hard-nosed catcher named John Stearns in the first round. But he wasn't in the organization long before Pope used him as trade bait.

At baseball's 1974 winter meetings in New Orleans, Pope set his sights on Tug McGraw, whose career many thought was on the down-turn after a rough season with the Mets. The price for Tug included Stearns and Del Unser, the Phillies' starting center fielder. Manager Danny Ozark and I opposed the trade, but Pope insisted we needed a closer if we hoped to break into the upper echelon. Stearns became a four-time All-Star with the Mets, an impressive individual accomplishment. But Tugger helped solidify our team.

In the following years, Pope followed up that trade with deals that brought in Garry Maddox from the Giants, Manny Trillo from the Cubs, and Bake McBride from the Cardinals. The free agent signing of Pete Rose in 1978 further helped build a championship-caliber team.

Pope also showed smarts in the trades he didn't make. In '74, we had a chance to swap catchers with the Detroit Tigers. We would have sent Bob Boone, then an unproven young catcher, to Detroit for Bill Freehan, who had already been selected for 10 All-Star Games and been awarded five Gold Gloves. But Pope's instincts told him to hold on to the younger backstop. After the multiplayer deal fell apart, Detroit general manager Jim Campbell fumed to the Detroit media, "I've never had an experience like that before. We wasted three days holding up players we might have been able to move someplace else. Then, bang! They pulled the rug right out from under us."

• • •

To do my job, I leaned heavily on our veteran scouts, Ruben Amaro Sr., Hugh Alexander, Tony Lucadello, Eddie Bachman, Wes Livengood, and Brandy Davis. I asked them to strongly consider every prospect's "head and heart," the qualities I believed separated good players from great ones. With the help of these scouts, I overhauled our entire scouting manual after the 1972 season. We developed a detailed grading system for prospects based on how much money a scout would be willing to pay to sign the player. We also updated our crosschecking system by which we compared players from different areas of the country. Pope brought our scouts into the draft era, and it was my job to hone our procedures for identifying the best talent in the country. I demanded that all my scouts do their jobs with the utmost thoroughness. For example, if one of them went to a high school or college game to look at a player, I required he submit a report on the entire roster.

I became close with Hughie, who had been working to identify baseball talent since the age of 20. His scouting career started in 1937 when he lost his left hand in an oil drilling accident in Oklahoma. That put an end to a promising playing career with the Indians. But Cleveland added him to its scouting department and had him shadow Cy Slapnicka, one of the team's existing scouts. Not long thereafter, Hughie went out on his own and found Cleveland a couple of future All-Stars. Years later, he moved over to the Dodgers, who, thanks to Hughie, signed players including Steve Garvey, Davey Lopes, and Don Sutton, among others. We pried Hughie away from the Dodgers in 1971, and it turned out to be one of the best moves we ever made. Nobody worked longer hours scouring the amateur ranks and other major league teams' rosters for talent. And nobody had a better eye for talent. He knew almost every minor league general manager in the country and often returned from his road trips with valuable pieces of inside information about available players.

But Uncle Hughie, as everyone called him, was more than just a scout. He also served as one of Pope's most trusted advisers. Pope rarely made a trade or brought up a guy from the minor leagues without first consulting Hughie. They'd sit in a room together, discussing personnel decisions and chain-smoking cigarettes until the air was blue.

As I told the *Philadelphia Inquirer* at the time of Hughie's death in 2000, "He ranks right there with the best people in the history of the franchise. He did as much as anybody to help the Phillies organization get where it was in the '70s and '80s."

Hughie quickly learned to cope with losing his hand, and with it, his dream of becoming a major leaguer. In the weeks following the accident, he stayed at home and pouted. Finally, his dad, who was an oil man, ordered him to get his ass out of the house. He let Hughie drive one of his old cars to a bar in Seminole, where Hughie had a few drinks. On his way home, he got a flat tire. Hughie stewed with anger. "How the hell am I supposed to change a goddamn tire with one hand?" he muttered to himself. But he figured it out, using his legs to help do the job.

That was Hughie—a man full of energy, ingenuity, and smarts.

Hughie never let his disability get in his way. When Sylvia invited him to our house for dinner soon after he arrived in Philadelphia, she served steak and corn on the cob. Much to the amazement of our wide-eyed children, Hughie managed to manipulate his knife and fork with only one hand. He became a regular guest at our home and shared wonderful stories of his baseball-related travels through America. He also taught our younger son, Doug, how to cheat at cards. It took me a while to figure out why Doug kept beating me, hand after hand. I should have known Uncle Hughie had something to do with it.

• • •

Some of the guys I worked with in Philadelphia had been friends and confidants since my early days in professional baseball. One of them was Ruben Amaro Sr.

As I look back over the course of the past five decades, I couldn't have asked for a better friend, ally, and like-minded baseball man than Ruben, who was an instrumental part of helping Pope and me revitalize the Phillies in the 1970s.

My first contact with Ruben came in 1958 when I was trying to throw strikes by him. He played shortstop for the Cardinals' top minor league affiliate in Rochester, and I was in my first full year of Triple-A ball, with Miami. During the off-season, the Cardinals traded Ruben to the Phillies. We became teammates in Buffalo.

In the early weeks of our friendship, our longest conversations took place when the infielders would gather around the mound during a game. Ruben liked to talk to the pitchers on his team, especially when they were in a jam. He would later tell me he was hesitant to engage me in these discussions at first. "You were a big, gigantic man with a big voice," he told me. "I was small and very quiet. I didn't know if you'd want me to mind my own business."

Once Ruben and I got to know each other, he realized I appreciated ballplayers who were thinkers and observers.

Off the field in Buffalo, Sylvia and I became close friends with Ruben. We supported him as he confronted racist landlords who didn't want to rent an apartment to a dark-complexioned Mexican, especially not one who was dating a lily-white girl from Philadelphia.

Our bond only increased in 1960 when he and I both got called up to the Phillies for the first time. Over the next few seasons, we went through the Gene Mauch/John Quinn wringer that turned a young and struggling ballclub into a winner. Then we both endured the highs and lows of the 1964 season in Philadelphia.

Ruben was traded to the Yankees after the 1965 season and finished out his career with the Angels in 1969, the year I finished my second season of managing minor league ball for the Phillies. Back in Philadelphia, I met with Pope to discuss organizational matters. It was then that I learned Ruben had accepted a managerial job with the Diablos Rojos del Mexico, the Reds of Mexico, and was on his way there. His family was a big deal in Mexico. Ruben's father, Santos, a native of Cuba, is enshrined in the Mexican Baseball Hall of Fame.

"Pope, we can't let him go," I said. "We could use a guy like that in our organization."

I didn't need to do much convincing. Pope liked the idea of hiring Ruben to manage our Triple-A team in Eugene, Oregon.

We somehow found out Ruben had stopped in Harrisburg to get an issue with his driver's license straightened out. Pope made a few calls, and suddenly there was an all-points bulletin out for a car with a trailer hitched to it and a Hispanic at the wheel.

Ruben was somewhere on the Pennsylvania Turnpike when he saw the flashing lights of a state trooper's cruiser. Ruben would later say he was cursing himself under his breath for getting a speeding ticket so early into his trek to Mexico. He rolled down his window to deal with the situation.

"Mr. Amaro?" the state trooper asked.

"Yes," Ruben replied, more than a little surprised at the personal greeting.

"Paul Owens of the Philadelphia Phillies asked that you give him a call right away."

Ruben pulled over and found a phone. Instead of driving to Mexico City, he headed for Eugene, where he served the organization as a player-coach in 1970.

Ruben went back to Mexico to manage in the winter and took some of our top prospects down there with him for some additional seasoning. He led that team to a championship. During a parade to celebrate the title, a horse stamped on his foot, completely shattering it. No longer able to play the game, he devoted himself to coaching and scouting full-time.

Thanks to Ruben, we later signed future All-Stars Julio Franco, Juan Samuel, and George Bell to professional contracts. Unfortunately, we lost Bell to the Blue Jays in the 1980 Rule 5 draft after Pat Gillick's scouts saw him playing winter ball in the Dominican Republic.

Baseball is all about calculated risk. Not all our signings in Latin America or elsewhere bore fruit. In 1974, we gave a two-year, $30,000 contract to a 14-year-old Puerto Rican kid we felt had star potential. The deal made Jorge Lebron the youngest player ever to sign with a major league team. I predicted he would be the next Cesar Cedeno, a talented outfielder for the Astros in the 1970s. Instead, Lebron never panned out. He played parts of three seasons in our minor league system before appearing in his last professional game at the age of 16.

Between the time we signed him and cut him, he fell severely out of shape—fat as a pig, in fact. He and Franco provide an interesting juxtaposition. Both "can't-miss" prospects, one played professionally until he was 16, the other until he was 49.

• • •

I got another chance to visit Cuba in the mid-1970s, when Delaware governor Pierre "Pete" DuPont arranged for a delegation from the state to travel to Havana. His wife, Elise, a State Department representative, led the group. My role was window dressing. Everyone knew Cuban president Fidel Castro loved baseball, so it seemed appropriate to bring a former ballplayer along. Mrs. DuPont's main goal on the trip was to convince Castro to allow two Cuban women to emigrate to the United States on humanitarian grounds. Unfortunately, Sylvia wasn't invited, depriving her yet again of a chance to visit Cuba.

I never met Castro, but I got to take an eye-opening tour of the country, which included a stop at the ballpark I played in as a minor leaguer. Elise DuPont returned home having secured the freedom of the women.

I never planned on getting mixed up in international intrigue while running the Phillies farm system, but if it meant landing a star player, I was willing to give it a go.

Not long after my Cuba trip, I was visiting friends in Easton, Pennsylvania, when Ruben tracked me down by phone with urgent news.

"One of the best young Cuban players wants to defect," he said. "His team's playing in a tournament in Mexico City right now. He'll sign a contract with us if we can get him to the United States."

The Cuban team's first-base coach, who was a friend of Ruben's, had agreed to help the young infielder evade the team's security detail long enough for us to grab him before the next day's game, his team's last in Mexico.

"What do you need me to do?" I asked Ruben.

"Make some calls and get the permission we need to make this happen," he replied.

I phoned Phillies owner Ruly Carpenter, who put me in touch with the organization's lawyers. I also called Elise DuPont for advice. Within a few hours, we had a green light from the State Department to proceed.

I called Ruben back to let him know he could signal his friend.

"Tell me when the thing is done," I told Ruben.

All the necessary people had been contacted. Everything was in place. In less than 24 hours, we were likely to have a top Cuban player in our farm system.

There was only one glitch: it rained like hell in Mexico City the next day. The Cuban team sat together at the stadium waiting to see if it would get the game in. The security detail sat with them. There was no opportunity for Ruben's friend to help the kid slip away.

The team flew back home with the kid in tow. Thanks to lousy weather, we lost our chance to defect a Cuban.

• • •

At spring training, I encouraged our minor league coaches to play basketball together at the end of a long work day. We put up a rim against a cement wall of our complex and waited until all the players had left before heading to the makeshift court. The competition got pretty intense. During one game, Mel Roberts, an outfield instructor who was several inches shorter than me, drove down the lane and attempted a layup. I blocked Mel's shot, and in the process, I fouled him so hard that he went flying into the cement wall face first. "I ain't driving anymore," Mel said after picking himself up off the ground. "From now on, I'm an outside shooter."

Though he was pushing 50, Granny Hamner, a roving instructor who played 16 seasons for the Phillies, was a constant menace. He tripped, shoved, and elbowed opponents in an attempt to create general havoc on the court. After a hard-fought game, we'd all go inside and polish off a case of beer and talk baseball.

As farm director, one of my favorite parts of the job was going around to our minor league sites to check out our kids. On those visits, I made it clear we expected them to take pride in their preparation and play and to respect what it meant to play for the Phillies organization.

I guess my reputation for demanding hard work spread quickly. Dickie Noles, who I took in the fourth round of the 1975 draft, later admitted he was "scared out of his pants" every time I showed up.

During his first year in the minors, Dickie showed up for practice one morning a little worse for wear after a night of drinking. I watched from the roof of the team's training facility as the coaching staff put the team through sprints. For the first round, Dickie ran hard. On the second, he moved noticeably slower. On the third, he really dogged it. "Hey, Noles, move your ass!" I yelled from my perch. He looked around trying to identify the voice. Then his gaze shifted upward to the roof. Our eyes met. Dickie turned around, went back to the start line, and proceeded to outrun almost everyone in the group, hangover and all.

• • •

After the long hours spent trying to improve our baseball team, our gang also squeezed in a little fun.

Okay, a lot of fun.

Our annual organization-wide Christmas parties, no wives allowed, typified the freewheeling good times that we had whenever we got together. We'd roll home every year from those parties at 3:00 or 4:00 AM knowing our wives would question us about what happened at the party, where we went after the party, and how we got home.

Pope had a favorite saying for times like these: "Dallas, you gotta have a good offense. It's your best defense." So when he got back to his New Jersey home, he'd get himself in a fluster and tell his wife,

Marcelle, "That goddamn Dallas Green! I'm never going out with him again. That son of a bitch kept me out all night! I couldn't get him to leave!" Meanwhile in Delaware, a similar scene played out in my bedroom: "Goddamn it, I couldn't get Pope to leave that party! I had to keep an eye on him, make sure he didn't hurt himself."

Sylvia and Marcelle, who Pope met in Belgium during World War II, would always compare notes later. "Did Paul have a lot of white hair on his socks when he got home?" Sylvia asked the day after one of the parties. "Yes, Dallas did, too." Then I'd have to explain why I had white hair all over my socks when I wasn't really sure why I had white hair all over my socks. I ended up blaming it on Pope's dog, Queenie.

Another year, the holiday party at the ballpark spilled over into a celebration at the house of a friend of a Phillies employee. We got a lift out there and, after a few hours, caught a ride back to the stadium parking lot. It was a typical mid-December night in Philadelphia, and I looked forward to the warmth of my car. There was only one problem. I couldn't find my car.

"Jesus Christ," I bellowed at Pope, "someone stole my car!"

"Mine, too!" he responded.

We took a minute to digest the bad news. Then we breathed a sigh of relief, and without exchanging a word, started walking to the hotel parking lot where we'd moved our cars before going to the after-party.

Pope escorted me back to my car, reminiscing about an eventful evening on the Christmas party circuit. He kept yakking as I tried to start the car. It took a good minute or two for my engine to turn over, and when it finally did, I only got a short distance before it cut out again. Pope came back over to check on the situation.

"Open the goddamn hood," he ordered. "I know what to do."

Pope had a lot of talents, but I didn't think car maintenance was one of them. In fact, I was pretty sure he didn't know a goddamn thing about fixing cars. And even though my dad had been a mechanic, none of his knack for auto repair rubbed off on me.

I decided to give Pope a chance to prove himself. The hood of the car popped open, and Pope took a long look inside. Lucky for us, one of Philadelphia's finest was out on patrol and saw Pope "working" on my car.

"Officer, you have to help this guy," Pope told the police officer. "He has to get home."

The cop, who recognized Pope, got out a pair of jumper cables and connected them to my battery. Pope, still fancying himself a car expert, reacted with disgust: "Goddamn it, you've got it on wrong! Let me see that!"

Pope rearranged the cables and took a step back to admire his handiwork.

"Okay, fire her up!"

I turned the key in the ignition…and the battery exploded.

The police officer sized up our predicament. "You gentlemen get home safely now. I'll catch you later," he said.

Pope and I went back to his car. I dropped him off in New Jersey and drove his car back to Delaware with another Christmas party story to tell.

• • •

We didn't just blow off steam and blow up car batteries. I'd like to think our work ethic as well as our ability to have a good time earned us respect around the majors. At the annual winter meetings, our suite became a command center for 14-hour workdays. Pope always left the door to the suite open so that anyone who wanted to talk about a trade or baseball in general could come in and bend our ears. We also worked to make sure all our minor league affiliates felt connected to the major league club. The officials who ran those teams were welcome to join in our discussions. While our wives were touring Hawaii or whatever locale hosted the meetings, we stayed holed up in our hotel room. Following these marathon work sessions, we'd get our fun in. Pope often spoke of the importance of "bounceability," which he defined as the capacity to stay up until the wee hours and arrive at work with little or no sleep, alert and ready to go. He had bounceability, and so did I.

Pope and I liked to engage in hijinks on our down time, but the most important thing in the world to us was making the Phillies organization the pride of baseball. People who disagreed with Pope on a baseball matter were likely to end up in a toe-to-toe confrontation with him and his finger in their chest. That's how we hashed things out. You'd have your say, and he'd have his. And by the end, you could be damn sure you'd settled on the right course of action.

By the late 1970s, we had put together a contending ballclub. In the eighth year after divisions were put in place for the 1969 season, the Phillies finally won the National League East. That breakthrough marked the beginning of an unprecedented period of prosperity in Phillies history.

Ozark, who beat out the likes of Richie Ashburn and Jim Bunning to land the managing job in 1973, was leading the team when it reeled off 101 wins in 1976 and 1977 and 90 wins in 1978. But after enormously successful regular seasons, we went a combined 2–9 in the postseason during that period. The Big Red Machine swept us in '76 and Tommy Lasorda's Dodgers beat us three games to one in both '77 and '78.

In baseball, "What have you done for me lately?" is a valid question. But so is "What have you done for me in your biggest games?"

Neither of the answers boded well for Ozark.

Despite three opportunities, Danny couldn't get the team over the hump into the World Series. And when we struggled to win games in 1979, Pope had seen enough. He fired Danny, and I took over as interim manager. We won a lot of games in September 1979, so I returned to the dugout the following season.

That, of course, brings us to 1980.

9

I FELT WE COULD OVERCOME the disappointment of 1979. In my opinion, that fourth-place season was an aberration. Not everybody shared my optimism. Most sportswriters picked the 1980 Phillies to again finish fourth in the National League East behind the Pirates, the Expos, and the Cardinals, the three teams that finished ahead of us the season before.

There had been some rough patches in spring training. Some of my ideas about conditioning and methods of motivating didn't go over well with cliques of veteran players that had been coddled by my predecessor, Danny Ozark.

At the end of camp, major league players went on a brief strike, wiping out the final week of the exhibition season. The players agreed to open the season as scheduled on April 9 but they threatened that another work stoppage would begin Memorial Day weekend if they couldn't work out an agreement with the owners on issues dealing with free agency.

During the mini-strike in spring training, all our guys chose to stay in Clearwater and continue working out. To me, that signified a dedication to making the 1980 season special. Fortunately, a Memorial Day strike didn't materialize.

"We're not going to out-talent anyone in the National League anymore," I reminded the team before we broke camp. "We're at the point where the rest of the league has caught up to us in terms of talent."

On Opening Day in 1980, we beat the Expos 6–3 at Veterans Stadium for our first season-opening win since 1974. A three-run home run by Greg Luzinski in the first inning got us off and running. Not normally a guy who showed much emotion on the field, Bull pumped his fist in the air as he rounded the bases. After the game, I told reporters I expected Bull to bounce back from an off year and regain the form that had established him as one of the league's best home run and RBI guys.

For one day, at least, the game looked easy. If only it had stayed that way.

• • •

I battled with my players the whole year. You've heard about player revolts that cause managers to lose the clubhouse? Well, in 1980, I lost the clubhouse almost every day. Luzinski, Mike Schmidt, Larry Bowa, Garry Maddox, and Bob Boone viewed me with suspicion or outright hostility. They scoffed at the "We, not I" signs I hung in the clubhouse in Clearwater. Who was Dallas Green to tell a team that went to the playoffs three out of the past four years how to conduct its business? They viewed my job as easy. Put the team on autopilot and watch the wins pile up. At the end of the day, they believed they ran the team.

They were missing one key point, however. As much as I liked winning games in April, it didn't amount to a hill of beans if we couldn't win them in October. I set out to develop a culture that valued that way of thinking. As a manager who had the complete backing of his general manager and owner, I felt confident I could accomplish that. It might take time, but I believed it would happen. Thankfully, the baseball season is long.

It helped that I had some of the big boys on my side from the beginning. Steve Carlton was happy as hell. Going into his 16th major league season, all he wanted was his first championship. And he didn't think Danny Ozark was capable of delivering one.

Pete Rose needed no motivation or babysitting to go out and compete with total pride and dedication; that was the only way he knew to play. He was the only Phillie to appear in all 162 regular season games in 1980.

Bake McBride and Manny Trillo didn't get too mixed up in the cliques, probably because they hadn't been on the team as long as some of the others. And I sensed Tug McGraw also had warmed up to me. On a rainy day in Clearwater, Tugger and I shared a light moment after a workout. I saw him sliding headfirst across the muddy infield and decided to join him. It was instinct on my part, but I think it showed I knew how to enjoy myself.

That made five veterans who weren't going to bitch and moan every time Dallas Green looked at them the wrong way or made a critical comment.

I knew baseball was fun when you're winning. And I saw no reason not to have a lot of fun in 1980.

• • •

Our offense carried us to a lot of wins in the first months of the season. Through May, we led the league in runs scored, mainly because Schmidt and Luzinski were first and second in the National League in home runs, respectively.

Starting pitching had emerged as a weakness, however. Dick Ruthven was returning from an injury. Nino Espinosa was sidelined by a shoulder problem. Larry Christenson underwent elbow surgery at the end of May. And Randy Lerch, though healthy, started the season 0–6. After his poor start, Lerch and I got crossways with each other. I sat him for 10 days to see if a little rest might reignite his competitive spirit. Though he won his next start, the time off didn't have a lasting effect.

That left us with Carlton—en route to 24 wins and his third Cy Young Award—and a lot of question marks.

Few things irritated me more than squandering a quality start by Carlton. Early in the season, Lefty pitched seven strong innings against the Mets, but despite having runners on base most every inning, we couldn't get on the scoreboard. After the 3–0 loss, I read the team the riot act: "You sons of bitches can't even play for a future Hall of Famer! You forget where you are! You forget what you're doing! We're supposed to have pride and character, but you don't show it! Well, if you can't show it for the best pitcher in the game, who the hell else are you going to show it for?"

Injuries and ineffectiveness prompted us to promote 23-year-old Bob Walk from Triple-A Oklahoma City at the end of May. He went out and won 11 games for us in '80, the third-most of any pitcher on the team.

Somehow, despite our pitching woes, we managed to go 17–9 in May. But we played only average baseball in June and July. With the Pirates and the Expos showing they were every bit as strong as we were, we couldn't afford to get stuck in a rut. The 1979 season had gotten off to a promising start, too. Then it fell apart.

As it turned out, the team's biggest headlines in July weren't generated by our play, but rather by a police investigation of the team doctor for the Double-A Reading Phillies. It was alleged he illegally supplied amphetamines to several members of the major league team. The players implicated in the media reports varied from story to story, so it's not worth mentioning any names here. But the scandal, if you want to call it that, prompted the *Philadelphia Daily News* to call us "The Pillies." Players' use of energy-boosting drugs was an open secret at the time. A year earlier, Pete Rose had admitted in *Playboy* that he popped "greenies" before games. Nobody wants to see the integrity of his team questioned like that, but I left it to the players to answer questions about the whole deal. It was their responsibility, not mine.

• • •

In early August, a few days after my 46th birthday, we went to Pittsburgh for a four-game series hoping to make a statement. Entering the series, we were 55–48 and in third place, three games behind the Expos. The Pirates were wedged between us and Montreal. If we could pull off a sweep at Three Rivers Stadium, we'd travel to Chicago to play a woeful Cubs team in no worse than second place. If we took three out of four, we'd be neck and neck with the defending champs and still nipping at the Expos' heels.

But two days and two losses later, the game plan had changed. Having lost precious ground in the standings, a Sunday doubleheader against Pittsburgh felt like a battle for survival.

Before the first game of the twin bill, Schmitty took it upon himself to call a players-only meeting. I had no problem with that. I felt our so-called team leaders weren't vocal enough in the clubhouse. If Schmitty felt he was finally ready to show some emotion that might motivate his teammates, I wasn't going to stand in his way.

Mr. Cool didn't have any magic words, however. We went out and committed three errors in a 7–1 loss to Jim Bibby and the Pirates.

As we drifted toward defeat, I decided it would be my turn to have a word or two with the team. Between games of the doubleheader, I kicked all the reporters out of the clubhouse and unleashed the angriest diatribe of my career. Even though the scribes had been banished to the hallway, they could still hear my words through the cinder blocks that separated them from the clubhouse.

"Get off your fucking rear ends and beat somebody!" I yelled at the top of my lungs. "You have to stop being so fucking cool! Can you get that through your fucking heads?! If you don't, you'll get so fucking buried, it ain't gonna be funny. Get the fuck off your asses!"

I could feel the blood rushing to my face as I proceeded with my R-rated screaming session.

In the short term, my appeal to the club was just as fruitless as Schmitty's. In the second game of the doubleheader, we committed two more errors and Pittsburgh beat us 4–1 to finish off the sweep. During the game, the raw emotions of the day bubbled to the surface again. With one run home for the Pirates in the bottom of the seventh inning, I ordered relief pitcher Ron Reed to intentionally walk Willie Stargell with first base open and Bill Madlock coming to the plate. After getting the signal, Ronnie stepped off the mound. Boone went out there to check on him. I could tell by the defiant look on Ronnie's face that he didn't want to follow my instructions. He ended up issuing the pass to Stargell, and the inning ended when Madlock grounded into a double play.

When Ronnie got back to the dugout, I got right in his face. I'm a tall man, but Ronnie, who had played in the NBA, had at least an inch on me. He was the strong, silent type who preferred a quiet chat in private. In other words, he was the opposite of me.

"What's your fucking problem?" I screamed at him.

We went toe to toe, each of us waiting for the other to throw the first punch. Fortunately for me, a couple of guys pulled us apart.

The disastrous series in Pittsburgh put us six games behind the Pirates and the Expos with less than two months left to play.

On our way out of town, I delivered a much calmer message for the press: "I'm just not going to let them quit on themselves. I won't quit on them. I'm sure the fans in Philadelphia won't quit."

That night, my coaches and I went out to dinner and, as we were wont to do, we tore the hell out of the place. We ate, we drank, and we were merry. It was a much-needed release from all the tension.

• • •

In 1980, our core group of players gave us a chance to win every night. Over the course of their careers, Schmidt had hit a lot of game-winning home runs, Rose had banged out a lot of three-hit nights, and Carlton had pitched a lot of shutouts. I hoped they and our other veterans would continue to perform at a high level.

But unlike Ozark, I planned to rely on young players to give us a positive jolt. If we didn't meet my expectations, I didn't want it to be because I had been afraid to shake up the status quo.

When Pope hired me as manager, it was with the understanding I wouldn't necessarily award playing time simply based on years of service. I helped build our farm system and knew we had several players in the minors who were ready to make an impact with the Phillies. The guys who were coming up through our minor league system were willing to run off a cliff for me. In a clubhouse where a lot of players wanted to throw me off a cliff, the loyalty and enthusiasm of those guys provided an essential balance.

One of those guys was Keith Moreland. I first encountered Keith in 1975 when he was a junior at the University of Texas, getting ready for a game between the Longhorns and SMU. On my recommendation, the Phillies took him in the seventh round of that year's draft. He later told me his brief interaction with me in Austin helped convince him to sign with the Phillies rather than return for his senior year of college. "You reminded me of my father," he said. "I had a feeling you were someone I should follow."

From the get-go, Keith showed he had a bright future in the game. In addition to natural talent, he hustled, played smart, and accepted new challenges without grumbling. A third baseman in college, he needed to switch positions if he wanted to play regularly for the Phillies in the near future. So, he learned to be a catcher.

Keith performed well in the low minor leagues, but he hit a bump in the road when he got to Double-A in 1976. One of my responsibilities at the time was negotiating contracts with our minor leaguers. Following his subpar months at Reading, I sent Keith what I considered a fair contract offer. He didn't see it that way. "I really worked my tail off last season, and I think I deserve a little more money," he told me. I didn't blink. "If you had worked your tail off, you'd be getting a little more money," I said. The conversation made me feel a little like John Quinn, who as Phillies general manager in the late 1960s gave me a similar, if less pointed denial, of a pay raise.

Keith went out the next season and worked his tail off. The following year he was promoted to Triple-A, where he continued to blossom.

With Boone struggling to find his hitting stroke in 1980, I decided to give Keith a shot to show what he could do. In July, he started getting a lot of playing time. And over the final months of the 1980 season, he hit well over .300.

Keith and Booney developed a harmonious relationship. Though he wasn't swinging the bat well, Booney remained a stellar defensive catcher. During games that Keith started behind the plate, Booney would sit next to him in the dugout and fill his head with knowledge about opposing hitters.

Lonnie Smith, a first-round pick in 1974, also gave us a boost by hitting .339 and stealing a team-leading 33 bases. Lonnie's play earned him a starting spot in left field on a lot of nights. That caused some friction between Luzinski and me. But Lonnie was hitting a hundred points higher than Bull, so what was I supposed to do?

The emergence of Moreland and Smith gave me additional options when filling out the lineup card. When it came to using young pitchers, however, I was acting out of necessity, not by choice.

In all, we got 24 wins from pitchers 23 or younger, including five in as many September starts from late season call-up Marty Bystrom. Originally, Marty was going to break camp with us, but a hamstring injury at the end of spring training forced him back to the minors.

After Larry Christenson went down, Marty, only 22 years old, got thrown into the middle of a major league pennant race.

He didn't blink.

On September 10, we trailed the Expos by half a game going into a two-game series at Shea Stadium. Marty pitched a complete game, shutting out the Mets and limiting them to just five hits. The next time out he pitched seven scoreless innings against the Cardinals. Over 21 days in September, Marty made five crucial starts and won every one of them, a level of success he never attained again in his career.

Marty kept his composure under sometimes difficult circumstances. In a September game against the Cubs, home-plate umpire Terry Tata squeezed him on several pitches. But the kid kept his cool, working around a season-high four walks to pick up a key victory.

Marty and the other young guys on the team had to pinch themselves when they looked around the clubhouse and realized Schmidt, Rose, and Carlton were their teammates. But while they had enormous respect for those guys, they weren't going to blindly follow them. The kids were Dallas Green guys, even if some of the veterans weren't.

• • •

We faced two possible scenarios after our August sweep at the hands of the Pirates. Either pent-up tension would continue to rise to the surface, causing us to stumble, or we would use the Pittsburgh series as a wake-up call and pull ourselves together.

The day after the sweep, we boarded a charter flight to Chicago, where we started a nearly two-month period that featured both of those scenarios.

Before the first game of the Cubs series, I had a one-on-one meeting with Ron Reed. I told him that my directives needed to be followed without protest. End of story. We didn't discuss our near-fight in the dugout. Nothing needed to be said about that. It was a case of two competitors letting their frustration get the better of them. No harm, no foul.

That afternoon in Chicago, I went back to Ronnie out of the bull-pen and gave him a chance to help us break a 10-game road losing streak. We led 5–3 going into the bottom of the ninth inning, but he coughed up a couple of runs, sending the game into extra innings. The Cubs scored the tying run after I ordered Ronnie to issue an intentional walk. He did so without protest this time.

The game was stopped because of darkness in the 14th inning, but we came back the next day and won the suspended game, as well as the regularly scheduled game. Schmitty hit two home runs and knocked in five RBIs in the two contests.

After a loss to the Cubs in the series finale, we went to New York and swept five games from the Mets.

But the road was still bumpy. I had a helluva time getting some of my players to buy into my program.

Luzinski played with hunger early in the season, but by the time he went on the disabled list in early July, he was hitting just .245. As he slumped, I started turning more to Lonnie Smith. And that's when Bull went to the newspapers and compared me to the Gestapo.

Bull wasn't the only disenchanted Phillie, of course. Bowa and Maddox were among those who disdained my tactics. I was too critical, in their opinion. Translation: they didn't like when I talked about obvious mistakes that everybody watching the game noticed. They thought I should have pretended that nothing happened, or at least kept my criticism out of the papers.

At the end of August in San Diego, Maddox lost two fly balls in the sun after choosing not to remove a pair of sunglasses from his back pocket. In that same series, Bowa also played shaky defense. We couldn't afford mental mistakes from two guys who were supposed to be team leaders.

Maddox didn't like his defensive prowess being questioned. By winning Gold Gloves every year from 1975 to 1979, he had earned his nickname, the Secretary of Defense. But he knew many Philadelphia fans still remembered his dropped fly ball against the Dodgers in the 1978 playoffs that may have cost the Phillies the series. I wasn't trying to pick at an old wound, nor did I want to hurt Garry's pride by bringing up haunting memories of '78. I just wanted him to wear his damn sunglasses! It was as simple as that.

• • •

Losing two straight to the last-place San Diego Padres was unacceptable. In a winner-take-all race, a team rarely backed into a division title. If we couldn't beat the likes of San Diego, either the Pirates or the Expos were going to leave us in the dust.

It didn't surprise me that Pope shared my concerns. San Francisco was our next stop after San Diego. On the short flight up the California coast, my mentor pounded a couple of drinks and stewed over the losses at Jack Murphy Stadium.

"Goddamnit, Dallas, we're playing like horseshit," Pope moaned. "I think I need to give these sons of bitches a kick in the ass."

At the hotel in San Francisco, his frustration mounted. We sat in his suite, had another drink, and discussed how to save the season from unraveling. Pope left the door to the room wide open, which gave us a clear view of the hallway. Well after midnight, pitchers Dickie Noles and Kevin Saucier walked by. They froze in place when they got to the open door. Big mistake. Pope let loose on them, not because they had missed curfew, but because they were Phillies players, and goddamn it, he wasn't enamored with Phillies players at that moment!

Before we called it a night, Pope said, "I'm going to talk to the club."

After the way he upbraided Noles and Saucier, it didn't surprise me that he wanted a crack at the entire team.

"Do you want the young kids in there?" I asked. It was September 1, and we had just called up some minor leaguers, including Bob Dernier and Mark Davis.

"I want *everybody* there," Pope hissed.

The next day, Pope marched down to the visitors' clubhouse at Candlestick Park and reamed the team for its poor effort and sloppy play. He singled out Maddox and Bowa for particular criticism. Before storming out, he gave out his hotel room number in case anybody wanted to come up and fight him later. Pope's tirade didn't make Maddox any less sulky, especially after I benched him for the entire San Francisco series. It didn't make Bowa any less of a complainer, either. But I think the message got across. We won all three games against the Giants to reclaim first place in the NL East.

• • •

John Vukovich, a utility infielder, hit just .161 in 66 plate appearances in 1980. And that was hardly an off-year. In fact, his career average was .161.

But every manager, especially one trying to fend off a clubhouse insurrection, needs a guy like Vuke on his team His leadership qualities made him as valuable as any .300 hitter ever could have been.

Drafted in 1966, he came up through the Phillies' system with Bowa, Luzinski, Booney, and Schmitty. Though he was a pretty decent hitter in the minor leagues, he could never hit a lick against major league pitching. His defense and work ethic were the reasons he kept getting shots in the big leagues.

In 1980, Vuke was my right-hand man among the players. He bought into the idea that I was only trying to accomplish what his teammates all said they wanted: a championship.

He wasn't afraid to get in the face of Bowa, Schmitty, or Bull if he felt they needed encouragement or a kick in the butt. That saved me from having to do all the berating. I knew Vuke represented my point of view well, and I trusted him to help spread the message.

If you had taken a clubhouse poll prior to the season, I'd guess that the majority of players would have voted to dump me. Five months into the season, with the Phillies in the thick of a pennant race, I'm sure a few holdouts felt the team was winning not because of Dallas Green, but despite Dallas Green. It would later be said that they may have been winning *to spite* Dallas Green.

The results were all that mattered to me. I wanted our guys to have chips on their shoulders and remember that we'd been picked to finish fourth in our division. They should have been a motivated bunch. Most had fallen just short of playing in a World Series several times. This might be their chance.

Pete Rose knew about October success. As a two-time World Series champion with the Reds, he had played on some of the best teams of the previous 50 years. In 1980, Pete hit .284, his lowest batting average since 1964, the year he hit the only grand slam of his career, off yours truly. Statistically speaking, it was a down year for Pete, though he remained a doubles-hitting machine.

From the bench, Vuke, my coaches, and I could only do so much to fire up the players on the field. By playing the game with unbelievable passion, Pete took on the role of an on-the-field surrogate. He inspired his teammates to succeed.

Between Vuke and Pete, we had two blue-collar ballplayers and natural leaders. The only difference between them is that one finished his career with 90 hits and the other with 4,256.

• • •

We trailed the Expos by half a game going into the second-to-last series of the season, a four-game set at home against the Cubs. Looking for the right chemistry in our lineup, I benched Luzinski, Maddox, and Boone for the series opener. The game was tied in the 15th inning when Chicago broke through for two runs. Down 5–3 and facing the prospect of falling further behind Montreal in the standings, we fought back with three runs in the bottom of the 15th. The tying run scored on a single by Maddox, who had entered the game a few innings earlier. He came home with the winning run on Manny Trillo's third hit of the night. After the game, Garry accused me of "managing for the press," whatever that means.

We went on to sweep the Cubs to pull into a tie with the Expos, who took three games in a row from the Cardinals.

That set up a final three-game showdown with Montreal over the first weekend of October. The first team to win two games was going to the playoffs.

Dick Ruthven came into the first game of the series with a career-high 16 wins. I counted on him to notch another one in Montreal. The Expos were depending on Scott Sanderson, also in search of his 17th win, to do the same.

It was a well-pitched game on a cold night. Ruthven pitched 5⅔ innings of one-run ball, and we were able to scratch out a 2–1 win, aided by Schmitty's 47th homer of the year.

It was our 12th one-run win since September 1.

A possible division-clinching game the next afternoon almost got snowed out. The snow then turned to rain. We sat around for hours waiting for a break in the weather. Most of our traveling party, including team staff and spouses, returned to the hotel. And we just sat. It was gut-wrenching. We were right where we wanted to be, needing to win just one baseball game to get back to the playoffs. Finally, the game started. It wasn't a thing of beauty. We committed five errors and stranded 12 runners on base that night.

We took a one-run lead in the top of the seventh but relinquished it in the bottom half of the inning. Things were tense. Sylvia, who had remained at the ballpark during the delay, was sitting with team officials behind our dugout when someone affiliated with the Expos threw a drink at first-base coach Ruben Amaro Sr.'s face as he came off the field. As Ruben tried to go up in the stands after the guy, Pope and team treasurer George Harrison were banging him over the head with their umbrellas. Before Ruben could join them, stadium security swooped in.

Trailing by a run in the ninth inning and down to our final out, we got a game-tying single from Boone. Schmitty then put the cherry on top of an MVP season, connecting on his 48th home run of the season off Stan Bahnsen in the top of the 11th inning. That gave us a 6–4 win and the National League East Division title. In a meaningless game to end the season, the Expos snapped our six-game win streak.

Our march to the NLCS, which included a 23–11 record in September and October, seemed like a cakewalk compared to Houston's. We clinched our division in the second-to-last game of the season. Houston and Los Angeles had to play an extra game to decide the NL West after the Dodgers swept the Astros to make up a three-game deficit over the final weekend.

Prior to the one-game playoff between the two teams, I opined that I hoped Houston won the game. We had played well against the Astros that season, winning nine of 12 games against them, and considering Schmitty was the only guy on our team who hit more than 19 home runs, I liked the idea of playing in the pitcher-friendly Astrodome.

Houston's victory in the tiebreaking game prevented a Phillies-Dodgers NLCS matchup for the third time in four years. I guess you have to be careful what you wish for, because the Astros ended up giving us all we could handle.

10

A DIVISION CROWN WAS NOT our ultimate goal in 1980. If it had been, Danny Ozark would still have still been managing the team. For the fourth time in five years, we had a chance to win the pennant and World Series. And that's what we planned to do.

As we prepared to meet the Astros in the National League Championship Series, I didn't get too carried away with clubhouse speeches. My mouth had roared plenty of times during the tumultuous season. Nothing more needed to be said. If we continued playing with the determination we showed in September and early October, we could beat anybody. I also didn't think it was necessary to bury the hatchet with Greg Luzinski, Garry Maddox, Larry Bowa, or any of the other players I clashed with during the season. I didn't hold any grudges, and I hoped they didn't, either.

Our sole focus had to be a formidable Astros team. Manager Bill Virdon's lineup may have lacked pop, but it featured guys who knew the value of sound, fundamental baseball. Houston's "nickel-and-dime attack," as an Associated Press reporter called it, was led by outfielders Jose Cruz and Cesar Cedeno. But it also included Joe Morgan, Enos Cabell, and Terry Puhl, all of whom stole more than 20 bases.

The Astros' real strength, however, was pitching. Joe Niekro won 20 games in 1980, and Nolan Ryan, Ken Forsch, and Vern Ruhle all had impressive seasons. Even without ace J.R. Richard, who started the All-Star Game just weeks before suffering a career-ending stroke, Houston had a staff that could frustrate opposing hitters, especially in a short series.

Fortunately, we had the best pitcher on either team, which gave us an advantage in the series opener. Steve Carlton hadn't pitched since notching his 24th win six days earlier, so he was well-rested.

The Astros hopped a red-eye flight to Philadelphia for Game 1 after winning their one-game tiebreaker with the Dodgers. A record crowd of more than 65,000 fans at Veterans Stadium turned out to give us an added edge.

The first game of the NLCS was a throwback to the first game of the season. Luzinski played hero in both. His two-run home run against Ken Forsch in the sixth inning erased a 1–0 Astros lead.

Carlton didn't have his best stuff in Game 1, but even his Grade-B stuff tied the Astros in knots. He scattered seven singles over seven innings before I lifted him from the game. Pinch hitter Greg Gross got us an insurance run by singling to score Maddox, who was starting for the first time in more than a week.

Tug McGraw, who carried a 26-inning scoreless streak into the game, blanked Houston over the final two innings to preserve our 3–1 win.

It was a mundane start to what turned out to be a wild series.

My postgame evaluation: we played sluggishly, but we won.

Bull, who had worked with hitting coach Billy DeMars to fix a glitch in his swing, told reporters he was ready to put a rough season behind him in order to focus on a larger objective. "I know the fans have been on me," he said. "But they've been on a lot of other guys, too. I know there's been talk about me being traded, but right now I want it out of my mind. My only goal is to get us in the World Series."

Well said, Bull.

• • •

Our work in Philadelphia wasn't done. We knew the importance of coming back the next night and winning Game 2, the last game of the series to be played at the Vet. We wanted to go to Houston needing to win just one of three games to advance to the World Series.

In Game 2, we had Nolan Ryan and the Astros right where we wanted them. Dick Ruthven held his own against Ryan, who exited the game in the bottom of the seventh inning with the score tied 2–2. But with the bases loaded and one out, Joe Sambito came in to strike out Bake McBride, and fellow reliever Dave Smith did the same to Mike Schmidt, ending the threat.

It was the first of several missed opportunities that changed the complexion of the series.

The teams traded runs in the eighth to keep the game deadlocked. In the bottom of the ninth, we again loaded the bases with one out. This time, Manny Trillo struck out and Maddox fouled out to send the game into extra innings.

Ron Reed, who had pitched a scoreless ninth, got knocked around in the 10th, giving up four runs. After scoring a run to pull within 7–4 in the bottom half of the inning, Schmitty came to the plate as the potential tying run with two outs. He got the green light on a 3-0 pitch from Joaquin Andujar but flied out to end the game.

Despite numerous chances to win, we let Game 2 slip away, stranding 10 runners on base in the final four innings. Our lack of clutch hitting obviously concerned me. If a team goes into a hitting rut during the regular season, there is time to recover. That isn't the case in a best-of-five playoff series.

After the tough loss, some reporters expected me to lash out at McBride for failing to score from second base on a one-out Lonnie Smith single in the ninth inning. Bake showed indecision as he rounded third, and after taking a wide turn, he returned to the bag.

"That's a very difficult thing for a base runner with only one out," I said after the game. "It's his judgment. He made a turn and stopped."

I made it clear we had no intention of folding our tent in Houston.

"We won nine of 12 against the Astros this year, so we had to beat them down there sometime," I said during the postgame press conference.

In fact, we had won four of six in the Astrodome, the so-called eighth wonder of the world. Now we needed to win two of three to avoid another exit in the NLCS.

• • •

In 1980, the Astros won 55 games at home, a win total that more than compensated for a losing road record. After taking Game 2 at the Vet, the Astros clearly liked their chances of winning the series. On the day off between games, a couple of Houston players told reporters their team was now in the driver's seat. I guess they didn't realize we were 21–10 in our last 31 road games.

I didn't see dejection or fatigue on the faces of my players. With more reporters than ever in the clubhouse, guys like Bowa and Schmidt stepped up and explained that the team had already put the tough Game 2 loss behind it. Rose and Tug McGraw stayed loose, with Tugger joking that the Phillies wanted to build suspense by letting the series play out a while longer. Pete cracked that MLB commissioner Bowie Kuhn was a very happy man, because the longer series meant more revenue for Major League Baseball.

With the off-day banter out of the way, we took the field for Game 3, the first home playoff game in Astros history, and also the first postseason game ever played in a dome. In the enclosed stadium, the roar of the crowd stayed trapped, creating a mind-boggling noise level.

The Astrodome lived up to its reputation as a pitcher's park that afternoon. We had a helluva time mounting any kind of an attack against Joe Niekro, whose knuckleball dipped and dived all day. We left runners in scoring position in each of the first three innings, continuing a disturbing trend from Game 2. After that, we didn't show much life again until the ninth inning when we stranded two more runners on base against Niekro. Fortunately for us, Larry Christenson and our bullpen did an equally outstanding job. The game remained scoreless after nine innings.

The most noteworthy event of the game to that point came in the sixth inning, when Cesar Cedeno of the Astros tripped over first base and broke his ankle, ending his season.

Joe Morgan opened the bottom half of the 11th inning with a triple. With nobody out, I instructed Tugger, who was in his fourth inning of work, to intentionally walk the next two batters to create a force play at any base. The plan didn't work. Denny Walling, a utilityman who got the start that day, hit a fly ball deep enough to score pinch runner Rafael Landestoy from third with the winning run.

Like I said, just because the Astros lacked superstars didn't mean they were easy to beat. And they knew it.

"You know, we don't have one guy who's going to bowl over another team," Enos Cabell told reporters after Game 3. "It takes seven or eight of us to do it."

I felt the same way about my team.

We hadn't quit when we found ourselves six games out of first place in early August. We didn't flinch when we went to Montreal the last weekend of the season needing two wins. And we weren't going to concede defeat now.

"I know we're in trouble," I said after Game 3. "I feel a little bit down right now. But we're going to get together in the locker room and try to regroup. We're just not getting any offense now."

Rose explained why he still had confidence. "They have to beat the best pitcher in the world to win the pennant," he said on his way out of the Astrodome clubhouse, referring to Lefty, of course.

That night, the Royals finished off a three-game sweep of the Yankees in the American League Championship Series. I hoped to be hosting Kansas City in the first game of the World Series in a few days.

• • •

In search of a hot bat in Game 4, I benched Bull, who went 0-for-5 in Game 3, in favor of Lonnie Smith. The game started off no differently than the previous two. We had plenty of chances to score off Astros starter Vern Ruhle, but we couldn't come up with a timely hit.

At least I got a workout in. In the fourth inning, the game was delayed 20 minutes while I argued with home-plate umpire Doug Harvey over a disputed triple-play call. We felt Ruhle hadn't caught the batted ball that precipitated the triple play. After the dust settled, the umpires inexplicably ruled it a double play when it should have been ruled a triple play or nothing. The inning continued, but we still didn't score. Both Virdon and I filed unsuccessful protests over the call.

Carlton lasted only 5⅓ innings. I had little choice but to lift him in the bottom of the sixth inning with the bases loaded, one out, and the Astros already leading 2–0.

Dickie Noles came in to face Luis Pujols, who hit a sacrifice fly that scored Gary Woods from third base. Or did it? My coaches and I had kept a keen eye on Woods, and we had no doubt that he left the bag way before the fly ball landed in Bake McBride's glove.

Dickie tossed the ball to Schmitty at third base to appeal the play. Third-base umpire Bob Engel stuck his thumb in the air to signify that Woods was out. The Astros' third run came off the board, and the double play ended the inning.

Ruhle kept us at bay for the first seven innings, which brought our scoreless streak in the NLCS to 18 innings. We had six outs to get our act together or our season was over.

I paced around the dugout trying to vent some of my nervous energy. All I could do was bark generic words of encouragement: "We haven't scored yet, boys! Let's go! We gotta get on base before we score!"

The team didn't need any motivation at this point. Every player in that dugout realized our plight. And they refused to go away quietly. Gross, Smith, and Rose singled off Ruhle to put us on the board in the eighth, forcing Virdon to dip into his bullpen. Dave Smith gave up another single to Schmitty, which tied the score at 2–2. Manny Trillo's sacrifice fly later that inning gave us a one-run lead. Trillo's sac fly actually should have been ruled a hit, allowing the inning to continue, since Astros right fielder Jeff Leonard merely trapped the ball instead of catching it. Instead, after I had another screaming session with the umpires, the moment simply became another footnote to a strange and exhilarating game.

Leading 3–2 entering the bottom of the ninth, I opted to stick with reliever Warren Brusstar, who had pitched a scoreless eighth. The ninth inning normally belonged to Tugger, but he needed rest after throwing a lot of pitches the day before. A walk, a sacrifice bunt, and a single allowed Houston to tie the score. For the third straight game, we were headed for extra innings.

In the 10th inning, I gave Bull a shot at redemption. With Rose on first base and two outs, the Astros had left-hander Joe Sambito on the mound. Playing the percentages, I had the right-handed-hitting Bull bat for McBride. Bull rewarded my faith in him by stroking a double to left field. On the crack of the bat, Pete took off and rumbled all the way around to score, bowling over Astros catcher Bruce Bochy in the process. Trillo followed with another double to score Bull.

Pete later said nothing was going to stop him from scoring that run: "They could have had a road block there, and I'd have broken the law and gone right through the road block, because I had to score that run. That gave us a lift. When I scored that run, guys started to say, 'Maybe things will go our way.'"

Another run put us up 5–3 going into the bottom of the 10th, and I turned to Tugger this time, hoping he had another inning in his tired arm. He recorded a one-two-three inning.

We had survived.

"It has been written that the Phillies have no character," I said after the game. "You would believe this team had no character only if you turned off your TV sets early. It was one of those frustrating games when we struggled early. And after they tied us in the ninth, we could have quit, but didn't."

• • •

We had battled for 166 games only to see the season come down to a single contest. I had a choice to make for Game 5. Should I start 17-game winner Dick Ruthven, who pitched well in Game 2, or should I roll the dice and go with rookie Marty Bystrom? My gut told me Bystrom.

"I'm giving you the ball tomorrow, kid," I told Marty the night before Game 5.

Though only 22, Marty had pitched in enough pressure-filled situations in his first month in the big leagues to show me he could handle this assignment. Little did anyone know, least of all me, that Ruthven would still play a big role in the outcome of Game 5.

We had experienced a lot since April. On some days we looked like world-beaters. On other days we played lethargically. For the first five months of the season, I honestly didn't know whether the players wanted a championship as badly as they said they did. There were days when I lost my cool with them. Pope got his licks in, too. At times, it appeared we might come apart at the seams. If we had played poorly in September and failed to make the play-offs, I'm sure all sorts of fingers would have been pointed my way. But we came together in the end, winning our division in the 161st

game of the season. It took us every one of those games to become a cohesive unit. Now we had an identity. We were battlers. And all 25 guys on the roster played a part in getting us where we were. Did the team finally decide to buy into my program? I guess you could say that. But more accurately, they bought into themselves. That was my program.

But all of that would mean nothing if we couldn't get another win in Houston.

• • •

If you were in the Philadelphia area and watched the 1980 NLCS on television, you were guided through it by two of the best broadcasters in the business, Harry Kalas and Richie Ashburn. Before Game 5, Richie made a prediction: "I think something unusual will decide this ballgame. It might be a bad play. It could be a check-swing base hit. But I don't think we're going to see your basic ballgame here. I don't think it's going to be boring."

Richie nailed it.

To get to the World Series, we had to go through Nolan Ryan. In his first season with Houston, Ryan hadn't put up the eye-catching totals in wins, complete games, and strikeouts he produced in eight seasons with the California Angels. But he was still one of the most feared pitchers in the game. At the age of 33, he already had compiled the third-most strikeouts in the history of the game. And dating back to the 1969 postseason with the Mets, when he was just a few months older than Bystrom was in 1980, he generally pitched well in the postseason. Considering we hadn't exactly pounded the ball in the first four games of the series, Ryan presented a major challenge for us.

I gave our young guys plenty of chances to prove themselves during the season, but for Game 5 of the NLCS, our fifth game in six days, I handed in a lineup card with the names of the eight position players who had started our season opener in April: Pete Rose, Bake McBride, Mike Schmidt, Greg Luzinski, Manny Trillo, Garry Maddox, Larry Bowa, and Bob Boone.

I felt a strong veteran lineup would help us against Ryan. In a season when so many players contributed to our success, it was only appropriate that I ended up using 20 of the 25 players on my roster that night.

• • •

Marty won some crucial games for us in September, but this was his first time pitching on the national stage. If that wasn't pressure enough, he'd be pitching in a loud and hostile environment. In each of the first four games of the series, the Astros got on the board first. To avoid adding to the list of challenges Marty already faced, I hoped we could jump out to an early lead in Game 5.

On the suggestion of Steve Carlton, Marty took the mound with cotton in his ears to help drown out the deafening roar of the Astrodome crowd. After Ryan set us down in order in the top of the first, Marty ran into immediate trouble. Terry Puhl led off with a single and, with one out, stole second. Marty retired Joe Morgan but yielded a run-scoring double to Jose Cruz. With Houston up early, the sold-out crowd at the Astrodome got that much louder.

Fortunately, we answered right back. With Maddox and Trillo in scoring position with two outs, Boone singled to center field to put us ahead 2–1.

The score stayed that way into the bottom of the sixth, thanks in equal parts to a workmanlike performance by Marty and two plays in the field that resulted in outs at home plate.

A defensive blunder by Luzinski in the bottom of the sixth allowed Houston to tie the score. Denny Walling hit a catchable line drive that grazed off Bull's glove for a two-base error. With one out, Alan Ashby drove in Walling with a single.

That was it for Marty. He gave me all I could have asked for, yielding just one earned run in 5⅓ innings. Brusstar got the final two outs of the sixth.

Ryan, meanwhile, seemed to be getting stronger as the game went on. From the third inning through the seventh, he faced the minimum number of batters.

Both teams knew the classic do-or-die mantra: there is no tomorrow. In reality, the winning team would get tomorrow off before squaring off against the Royals. The loser would have 120-some tomorrows until spring training.

The circumstances prompted me to get creative with my choice of relief pitchers. Our bullpen had logged a lot of innings in the series, so I turned to Game 3 starter Larry Christenson, pitching on one day's rest, to give me an inning.

Puhl, who went 10-for-19 in the series, again led off an inning with a base hit. Cabell sacrificed him to second, where he stayed on a ground out. We were one big out away from keeping the game deadlocked, but Houston mounted a rally. After Cruz walked, Walling singled to right to score Puhl. Christenson then uncorked a wild pitch that brought Cruz home. Ron Reed came in and surrendered a run-scoring triple to Art Howe. When the inning finally ended, the Astros led 5–2.

Just like the night before, we were six outs away from 120 tomorrows. Ed Wade, the Astros' public relations director, left the Astrodome press box and started making preparations for the postgame press conference. "With Ryan on the mound, I thought we had it wrapped up," the future Phillies general manager said.

Some dugouts might have gotten quiet at this point. But ours was buzzing with energy. Everybody in a Phillies uniform wanted a piece of the action. Out in the bullpen, Dickie Noles was nearly coming out of his skin. He had pitched well in Games 3 and 4, so I had him get loose in both the sixth and seventh innings before deciding to sit him back down for good. Between innings, Dickie came down from the bullpen and paced furiously from one end of the dugout to the other, making sure I saw him each time he passed. On his third time by, he stopped in front of me.

"What's the matter, you don't trust me?" he yelled. "Put me in the game!"

I respected Dickie's fire, and always had, but at that moment I had more pressing concerns.

"Get your ass back to the bullpen, Dickie!" I screamed at him. "I'll let you know if I need you!"

Dickie wasn't alone. Everybody in the dugout wanted to grab a bat. It was a controlled intensity, however. And that was important. With Ryan very much in control, we would have played right into his hands if our guys got overeager at the plate. We couldn't bank on erasing the deficit with a long ball. Home runs had been few and far between in the series. In fact, Bull's homer in Game 1 stood as the only one hit by either team. To win this game, we needed to chip away at the lead.

Before Bowa led off the inning, Rose told him, "Get on base, and we'll win this thing." Bowa proceeded to dump a single into center field.

What happened next had a profound impact on the outcome of the game. Booney hit a grounder back to the mound. The ball, which wasn't hit hard, ricocheted off Ryan's glove and fell into no-man's land for an infield single. If Ryan fielded ball, the Astros would have easily turned a double play, making a Houston–Kansas City World Series that much more likely. But as it stood, we had runners on first and second with nobody out.

• • •

The roar of the fans in the Astrodome made it difficult to talk to anyone. That led to a lot of interior monologues in the dugout and on the field.

From the third-base coaching box, Lee Elia had a perfect view of the unfolding events through the eyes of our team. After each pitch, Lee looked to the bench for a sign. These glimpses of a team on the brink provided him with his most lasting memory of the 1980 season. "I looked in there and saw the faces of guys who had been fighting all year to accomplish something this team had never done before," Lee recalls. "I'm looking at Dallas Green, Bobby Wine, Pete, Schmitty. I see the tension and the pressure. I see Dallas on the top step, refusing to accept that the season may be coming to an end. I'm also thinking to myself, *You're the only person who has this picture.*"

What was going through my mind? Memories of the 1976, 1977, and 1978 seasons were certainly in there somewhere. I hated to think we might be headed for the same fate as those teams. If we didn't at least reach the World Series, I wouldn't return as manager, and the team would be broken up.

Bobby, who had experienced the three previous playoff losses as Danny Ozark's chief deputy, couldn't help but think, *Oh no, not again. Almost, but not quite.* Like me, Bobby was also haunted by ghosts of 1964, the year we were teammates on a Phillies team that seemed destined for the World Series before famously flopping.

Sylvia and our four children nervously watched the final innings at our home. They had attended the two games at the Vet, but like so many Phillies fans, were now glued to their TV, praying for a miracle. Sylvia hoped she wouldn't have to face a classroom full of disappointed students the next day. And she hated to think that our kids might get taunted at school if their dad's team didn't pull the game out.

• • •

Ryan, chomping on his chewing gum, stared in at Greg Gross. Historically, Ryan was nearly unbeatable when taking a lead past the seventh inning. In nearly 3,000 career plate appearances to that point, Greg had bunted for a base hit just a few times. But with the infield playing back, Greg squared around on Ryan's first pitch and dropped a perfect bunt up the third-base line. He easily beat it out for a hit.

With the bases loaded and nobody out, Rose, a .382 career hitter against Ryan, came to the plate. Pete worked the count full, fouled off a pitch, and then took ball four. Pete defiantly slung his bat toward the dugout and trotted to first base as Bowa crossed home plate to cut the Houston lead to just two runs.

Bill Virdon decided to end the night for Ryan. With the bases still loaded, Joe Sambito got pinch hitter Keith Moreland to ground into a force out at second, but a run scored on the play to bring us even closer.

Virdon saw the game slipping away, so he called on Ken Forsch, normally a starter, to face Schmidt with the go-ahead runs on base. Forsch struck Schmitty out on three pitches.

In desperate need of a clutch two-out at-bat, I called on a guy who hadn't had a postseason hit during his 13-year major league career.

Del Unser sized up Forsch from the on-deck circle before coming on to pinch-hit for Ron Reed. First-pitch swinging, he stroked a game-tying single to right-center field.

The enthusiasm level in the dugout was now off the charts. And the Astrodome suddenly quieted. Pete was slapping fives with anybody within arm's reach. Bowa was jumping up and down like a kid. John and George Vukovich (no relation) and Keith Moreland were hooting and hollering.

The excitement reached an even higher level when Trillo ripped a two-run triple. We had entered the inning trailing 5–2. After Maddox flied out to retire the side, we led 7–5.

• • •

At 36 years of age, Tugger wasn't a kid. After losing time to injury in July, he became a real workhorse in September. And he had pitched in each of the first four games of the NLCS, including three innings in Game 3. He needed a day off. Everyone in our beleaguered bull-pen did. But given the circumstances, I chose to bring him in to help hold the lead. My other option was Dick Ruthven, my would-be Game 5 starter. Like Noles earlier, Ruthven was champing at the bit to get in the game. But he hadn't pitched in relief all year. And I believed Tugger had at least one more inning left in his arm. If he looked sharp in the eighth, I would consider keeping him in for a six-out save. If not, Ruthven would still be available to pitch multiple innings in a tie game. In a series where no lead was safe, I felt this was a sound strategy.

But Tugger couldn't get the job done in the eighth. Craig Reynolds reached base on an infield single, and Puhl soon followed with his fourth hit of the game. With runners on first and third and two outs, Rafael Landestoy singled in a run. Jose Cruz followed with another single that tied the score at 7–7.

We had punched and the Astros had counterpunched. Now it was our turn to try and put Houston on the mat once and for all. We got runners on first and third in the top of the ninth against Frank LaCorte, but George Vukovich, pinch-hitting for Tugger, grounded out to end the threat.

As planned, I brought in Ruthven for the bottom of the ninth. I'm sure a lot of our guys had their hearts in their throats at that point. I know I did. Few teams in baseball manufactured runs better than Houston, and all they needed now was to scratch a lone run across.

We hadn't had a one-two-three inning all game. But when we needed one most, Ruthven delivered, retiring Dave Bergman, Ashby, and Reynolds to preserve the tie.

It was only fitting, I guess, that a series that had already featured the most extra-inning games in NLCS history wouldn't be settled in only nine innings.

In the top of the 10th inning, Schmitty struck out, making him 0-for-5 on the day with three strikeouts. It turned out to be his last at-bat of a disappointing NLCS in which he had only one extra-base hit and one RBI.

But this series was all about the unexpected. With one out, a role player came up big again. Unser smacked a ball to first base that took a nasty hop and sailed over Bergman's head and into the right-field corner for a double. Unser remained on second after Trillo flied out. The responsibility of bringing him home fell on the shoulders of Maddox, who, like so many of the Phillies, had only tasted playoff defeat. Garry and I didn't always see eye to eye during the 1980 season, but we had become united in our goal of seeing this series to a successful conclusion.

On LaCorte's first offering, Garry hit a sinking fly ball to center that fell under Puhl's glove for a go-ahead double.

This time, the lead held. Ruthven came back to pitch the 10th. With two outs and nobody on, Enos Cabell lifted a lazy fly ball to center. Garry loped over and squeezed it for the final out. His teammates carried him off the field, one of several mini-celebrations that broke out all over the infield of the Astrodome.

Pope and I hugged and cried all the way to the clubhouse and continued blubbering as the players celebrated one of the most thrilling playoff series in baseball history.

• • •

Whether we won or lost, I would have considered Game 5 one of the greatest playoff games ever. As a whole, the series had enough twists and turns to keep even casual fans on the edges of their seats. It represented the game at its best.

Trillo, whose career year in '80 included eight hits and four RBIs in the NLCS, was named MVP of the series. But five or six other guys easily could have won that honor. Our victory was a total team effort.

I'll always remember the harrowing intensity of that Houston series. We celebrated our victory with a jubilance normally reserved for teams that have just won the World Series. But after weathering so many storms against the Astros, I don't think anybody in the Phillies organization felt our run could possibly end. The screaming and the yelling and the champagne in Houston gave us a much-needed release from six days of pure anxiety. That series was memorable, but it was never fun.

On the other hand, with the monkey finally off our back, the World Series had the potential to be a blast.

11

AFTER OUR EPIC FIVE-GAME victory over the Astros in the National League Championship Series, Pete Rose told me he thought the World Series would be "a piece of cake."

The Royals were actually favored to beat us, however. Kansas City had six more wins than we did during the season and had just come off a sweep of a Yankees team that won 103 games in 1980. Those who liked the Royals' chances figured we had spent a season's worth of energy and emotion in the battle with Houston. We had a couple of things in common with Kansas City. Like us, the Royals had lost three straight League Championship Series between 1976 and 1978. And like me, the Royals were led by a rookie manager, Jim Frey.

With so much on the line, a rookie pitcher making his postseason debut got the start for us in Game 1. Our series against the Astros, which forced me to use starters as relievers in multiple games, had badly depleted our pitching resources. I could have opted to go with Steve Carlton on two days' rest in Game 1 at Veterans Stadium, but the risk was too great. Lefty had pitched 304 innings during the season, more than anyone else in the majors, and was a much better pitcher on regular rest. I took a chance and gave the ball to Bob Walk, one of the few players not to appear in the Houston series.

Walk won 11 games during the season but hadn't been too sharp in August or September. Marty Bystrom's tremendous run in the final weeks of the season earned him a start over Walk in the NLCS. I hadn't considered using Bobby in relief, either. He was a bit of a flake, and I didn't know how well he would handle the tension of pitching in the playoffs.

Now he was the only fresh arm we had. I hoped he could keep things competitive in the most important start of his young career.

By the time we came to bat in the bottom of the third inning, my decision to start Bobby wasn't looking good. The Royals already led 4–0 behind a pair of two-run home runs by Willie Mays Aikens and Amos Otis. Early on, it looked like Royals starter Dennis Leonard, a 20-game winner during the season, might send nearly 66,000 fans at the Vet home disappointed.

But unlike the series against Houston, this time we didn't wait until the late innings to mount a comeback.

With one out in the bottom of the third, Larry Bowa singled and shocked the hell out of all of us by stealing second. We had been trying all year to get him to run more. And he finally got the message in a World Series game we trailed by four runs! The steal shocked the hell out of the Royals, too, and in my opinion, it kick-started our offense. We pounced on Leonard for five runs that inning, three of them coming on a blast by Bake McBride, a left-handed hitter I inserted in the clean-up spot to provide a cushion between righties Mike Schmidt and Greg Luzinski.

A run apiece in the fourth and fifth innings expanded our lead to 7–4.

Walk settled down after his rocky start, giving up just one hit between the third and seventh innings. But another two-run shot by Aikens in the eighth kept the Royals close.

With the score 7–6 and nobody out, I had to deprive Tug McGraw of a much-needed night of rest. For the sixth consecutive game in the playoffs, I called on him to help secure a win. And that meant I needed six outs from him.

Tugger gave up a hit in the eighth and breezed through the ninth to shut the door on the Phillies' first World Series victory in 65 years.

Walk gave up three long balls, but he helped himself immensely by keeping Royals speedster Willie Wilson off the bases. Wilson, a .326 hitter who led the majors in runs scored, went 0-for-5 in Game 1. Walk also held George Brett, who flirted with .400 for much of the season, to just one hit in four at-bats.

Other than having to use Tugger yet again, I felt upbeat about Game 1. Walk gutted out seven innings, giving everyone in the bullpen not named McGraw the night off. And our bats helped make that possible. I wouldn't have been able to stick with Walk as long if our offense hadn't staked him to a lead.

Before every game of the playoffs, pitching coach Herm Starrette checked with everyone on the staff to see how they felt. A long season takes its toll on the body, but having come this far, nobody in the bullpen wanted to say anything that might discourage us from using them. I knew I was wearing Tugger out. But with a game on the line, I wanted a guy on the mound who showed no fear. That was Tugger.

"Certainly I was tired," he told Philadelphia sportswriters after Game 1, "but there's always room to reach back for a little extra. I don't have enough brains to realize how important this is. I just enjoy myself. Emotionally, I can't get enough of it."

• • •

I liked that we were playing with confidence, but I didn't want us to get too relaxed.

"I'm not saying what I'll do," I said before the series. "But I don't think I'll wait for a guy to be 0-for-12 before I make a lineup change."

Under the rules at the time, every game of the World Series was played either with or without the designated hitter, no matter the ballpark. Even-numbered years were the ones when the DH was used, so that meant I had a spot in the lineup for an extra bat. In the series opener, I used Bull as our DH and put Lonnie Smith in left field. When Bull's name was nowhere to be found in the Game 2 lineup, my statement was interpreted as a commentary on his performance.

My decision to stick with Lonnie in left and use Keith Moreland as our DH was at least partly based on the fact that Bull had come down with a mild case of the flu. A lot of people didn't buy it. Mindful of our battles during the season, many interpreted the lineup adjustment as my way of punishing Bull for his 0-for-3 performance in Game 1. To this day, a lot of people cite his absence in the second game against the Royals as evidence that I had it out for Bull.

It's hard for me to accept the allegation that I would bench a guy in the World Series purely out of spite. For several seasons, Bull had been a big part of our offense, and maybe he deserved more playing time than I gave him in the playoffs. But by fielding a team I thought gave us the best chance to win that night, I was simply following the blueprint of the season. Under the circumstances, I felt Moreland and Smith could help us more at the two positions Bull could have played.

• • •

I hoped to avoid a repeat of the NLCS, in which we split the first two games of the series at the Vet. With Carlton facing Larry Gura in Game 2, we needed to win or risk giving the Royals a big boost in momentum as the series moved to Kansas City for the next three games.

Lefty held the Royals without an earned run over the first six innings of Game 2, then suddenly lost his command of the strike zone. Three walks in the seventh inning contributed to three Kansas City runs that gave the Royals a 4–2 lead.

Every baseball writer in the press box waited to see how we'd respond. Either way, they had a ready-made lede to their game stories.

Another late-inning rally by the Phillies would solidify our reputation as the Comeback Kids. If we fell short, however, there'd be a lot made about our run of improbable victories coming to a screeching halt.

We got the newspaper headlines we wanted.

Bob Boone led off the eighth with a walk against Royals closer and AL saves leader Dan Quisenberry. Del Unser, pinch-hitting for Lonnie Smith, smacked a double to drive home Boone. A double by Schmidt and singles by McBride and Moreland later in the inning brought in three more runs.

I can't say enough about the contributions of our role players during the 1980 postseason. Del Unser, who delivered two critical hits in Game 5 of the NLCS, came through again in the World Series. He and Greg Gross were among the most prepared players on the team. Each would spend a lot of time in the clubhouse watching game tape and live games on TV to pick up on the tendencies of opposing pitchers. Before the World Series, they studied Quisenberry, knowing that as left-handed hitters, they'd likely be called on to face him in the late innings. That preparation had paid off for Del in Game 2.

With a 6–4 lead entering the ninth, I normally would have called for Tugger. But there was no question that he needed a night off. Ron Reed, who saved nine games during the season, came in to try and get the final three outs. He brought the tying run to the plate but got out of the inning unscathed.

We would have cruised to victory in Game 2 if Carlton hadn't walked six batters. In my postgame remarks, I attributed Lefty's inability to get a proper grip on his slider to the fact that the game balls were unusually slippery. I said I'd be contacting the commissioner's office with a formal complaint. Even though we won, I felt I needed to stick up for my ace.

In winning the first two games at home, we had put the Royals in a bind. They had to win two of three games at Royals Stadium to prevent us from celebrating a championship on their field. And even if they swept the middle three games of the series, we'd still have a shot to win the title back at the Vet.

• • •

Bull's illness kept him from traveling with the team to Kansas City, but when he showed up, he fumed that I didn't even ask him how he felt. I left the Game 2 lineup unchanged for Game 3, which pitted Dick Ruthven against Rich Gale.

I couldn't have asked for more from Ruthven, who gave up three runs in nine innings. Unfortunately, we went cold in the clutch. Despite 14 hits and six walks, we only scored three runs. In the process, we tied a World Series record by stranding 15 runners on base.

The game went to the 10th inning tied 3–3. I hoped Tugger, who was pitching on two days' rest for the first time that postseason, could keep the Royals scoreless long enough for us to pull the game out. But with two outs in the 10th, Aikens singled home Wilson with the winning run.

Talk about a frustrating loss. We had the Royals where we wanted them but couldn't put them away to go up 3–0 in the series.

"We had a chance to crush this team tonight, but we just passed it up," I lamented after the game. "We had the game if we can come up with that one clutch hit."

The defeat gave us our first taste of adversity in the World Series. Our response to that setback would be critical. But Game 4 didn't start any better than Game 3 had ended. The Royals jumped all over Larry Christenson for four runs in the first inning. It just wasn't Larry's night, and he recorded only one out before I pulled him from the game. He even committed an error on a would-be pick-off play at first base. His father was in a coma with a brain aneurysm, so L.C.'s thoughts may have been elsewhere. Dickie Noles and Kevin Saucier hadn't pitched since the NLCS, but it appeared I'd need multiple innings from one of them. Dickie had been warming up for just a few seconds when bullpen coach Mike Ryan asked him if he was ready. "Ready!" responded Dickie, not about to pass up a chance to pitch in the World Series.

Dickie got us out of the inning, but we still had four runs to make up. When he went back for his second inning of work, the score was 4–1…at least for a little while. Dickie retired the first two hitters, but Aikens added to the Royals' lead with yet another home run. As the ball sailed out toward right field, Dickie turned and watched it clear the fence. When he turned back around, he saw Aikens still standing at the plate, admiring his fourth homer of the series. This didn't escape Dickie's attention. "Willie, you better start running, or you're gonna get hit next time!" he shouted.

Back in the dugout between innings, Dickie started talking to Moreland, Bystrom, and Walk. I didn't hear exactly what was being said, but I had a pretty good idea of the general topic. Somebody was going to pay for Aikens' showmanship.

A couple of innings later, Aikens was in the on-deck circle when George Brett pissed Dickie off by taking his time getting in the batter's box. During the day off before Game 3, Brett underwent minor surgery to lance a swollen hemorrhoid. Maybe he wasn't feeling himself, or maybe he was just trying to get under Dickie's skin. After each of the first two pitches, both strikes, he stepped out of the box and made Dickie wait some more. At that time in his life, Dickie was easy to agitate, so he decided to throw his 0-2 pitch high and tight. The order didn't come from the bench, but I was pleased with the outcome.

The ball sailed up and under the chin of Brett, who dove to the ground to avoid being hit. For a couple of seconds, an eerie silence came over Kauffman Stadium. Then, in unison, more than 40,000 fans started booing like crazy.

Royals manager Jim Frey raced out of the dugout screaming bloody murder: "He was trying to hit him! He was trying to hit him!"

Jimmy tried to sidestep home-plate umpire Don Denkinger to go out after Dickie.

Pete Rose viewed the outburst with amusement. "Jimmy, get your ass back in the dugout!" Rose yelled. "If he wanted to hit him, he would've hit him!"

When play resumed, Dickie struck out Brett. Then he struck out Aikens. As we left the field, a fan threw an object that grazed Pete. It turned out to be a wadded-up paper cup, but we didn't really care what it was. A bunch of our guys jumped out of the dugout looking for the guilty party.

We still trailed the Royals by four runs, but we showed some fight that afternoon. We cut the lead to 5–3 in the eighth, and that's how the game ended. The series was now tied.

Though we didn't win the game, I liked that the team showed a little fire. In my playing days, no one thought twice if a pitcher brushed back a hitter, especially one whose team was getting a little too comfortable at the plate. Nobody questioned why it happened because the answer was obvious.

After the game, Aikens made no public apologies for standing at home plate to admire his home runs: "When I hit a baseball well and I know it's going out, I like to watch and get some enjoyment out of it."

Dickie sent the Royals a message, but now we needed to send them an even stronger message by stopping Aikens' power surge.

• • •

We proved earlier in the World Series that we could win two games in a row at home, but I hoped that wouldn't be necessary. It was time to thwart Kansas City's momentum.

The next game summed up our season well.

I again put my trust in 22-year-old Marty Bystrom to pitch in a high-pressure situation on the road. And just like in the decisive game of the NLCS, Marty kept us in the ballgame, giving up three runs in five innings. When Marty departed, the game was tied 2–2, but Reed allowed an inherited run to score, giving Kansas City the lead.

After Larry Gura put two men on base with one out in the top of the seventh, Frey gave him the hook. In came Dan Quisenberry to try for an eight-out save. Though that would be unheard of in today's game, Quiz was no stranger to multi-inning outings. In tying Goose Gossage for the AL saves title in 1980, he often pitched three or more innings in a game.

Quisenberry's side-winding sinker got Kansas City out of trouble in the seventh. For the second time in three days, I turned the game into a battle of closers by bringing in Tugger for what I hoped would be a nine-out win. He kept the game close. We still trailed 3–2 going to the ninth.

To that point, we had mustered little offense against Quisenberry. Our only base runner against him reached on an error by Brett. The first five outs he registered all came on ground balls, a sign his sinker was working that afternoon.

In the ninth, we finally got to him. Schmitty, who had provided our only scoring of the night with a two-run homer in the fourth, started us off with an infield single that skipped off Brett's glove. By squaring to bunt a couple of times earlier in the series, Schmitty had planted the idea of a bunt in Frey's head. So there was Brett, playing a few steps in to guard against a possible bunt by a guy who hit 48 homers during the season and one earlier in the game. If Brett had been playing at normal depth, he likely would have made the play.

Lonnie Smith had pinch-run for Luzinski, who was back in the lineup, earlier in the game. Now I felt I had a better option than Lonnie sitting on my bench. I wanted to give Del Unser and his hot bat a shot at Quisenberry. In the NLCS, Del knocked in the tying run and scored the winning run in the series-clincher in Houston. And his double in Game 2 of the World Series helped key a win.

Much to our enjoyment, he came through again in Game 5. His double down the first-base line scored Schmitty from first base and tied the score. Two outs later, with Unser standing on third, Manny Trillo hit a liner that bounced off Quisenberry's glove for an infield single to put us ahead 4–3.

With Brett and Aikens due up in the bottom of the ninth, Tugger had his work cut out for him. A leadoff walk to Frank White didn't make his job any easier. Tugger had thrown just 24 pitches coming into the inning, so I chose to stick with him. A three-pitch strikeout of Brett gave me confidence he had enough in the tank to finish the game. A four-pitch walk to Aikens had the opposite effect.

The Royals had the tying and winning runs on base and Hal McRae, a veteran in his sixth postseason who was hitting close to .500 in the series, coming to the plate. He hit a towering drive down the left-field line that barely curled foul. After we all breathed a huge sigh of relief, Tugger got him to ground into a force out, giving Kansas City runners on first and third with two outs.

Aikens' four home runs in the series had grabbed a lot of attention. But he wasn't the hitter I most feared in the Kansas City lineup. That distinction belonged to Amos Otis, whose 11 World Series hits in 20 at-bats to that point included three home runs. Before the game, I chatted with Boone about what to do if Otis came up in a pivotal situation in the late innings. If it was feasible, I wanted to intentionally walk him. If not, I didn't want to give him anything to hit. With runners on the corners, an intentional pass would have put the winning run in scoring position and given Tugger no margin for error.

Maybe Otis would be overzealous and swing at bad balls. Not a chance. Tugger threw four pitches in a row out of the strike zone, and Otis took his base.

The bases were loaded for Jose Cardenal, a former Phillie who didn't have a hit yet in the series. A walk would tie the score, and any hit that reached the outfield would likely win it for Kansas City. The stakes of this Game 5 weren't as high as Game 5 of the NLCS—the series wouldn't end with a win or a loss. But the team that pulled this game out would have a distinct edge when the series shifted back to Philadelphia.

Tugger's pitch count was up to 42. He reached deep for a few more good screwballs and got Cardenal to strike out to deliver that nine-out win I'd been looking for.

Tugger, one of the few guys on the team who showed no inhibitions in front of the press, uncorked a real doozy of a quote after the game: "When I was out there, I had a feeling of guilt, because I was out a little late last night," he told the reporters huddled around his locker. "I had a couple of extra beers to relax me, and then my wife relaxed me."

He went on to explain what was going through his mind before Cardenal's at-bat: "I looked at the scoreboard and saw that Jose didn't have a hit in the series. I was just praying that this wasn't going to be one of those fairy tale stories where Jose Cardenal came back to haunt the Phillies with a two-run single in the bottom of the ninth. Thankfully, that plot wasn't written."

From the day in August 1979 that I came down from the front office to manage the Phillies, this was the situation I hoped we'd be in. With one more win, the Phillies would be World Series champions for the first time. Even better, the celebration would take place in our home stadium in front of our long-suffering fans.

• • •

Close to 11:30 PM on October 21, 1980, Tug McGraw found himself in a familiar setting, pitching in a tense situation with the ballgame on the line. We led the Royals 4–1 in the top of the ninth of Game 6, but Kansas City had the bases loaded and only one out.

How badly did Philadelphia want a championship? So badly that the Philadelphia Police Department stationed mounted officers on the field to preserve order if Tugger recorded the final two outs. Also surrounding the dugout were police officers with German shepherds.

Steve Carlton had staked us to a lead by pitching seven-plus strong innings. Now Tugger was trying to seal the deal. He started the ninth by striking out Otis. But I could tell he was laboring. We had played 11 postseason games, and he had pitched in nine of them. Before White came to the plate, I wondered whether Tugger had finally run out of gas. Reed was warming up in the bullpen and was ready to come in at my signal. I stood on the top step of the dugout debating whether to walk out to the mound and take the ball from Tugger.

And there I stayed.

Tired and prone to bouts of wildness, Tugger was lucky White came up hacking. He lifted the first pitch high into the air in foul territory behind home plate. Bob Boone flipped off his catcher's mask and gave chase. I saw the ball go up but lost sight of it as it descended near our dugout. It looked like a routine play, so I waited for confirmation from the crowd that we had recorded the second out of the inning. Instead I heard the collective gasp of 66,000 people, followed immediately by thunderous cheers.

What the hell just happened? I wondered. I looked up at the stadium's video screen to get the answer.

Pete Rose, who ran in to make a play on the ball, ended up an arm's length away from Booney but backed off at the last second as Booney looked up and prepared to make the catch. What followed became a staple of every highlight reel of the 1980 World Series. The ball hit the middle of Booney's glove and bounced back out. Pete instantly reacted, lunged, and picked the ball out of the air just as it was about to hit the ground. Instead of White getting new life and Tugger having to throw more pitches, we got an enormous second out. To this day, Boone insists it should have been Pete's play all the way.

As a kid born and raised in Delaware, I grew up a Phillies fan and was fortunate enough to begin my major league career with the team in 1960.
(AP Images)

After taking over as Philadelphia's manager in 1979, well, let's just say I wasn't one to mince words, especially when it came to making my feelings felt to the umpires. (Getty Images)

Ruben Amaro, Pete Rose, and I celebrate winning the 1980 National League pennant thanks to a Game 5 victory in the NLCS against the Houston Astros. (AP Images)

That's Ruly Carpenter and me in 1981, shortly after Ruly announced that his family was putting the Phillies up for sale. Everyone in the organization took the news hard. (AP Images)

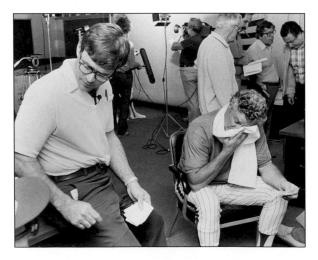

Dreams really do come true. This shot was taken after we won Game 5 in Kansas City in the 1980 World Series. We finished the Royals off two days later to claim the Phillies' first championship. (AP Images)

Our World Series victory was extra sweet for me because I was able to share it with my longtime friend and mentor, Paul Owens. Pope demonstrated enormous faith in me throughout my career, and for that I am forever grateful. (Philadelphia Daily News)

When I took over the front office of the Cubs, I brought Lee Elia from Philadelphia to be our manager. Letting him go in just his second season at the helm was the toughest personnel decision I had to make in my career.
(Chicago Cubs)

Leon Durham, Ryne Sandberg, Lee Smith, and Mel Hall were a huge part of the success we had in Chicago. Hall was valuable even as he left town—he was part of the package I sent to Cleveland in 1984 in exchange for Rick Sutcliffe.
(Chicago Cubs)

I hired Jim Frey, the skipper of the Royals when the Phillies beat them in the 1980 World Series, to manage the Cubs in 1984. He won the Manager of the Year Award for guiding the Cubs to their first postseason appearance since 1945. (Chicago Cubs)

After a disappointing 1985 season and a lackluster start in 1986, I relieved Frey of his duties. In 1987, the Cubs did the same thing to me. (Chicago Cubs)

After serving as general manager of the Cubs from 1982 to 1987, I went back to the dugout in 1989 to manage George Steinbrenner's Yankees. We had our share of disagreements, but I respected his commitment to putting a winning team on the field. (USA Today)

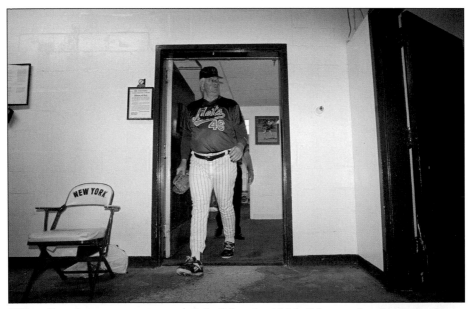

When I took over as manager of the Mets in 1993, I knew that I was in for a challenge. The team was 18 games under .500 when I walked through the door. (AP Images)

My wonderful wife, Sylvia, with whom I've shared my life since we met in 1955.

Sylvia and I were blessed with four wonderful children: Kim, Doug, John, and Dana.

No family should have to endure what my son, John, his wife, Roxanna, and their son, Dallas, have in losing their beloved daughter and sister, Christina-Taylor. My granddaughter was shot and killed in the Tucson, Arizona, massacre that also resulted in the shooting of U.S. Representative Gabrielle Giffords in 2011.

Attending the funeral service for Christina-Taylor truly tested the strength and fortitude of our family. I can only hope that my granddaughter's story can inspire others to take action and live life to the fullest. (AP Images)

The only man who stood between us and a championship was Willie Wilson, whose World Series struggles belied how dangerous he could be. Tugger would later admit all his postseason innings finally caught up to him in the ninth inning of Game 6 of the World Series. Suddenly, it hurt like hell for him to throw a screwball, his best pitch. But that's what he offered the left-handed-hitting Wilson to start the at-bat. The pitch started outside and broke back over the plate for a strike.

Booney, who called a game better than anybody, wanted Tugger to throw another screwball. But Tugger didn't think his arm would cooperate, so he shook him off and threw a slider. Wilson fouled the pitch off his foot. The third pitch of the at-bat was a not-so-fast fastball that sailed a little high for a ball. Tugger had thrown three different pitches to Wilson and had him guessing now. On the fourth pitch, Tugger came in with another fastball.

Wilson swung through it to end the game.

Tugger danced off the mound and leapt in the air. Fireworks exploded over the stadium and the words *World Champions* blinked on the scoreboard as we raced out of the dugout and swarmed him.

In the clubhouse, Pope and I hugged each other and cried like babies. I composed myself long enough to take a congratulatory phone call from President Jimmy Carter. The victory was a culmination of everything Pope and I had experienced together as Phillies since 1956. He had trained me well, and it felt wonderful to help bring him and the organization a championship. I was ecstatic.

In his postgame comments to reporters, Tugger, his left arm wrapped in ice, deflected attention away from himself. "Dallas lined out his program of what Phillie baseball should be," he said amid the mist of champagne. "He told us we had to be a team with character, that we had to look in the mirror. He was just an average player at best, and where he got his 'Phillie baseball' is beyond me. But he had confidence in his ideas, and he backed his people. It took us a few months to catch on, but then we did."

Schmitty, who got us rolling in Game 6 with a two-run single in the third inning, earned World Series MVP honors. He had shaken off a subpar NLCS to go 8-for-21 against Kansas City. Carlton won three games for us in the postseason. When we needed them, our stars came through. But the championship wouldn't have been possible without our bench and bullpen.

We celebrated through the night and went straight from the ballpark to a ticker-tape parade down Broad Street and into John F. Kennedy Stadium. Pope, Ruly Carpenter, and I clutched raised hands in the air aboard the Phillies' truck. In my speech at the stadium, I uttered words that could only be said in October: "You people are beautiful, and this team is beautiful."

We had reached the top of the mountain. For two lifelong baseball guys like Pope and me, there was no better feeling. Back in those days, baseball could still boast that it was the country's most popular sport. Almost 55 million people watched Game 6 of the '80 World Series, the largest audience in postseason history. And all those viewers got to witness the Phillies' first title in franchise history. Unfortunately, due to a Major League Baseball restriction on local broadcasts, Harry Kalas and Richie Ashburn didn't get to call any of the World Series games.

I wondered if I would hear from my former manager, Gene Mauch, in the weeks following our triumph. Gene was between jobs at the time, having been fired by the Twins during the 1980 season. I thought he might call to deliver a quick congratulations. But my phone never rang.

Ironically, I didn't win the *The Sporting News* Manager of the Year Award that season. In a vote taken before the start of the playoffs, baseball writers gave the award to Bill Virdon of the Astros.

• • •

Sylvia was a trouper during that amazing season, rarely missing a home game. After teaching high school all day in Newark, Delaware, she'd drive 15 miles to our home in West Grove, Pennsylvania, and pick up our youngest son, Doug. Then they'd drive 40 miles from our home to the ballpark. By the end of the season, she was equal parts exhausted and thrilled.

Our lives changed after winning the World Series. There began to be a lot more demands on my time, and everyday outings were no longer quite so routine. If we went to the Christiana Mall in Wilmington, 50 people would line up for autographs while we were eating french fries in the food court.

Our fans sure were thrilled with our championship.

I guess the alternative is the last-place manager who's met with indifference or jeers when he visits the local mall. Given a choice between the two, I'll take my experience every time.

12

IN ADDITION TO BRINGING a ton of satisfaction to me, the Phillies, and the city of Philadelphia, winning a World Series had the unforeseen benefit of helping me graduate from college.

In 1955, following my junior year at the University of Delaware, I signed a free agent contract with the Phillies. At the time, I was several courses short of getting my degree. During my playing career, I took classes during the off-season, but when I became the Phillies' minor league director in 1972, I decided I probably didn't need the diploma to fulfill my career goals. With the passage of time, however, I got to thinking about my four kids and the messages I wanted to convey to them through my actions. By finally getting my degree, I would be able to impart two lessons in one: the value of education and the importance of finishing what you start.

With Sylvia's prodding and after discussing the situation with administrators at the University of Delaware, it was decided I could obtain the final credits required for graduation by completing a special project for labor relations professor Arthur Sloane. On top of being a brilliant mind and an accomplished author, Sloane was also a real baseball nut. I had already appeared as a guest lecturer in his class, speaking to students about the influence of the Major League Baseball Players Association on the economics of the game. For my project, Professor Sloane tasked me with writing a paper on what I did to change the Phillies in 1980. I wrote the essay, and with that, obtained my degree in business administration.

I wasn't your typical manager. I won a World Series in my first full season as skipper of the Phillies. I also became only the third former major league pitcher to manage a team to a championship. It's a rule of thumb in baseball that retired pitchers become pitching coaches, not managers, probably because pitchers are so focused on mastering their own craft that they develop tunnel vision. Until someone misses a cut-off man behind them or fails to score on a double because he doesn't run the bases properly, pitchers tend not to think too much about what's going on around them. I was never like that. I learned how to bunt, field my position and hold runners, run the bases, and take signs. I schooled myself on the intricacies of baseball. I faced enough obstacles as a player, and I didn't want a lack of fundamentals to be one of them.

None of the coaches on my staff in 1980 were standout major leaguers. Ruben Amaro, who hit .234 in 11 major league seasons and got some MVP votes in 1964, had the most successful career. Herm Starrette, our pitching coach, won just one game in three seasons. Mike Ryan (.193 in 11 seasons), Lee Elia (.203 in two seasons), Bobby Wine (.215 in 12 seasons), and Billy DeMars (.237 in three seasons) were, like me, mediocre at best during their playing careers. But they were all outstanding teachers who contributed significantly to our championship.

A relatively small number of Hall of Fame players have managed in the majors. At least in recent years, that's a result of star players retiring with so much money that they don't need to continue working. But managers and coaches who struggled as players bring a valuable perspective to a team. They tend to be hard workers who know how to handle adversity.

Despite my successful transition from the front office to the dugout, the plan was still for me to take over as Phillies general manager when Paul Owens decided to retire. At the age of 56, Pope wasn't at that point yet, so I agreed to return as manager for the 1981 season. We had righted the ship and won a World Series, and I saw no reason why we couldn't repeat as champions. I loved almost everything about the Phillies organization and wanted to see it remain as successful as possible.

• • •

I say "almost everything," because, dating back to my playing days, one thing the organization had always struggled with was stinginess. As a player I fought tooth and nail to earn an additional $500, only to be denied the raise. After 10 years in the front office, I was still only making around $40,000 a year. As manager, I got bumped up to $75,000. Pope helped reinforce the organization's reputation for frugality by never making hay about his own salary, which paled in comparison to his counterparts around the majors.

"Jesus Christ, Pope, you don't get a raise, so no one else gets a raise!" I'd playfully scold him.

My family was doing fine, but with four kids to put through college, a few extra bucks wouldn't have hurt. After winning the World Series, I was sure I'd be in line for a sizable pay increase. I thought a salary of $120,000 was a reasonable expectation. I bounced that number off Pope, who went to team treasurer George Harrison for approval. We were having a ball at the 1980 team Christmas party when Pope reported back to me with disappointing news.

"That goddamn George Harrison!" Pope bellowed. "He won't give an inch. He's willing to give you $90,000."

Thanks to the party, I was very much feeling the yuletide spirit, but not to the point where I couldn't identify an insult when one was slapping me in the face. Pope and I had already gone a few rounds with George over the issuance of World Series rings. We rightfully believed the championship came about due to the efforts of everyone in the organization, from the scouts to every player on the roster.

But George decided he was only going to give rings to the top front office people, the manager, and the starting players! Bill Giles, who was the Phillies vice president at the time, intervened on our behalf. Everyone got a ring, though not everyone got the *same* ring. Some had fewer diamonds than others.

Still sore about that battle, I let my feelings be known.

"You gotta be shitting me, Pope!" I responded. "We just won the first goddamn World Series in almost a hundred years, and this son of a bitch is holding me up on a few thousand dollars?"

In the days that followed, I pouted like hell. But the Phillies didn't budge. Pope told me he could go behind George's back and find a way to get me almost to $100,000. I wasn't happy, but I asked Pope to go ahead and do that, and I signed a one-year contract for close to six figures.

By the time we got to spring training in 1981, I had put that whole deal behind me. Another situation took precedence.

It shocked us all when Ruly Carpenter announced his family was putting the Phillies up for sale, citing concern over the escalating costs of operating a major league team. Part of that had to do with free agency. Atlanta's signing of Claudell Washington to a five-year, $3.5 million contract after the 1980 season really turned off Ruly's dad, Bob. He and his son both realized that many players would soon command million-dollar salaries. The growing disagreements between owners and the players union threatened to come to a head in 1981. A strike loomed if they couldn't work out their differences.

Ruly, who took over as team president at the age of 32, was liked by everyone in the organization, including the players, and we all took the news hard. I felt a lot better when I found out Giles was leading a group that planned to buy the team. We had all been around Bill long enough to know he was a stand-up guy. As much as I hated to see the end of the Carpenter era in Philadelphia, I understood that business was business.

• • •

Despite the uncertainty over our ownership situation, it was just like old times at spring training. Pope, Hughie Alexander, and I spent most of our time away from the baseball field at a Clearwater hang-out called the Island House. An incident took place there one night that said a couple of things about Pope: one, winning a World Series hadn't changed him a bit; and two, he would always be fiercely loyal to the Carpenter family.

We were in the Island House around dinnertime when we saw former Phillies pitcher Russ "Monk" Meyer sitting at the bar. Pope invited him to join us at our table, where we proceeded to reminisce about Phillies baseball in the 1950s. Russ had a pretty decent career, winning 94 games in 13 seasons and playing in three World Series, one with the Phillies and two with the Dodgers. He was also noto-rious during his playing days for losing his cool on the mound if he didn't pitch well or if errors were committed behind him. Those out-bursts led to a revised nickname: Mad Monk. Once, while pitching for the Dodgers against the Phillies, he got into a heated argument with the home-plate umpire over balls and strikes. Monk got so upset that he heaved his resin bag high into the air. A few seconds later, it came down squarely on his head. That self-inflicted wound earned him an ejection from the game. Back in the dugout, he was caught by television cameras spewing profanity and making obscene gestures toward the umpire.

In Monk and Pope, we had two volatile personalities at the table.

The conversation eventually turned to the Carpenter family's impending sale of the Phillies. After a few drinks, Monk started rail-ing against Bob Carpenter, who ran the Phillies in Monk's playing days. It started off slowly and built to a crescendo. Monk went on and on about Mr. Carpenter's cheapness, mistreatment of players, and lack of baseball knowledge.

Mr. Carpenter had hired Pope and put me through college, so obviously we had different feelings about the man. Monk was our guest at the table, so I held my tongue. Pope let it go for a while, too. But when Monk kept bashing away, Pope issued an ultimatum: "Knock it off, Monk, or I'm going to knock you on your ass!"

"Bob Carpenter was a cheap son of a bitch," Monk growled slowly.

As promised, Pope turned to Monk and nailed him in the face. Monk fell off his chair, and Pope went down after him. Everybody in the crowded restaurant turned to see what all the commotion was about. I'm sure they were taken aback to see the Phillies general manager and some other guy underneath a table swinging at each other and wrestling around.

Hughie and I figured we needed to intervene, so we got on the floor and tried to separate them. We might have been better off staying in our seats. In the confined space underneath the table, Pope took a swing at Monk and accidentally hit Hughie right in the jaw. So Hughie, one hand and all, started fighting with Pope!

With all the jostling of the table, a couple of glasses fell and shattered on the floor. That noise, like a bell in a boxing ring, seemed to signify the end of the round.

I got Hughie calmed down, but Pope was a little harder to bring under control. He and Monk wanted to continue the bout outside. I decided the best course of action would be to keep Pope with us and get Monk the hell out of the restaurant. Once that was accomplished, however, Pope directed his anger at Hughie, whom he accused of trying to help Monk. When he finished his tirade, Pope stormed out of the restaurant, too.

Since we were regulars, and the restaurant staff knew we didn't ordinarily cause so much trouble, they let Hughie and me stay. He and I returned to the table and had another couple of drinks. After about an hour, the door of the Island House swung open and Pope came back in. We noticed someone was behind him, and they both seemed to be having a good old time.

It was Monk Meyer. He and Pope had their arms around each other's shoulders and were suddenly best buddies.

Whether identifying the potential of a player who went on to become the best third baseman ever to play the game or crawling through a Chicago restaurant to illustrate a story about a lion, Pope worked hard, and he most definitely played hard. We all did.

• • •

In our pursuit of back-to-back titles, we kept the team largely intact—with one notable exception. My relationship with Greg Luzinski hit a low point during the postseason after I benched him a couple of times. Years would pass before he and I mended fences. The sad part about it was that I liked Bull. He and I had gotten along well when I managed him in the minors in 1968. What changed? Simply put, I think Bull had become complacent and stopped working on his game. He also wasn't focused on keeping his weight down.

Pope sold Bull to the Chicago White Sox, and to fill the void in left field, we traded Bob Walk to the Braves for veteran outfielder Gary Matthews. I had always liked the way Matthews played, and Bobby was a high-strung, high-maintenance kind of pitcher. Though he was coming off an 11-win season, which included a gutsy performance in Game 1 of the World Series, we weren't sure how high his ceiling was. Plus, we felt we needed Sarge more than we needed Bobby in order to compete for another title.

Sarge hadn't played on a lot of winning teams, but he exuded the qualities of a winner. I liked his hustle and businesslike approach to the game. I also knew he had been taught the game the right way. No organization groomed outfielders better than the San Francisco Giants, who took Gary in the first round of the June 1968 draft. That same year, they selected another outfielder—Garry Maddox—in the second round of the January draft. Now we had both on our team.

• • •

For the first two months of the 1981 season, we were in and out of first place. A June 10 win against Houston that improved Steve Carlton's record to 9–1 put us two games ahead of the Cardinals in the National League East.

It was the last game played before the players went on strike.

Among the squabbles that led to the strike was a proposal by owners to compensate teams that lost players to free agency. But it was about more than any single issue. There was a lot of antagonism between the two sides in the years leading up to the strike, and it was bound to boil over sooner or later.

The whole situation felt like a double-edged sword for me. I was a player rep for the Phillies during an era when the pendulum was totally on ownership's side. As a front office guy in the 1970s, I had a different view of the game. I learned what it took to run a successful organization. By the early 1980s, I saw that the pendulum had swung the other way. I empathized with owners who feared the union was becoming too mighty.

The power shift away from the owners started in 1966 when Marvin Miller became executive director of the union. Having worked previously on behalf of America's auto and steel workers, he had impeccable credentials. Before Marvin, there was no such thing as collective bargaining in baseball. When I was a player rep in the early 1960s, our most significant lobbying effort was for a television in the Connie Mack Stadium clubhouse.

Under Marvin's leadership, the floodgates of free agency opened, putting an end to the days when owners and general managers controlled players' destinies. At the time of the strike, the players were well on their way to running the game themselves.

I respect what Marvin did for the players union. He was a marvelous negotiator and a tough sucker. Our lawyers could not match up with him at all. A couple of the Phillies—Bob Boone, who was the National League player representative, and Larry Bowa, who was the team's player rep—got closely involved in the labor negotiations.

By the second week of August, enough issues had been resolved to the union's satisfaction to put an end to the strike.

With a bitter taste in my mouth, I went back to trying to defend our title.

• • •

In light of the strike, which bit a two-month chunk out of the season, Major League Baseball cooked up a revised plan for the playoffs and World Series. It went like this: the four teams leading their divisions before the strike would automatically advance to an opening round of the postseason. In our case, we would play whichever National League East team posted the best record in the "second half" of the season. If that turned out to be us, then we'd play the team that had the second-best record in the second half.

When play resumed, I told the press we didn't view the rest of the schedule as exhibition games. Maybe that was lip service on my part. I wanted us to stay hungry, but as we went on a six-game losing streak at the end of August, I realized our players were just going through the motions. It didn't matter how they performed, because they were already in the postseason.

After a while, going 0-for-4 at the plate didn't hurt. Losing a game didn't sting. The media started pounding me. It reached the point where I couldn't keep up the charade any longer. "It's a horseshit rule," I told Jayson Stark, who was covering the Phillies for the *Philadelphia Inquirer*. "We're in the playoffs. So, yeah, I want them to play hard, but they have no incentive to win."

That on-the-record quote was preceded by a more colorful rant, prompted by Jayson's question about whether the team lacked motivation. It started with a "Fuck you, Jayson!" and went from there. Another writer, I think it was Hal Bodley, recorded the outburst, which included 30 or 40 variations of the word *fuck*. Sylvia took a transcript with her to school the following day. The English teachers had a ball noting how I utilized the f-word as a noun, verb, adjective, adverb, and gerund.

We went 25–27 in the second half of the season and limped into a division playoff against the Expos, the second-half winner of the National League East.

• • •

In fairness to my players, my attention during the second half wasn't squarely on the field, either. While serving a five-game suspension in late August for bumping an umpire, I took a call from the Tribune Company, the new corporate owners of the Chicago Cubs.

Initially, they contacted Ruly Carpenter, who had yet to turn over daily operations of the Phillies to Bill Giles, seeking permission to talk to me about a job.

I had no intention of leaving Philadelphia. But this was a time of transition for the Phillies. With Ruly on his way out, I figured it wouldn't hurt to at least listen to what the Cubs had to say.

Andy McKenna, the liaison between the Tribune Company and the Cubs, told me the company wasn't interested in me managing the team. They wanted me to be their general manager.

McKenna flew into Philadelphia and met me at the Holiday Inn across from Veterans Stadium. It was there that he spelled out his vision for my future with the Cubs.

"We like what you did with the Phillies' minor league system, and obviously we're impressed by what you accomplished last season," McKenna told me. "We think you'd be perfect for the Cubs."

At the end of his pitch, he proposed scheduling a follow-up meeting between him, me, and Tribune president Stan Cook.

"When the Phillies are in Chicago later in the season, let's have dinner and discuss this further," he said.

The talks were in an early stage, but I realized they couldn't continue without the participation of my wife. Intrigued enough by the idea, I agreed to the chat with Cook in late September. The Tribune Company agreed to fly Sylvia to Chicago for the meeting. But rather than just booking her a ticket on a commercial airline, they flew their corporate jet to Wilmington to pick her up. Sylvia finished teaching school on a Friday afternoon and boarded the Tribune plane for the short flight to Chicago. That was the first clue I got about the Tribune Company's largesse.

By the time Sylvia arrived, we had polished off a matinee victory over the Cubs. A few hours later, we were at Cook's house for dinner. The conversation that night dealt mostly with my ideas about how to build an organization and my general philosophy of the game. I have to say I laid my BS on them pretty heavy that night.

Whatever I said must have convinced them that I was their guy, because on the limousine ride back to the hotel, McKenna cut to the chase. "Here's what Chicago's willing to do," he told me, launching immediately into dollars and cents. The numbers knocked our socks off. It was a helluva lot more than the nearly $100,000 I was making with the Phillies. Some covert inquiries in the following days about other executive salaries around baseball led me to believe the Cubs were willing to make me one of the highest-paid general managers in the game. This surprised me. I'd never been a GM before, after all. But I knew I was up to the task. And the Tribune Company obviously had studied my background enough to reach the same conclusion.

I was still very much on the fence about leaving the Phillies, however.

Sylvia and I discussed it. Pope and I discussed it. But I didn't make any final decisions. We still had postseason baseball to play. As we were preparing to take on Montreal, news leaked that I was a candidate for the Cubs job. I didn't confirm the reports. That would have turned a rumor into a fact and created a major distraction.

• • •

The Expos were making the first playoff appearance in their history in 1981. We opened our best-of-five series with two losses at Olympic Stadium before returning to Philadelphia to try and reel off three consecutive wins.

We almost achieved that. Two wins at the Vet evened the series. We had Steve Carlton, who was between his third and fourth Cy Young Awards, pitching in Game 5, so I liked our chances of making a return trip to the National League Championship Series. But the Expos and starting pitcher Steve Rogers whipped our ass. We couldn't touch Rogers, who shut us out 3–0.

If not for the strike, I am convinced we would have won another World Series. Now, my future in Philadelphia was up in the air. I hadn't expected to manage the Phillies as long as I did, and the allure of being a general manager was strong. The more I thought about it, the more I realized it might be time for a change.

As we did at the end of every season, Pope and I went down to Clearwater to check out our minor leaguers in the Florida Instructional League. But this time, we had other business to discuss. And we aired things out pretty good. We were friends who didn't hide anything from each other. I needed to know whether the new Phillies ownership still planned to have me succeed him when he retired.

"Giles wants you to continue managing, but the other stuff hasn't been ironed out yet," Pope told me. "As far as I'm concerned, you'll be the guy, but I'm not going to have the same pull as I had with Ruly."

I appreciated Pope's honesty. We had known each other for 25 years. And in the end, I knew he wanted what was best for me.

With that, I resumed my conversations with the Cubs.

• • •

I turned the Cubs down three times before I finally said yes.

Having been interested in an escape from city and suburban life, Sylvia and I purchased a 60-acre farm in West Grove, Pennsylvania, which was about an hour from Philadelphia. Sylvia was happy teaching in the area. The youngest of our four children was about to enter high school. And after the 1980 World Series, we felt even more attached to Philadelphia.

After several conversations with Sylvia, I decided against the move to Chicago. I called McKenna and explained about the farm and everything else. He listened to what I had to say and told me he'd get back to me. And he did. He upped the offer with stock options and some of the usual bullshit that corporate guys usually receive. Still, I said no. "Andy, I'm sorry, but we just can't make it work," I told him.

With his repeated attempts to woo me, McKenna had made it abundantly clear I was the guy the Cubs wanted. Each time he contacted me, I thought a little bit more about the job. I guess his persistence was paying off.

He called back a little while later. "I'm coming in," he informed me. By that, he meant he was going to board the Tribune jet and pay me another visit. I picked him up at the Wilmington airport, which was closer to West Grove than Philadelphia, and brought him out to the farm. I wanted him to see what we had and would be giving up if I took the Cubs job. With his starched shirt and perfectly knotted tie, McKenna was anything but a farm guy. Sylvia and I were decked out in our sloppy stuff. Shortly after we pulled up, one of our cows got loose, and I had to get her back in the pen. McKenna watched all of this unfold with big-city bemusement.

Over lunch, he attempted to further sweeten the deal. He showed me photos of a very stately house in the Chicago area.

"We'll buy you this house or let you pick out any house you want," he said. "If you decide to sell it at any point, you can keep any windfall you get from it."

That got us a little bit more excited—but I still turned him down.

McKenna left the farm disappointed. But that son of a bitch kept coming back to me. A few days later he called while on his way to South Bend for a Notre Dame football game. "I'm not giving up," he said. "I think you belong in Chicago. I know you do. We can make it work."

He rattled off all the components of the offer: the money, the stock options, the house, and the control I would have over all baseball decisions. "Just think about it," he pleaded.

I went back to Pope and told him what the Cubs were willing to give me.

"Dallas, you have to take it," Pope said. "This is crazy. You're not going to make that kind of money here or anywhere else. I know you love everything about the Phillies and your farm, but Chicago is a great city, and you'll love it. Wrigley Field is special and so is Chicago. You've got to take it."

The Phillies were a part of me. But I finally said yes.

13

I DIDN'T PLAN ON LEAVING Philadelphia empty-handed. After accepting the Cubs job, I sat down with Paul Owens to discuss which members of the Phillies I could take with me. Lee Elia and John Vukovich were at top of my wish list.

I wanted Lee, an old friend and Phillies coach in 1980, to manage the Cubs. And I knew Vuke, who retired as a player after the 1981 season, would make a wonderful coach. Both had been trained the Phillies way. The three of us had experienced a World Series victory, and together I hoped we could instill a winning culture in Chicago, where the Cubs had lost a lot of games in recent years.

Lee had only managed at the minor league level, but he had the baseball smarts, passion, and work ethic to whip a major league clubhouse into shape.

He and I went way back. We both attended the University of Delaware, though not at the same time. Lee entered school as a freshman the same year I signed professionally with the Phillies. When I returned to campus to take winter courses during the off-season, he and I got to know each other a little bit. Lee, a Philadelphia native, was a helluva athlete, and like me, a recipient of scholarship money from Phillies owner Bob Carpenter's Friends Foundation. At Delaware, he played baseball, football, and basketball. A knee injury in college likely kept him from having a more successful professional baseball career. Also like me, he played more games in the minors than the majors.

Nine years after I signed with the Phillies, I played with Lee at Triple-A Little Rock, where I pitched and he played shortstop. We drifted apart again after that season but were reunited in the early 1970s when Lee joined the Phillies as an infield instructor and third-base coach for a minor league team managed by Jim Bunning. Before taking that job, Lee was out of baseball and selling insurance.

When I became the Phillies' farm director, I tapped Lee to manage teams at almost every level of the organization. Then in 1980, I asked him join the major league coaching staff.

I was convinced Vuke would be a valuable asset to Lee's staff. As a player on the '80 Phillies team, he assumed a vital leadership role. Whether reminding Greg Luzinski to watch his weight or telling Larry Bowa to shut his trap, Vuke got players to listen.

"You can have Lee and Vuke, but that's it," Pope told me.

"I want Gordie, too," I replied.

Gordon Goldsberry, the Phillies' West Coast scouting supervisor, had outstanding baseball instincts. I wanted to name him director of minor leagues and scouting for the Cubs.

"Okay, but nobody else!" Pope yelled.

So that's who I satisfied myself with—at least at that moment.

As it turned out, I hired many more people I considered assets after the Phillies decided to cut loose several so-called Dallas Green guys. They included coaches and scouts Jim Snyder, Tom Harmon, Glen Gregson, Erskine Thompson, and Brandy Davis, all of whom I welcomed to Chicago with open arms.

• • •

The Tribune Company, which owned the Cubs, liked five-year plans. But when I got to Chicago, I wasn't looking five years into the future. I intended to change the culture of the Cubs right away. That meant getting my people to contemplate what it would take to win a championship. Anyone incapable of thinking in those terms wasn't welcome in the Cubs executive offices.

I recognized we faced an uphill battle. The Cubs hadn't played postseason baseball since 1945. During the Wrigley family's decades of ownership, the Cubs' mantra was, "Open the doors, and they will come." Ownership didn't really care what kind of product it put on the field. Wins and losses stopped mattering.

During the strike-shortened 1981 season, the Cubs went 38–65 and drew an average of fewer than 10,000 fans per game. The team was losing *and* the people weren't coming anymore to watch games. Contrary to the Wrigley way of thinking, I equated bad baseball with bad business.

I brought in people who subscribed to my way of thinking. Our new media relations guy had no prior experience working in the major leagues, but I sensed he and I were on the same wavelength. The gamble paid off. From the get-go, Ned Colletti, who had been a sportswriter in Philadelphia, did a bang-up job for us. Ned worked his way up the ranks, and in 2005, he became the general manager of the Dodgers.

Ned understood the Cubs organization needed to do better at selling itself. So did the husband-and-wife team I brought in to help run our business operations.

Bing and Patty Hampton were principal owners of the Phillies' Triple-A affiliate in Oklahoma City. As the club's farm director, I witnessed their creativity through the lengths they went to promote the 89ers via theme nights, giveaways, and in-game events. I wanted them on my team in Chicago.

The hiring created an unusual situation, because Bing and Patty intended to hold onto ownership of the 89ers while working for the Cubs. Some questioned whether that meant they'd be working for two organizations at the same time. But Major League Baseball commissioner Bowie Kuhn allowed it on the condition that Bing and Patty avoid direct contact with the Phillies while serving me.

• • •

While I was busy assembling a front office team in Chicago, I made sure the Cubs players knew I hadn't forgotten about them.

Soon after my arrival, I sent a letter to every player spelling out my expectations for spring training. I ordered them to come to camp in shape and ready to work on fundamentals. The letter, which got leaked to the press, challenged the players to ask themselves whether they truly had a desire to be successful or whether being a Cub was more about enjoying good times at the bars and restaurants on Rush Street.

I was upset that a private communication got leaked, but before long, I was telling the whole world how I felt. In an interview with Phillies broadcaster and *Philadelphia Bulletin* columnist Richie Ashburn a few months later, I said, "From top to bottom, the Chicago Cub organization was a disaster area, even worse than I thought when I first took the job. I could find absolutely no direction and very little organization."

At first, the Chicago sports pages ran stories with hopeful headlines like, "Can Dallas Green Turn the Cubs Around?" But once I started sharing my views about the sorry state of the organization, the news became, "Green Says Cubs Are a Mess."

The Cubs' history of losing carried with it the advantage of giving us free rein to make moves that might take the team in a positive direction. We had a few promising young players in catcher Jody Davis, outfielder Leon Durham, and pitcher Lee Smith, and an established major league first baseman in Bill Buckner, but otherwise the cupboard was bare at the big league and minor league levels. Years of poor scouting and drafting had left the organization in bad shape.

I told my staff to shake up the mix, even if that meant trading shit for shit. If we netted a few quality players, even by accident, then we'd be better off than we were before. I also told them we wanted inventory and to always ask for that extra guy in trades.

• • •

I had looked to Philadelphia for people who could help the Cubs behind the scenes, and it made sense to turn to my former team for on-the-field talent, too. Between Gordie and me, we knew just about every piece of inside information about current Phillies players and kids in the organization's farm system. For a Phillies team with designs on making the postseason, the Cubs were an ideal trade partner. We had expendable veterans who could help them win in the short term.

In December 1981, we got the ball rolling by trading starting pitcher Mike Krukow to Philadelphia for pitchers Dan Larson and Dickie Noles and catcher Keith Moreland. Though we gave up our most consistent starting pitcher from the season before, just like that, we had three guys with World Series rings.

On the day of the trade, Keith was out playing golf. After coming off the links, he retired to the clubhouse and downed a couple of beers. The only way to call someone in those days was on their home phone. When Keith arrived home that night, his wife met him at the door with a frazzled look on her face.

"You've been traded to Chicago!" she said. "Dallas has been trying to get a hold of you all day."

When Keith called me back, I laid out my vision for him: "We're going to turn things around in Chicago. I know you know what it takes to win, so saddle up and come along."

Dickie found out about the trade as he was driving home from a bar in Charlotte, North Carolina. He was pulling out of a convenience store parking lot when a man beckoned him to roll down his window. The man happened to be former major leaguer Tommy Helms, who shared both a hometown and a penchant for late nights with Dickie.

"Good luck in Chicago!" Tommy shouted.

"Chicago?"

"Yeah, you've been traded to the Cubs. You didn't know that?"

Dickie sat in the parking lot and smiled. He didn't want to leave Philadelphia but was ecstatic about joining me in Chicago, knowing what we could accomplish together.

That trade worked out pretty well for us.

But it was my next trade with the Phillies that resonates in Philadelphia and Chicago to this day.

• • •

I knew from stories in Philadelphia-area papers sent to me by my best friend, Clyde Louth, that veteran shortstop Larry Bowa and owner Bill Giles were in a heated dispute over Bowa's contract. Bowa wanted a three-year extension that Giles and Pope didn't think he was worth. After 16 years in the organization, it was clear Bowa's days as a Phillie were over.

This put the Phillies in a jam. They had designs on competing for a second championship in three years, but they needed a proven shortstop to have a realistic shot at that. It just so happened I had a guy who fit the bill: Ivan DeJesus. Even though he had a dreadful year at the plate in 1981, he was a career .257 hitter to that point and just two seasons removed from stealing 44 bases.

Bowa and I didn't always get along in Philadelphia, but his opinion of me improved a lot after he got a World Series ring in 1980. His dedication to the game was second only to Pete Rose among players I knew. Though he had lost a step on the base paths and some range at shortstop, he still knew how to play championship baseball.

Gordie and I were willing to trade for Bowa, but we agreed the Phillies were going to have to throw in at least one other player to make a deal worth our while. We needed inventory. And the fact that DeJesus was seven years younger than Bowa gave us leverage to ask for an additional player.

In January 1982, Bowa went on a Philadelphia radio station and said his agent told him the Phillies had agreed to trade him, infielder Luis Aguayo, and outfielder Dick Davis to the Cubs for DeJesus and pitcher Bill Caudill.

His agent was wrong.

Gordie and I wanted a young player who could be a building block for the Cubs' future. We agreed that 22-year-old Ryne Sandberg had that potential. Gordie had scouted him in high school, and I had picked him in the 20th round of the 1978 draft. Sandberg only had six major league at-bats to his name, but we were confident he had all the skills to thrive in the big leagues. He was a tremendous all-around athlete, with great speed and hands. He had mostly played shortstop in the minor leagues, but we felt he could adapt to any infield position.

Pope and the Phillies liked Sandberg, too. But as negotiations continued, we hung tough.

It helped us that the Phillies had middle infielder Julio Franco in their minor league system. Pope went on the record saying he thought Franco, and not Sandberg, was the team's shortstop of the future. That left one fewer infield position Sandberg could play for the Phillies, who were likely going to send him back to Triple-A for another year.

The talks went on for weeks. There were other talented players in the Phillies system, including Len Matuszek, a slugging first baseman who had hit for power and average. But first base was one of the few positions where we didn't need help.

We held out until Pope agreed to give us Sandberg.

All the newspaper stories about the trade mentioned Sandberg in passing. He was a prospect, a throw-in, a deal-sweetener.

Ryno jumped right into our starting lineup as a third baseman in 1982. His eventual development into a perennial All-Star and Hall of Famer at second base now makes that deal look like one of the most lopsided in baseball history. But in the short term, the trade benefited the Phillies. DeJesus helped them get to the 1983 World Series. They got what they wanted, and so did we.

The trade for Sandberg was a sound baseball decision. Every now and then, such decisions make general managers look like geniuses.

• • •

With all the Philadelphia transplants in Chicago, it didn't take long for the Cubs to be nicknamed "Phillies West" and the "Cubillies." I threw fuel on the fire by never missing a chance to tell Chicago fans how much the Cubs could learn from the Phillies' way of doing business. They resented the hell out of me for that.

It would be a couple more years before some strategic trades and Ryno's emergence as a superstar helped the Cubs shed their losing ways. For the time being, we had to try to drum up interest in the team based on a belief that better days lay ahead, even if they might take a while to arrive.

I tried to make it clear that I didn't think there was anything lovable about losing.

With that in mind, Bing Hampton came up with a hell of a slogan for the Cubs: "Building a New Tradition." It was a way for us to hedge. The new tradition of winning wouldn't take hold overnight. A blind man could see that. But it was being built…or so we hoped.

Not everybody embraced the idea of the Cubs as winners. Some so-called fans actually liked the decades of losing. Studs Terkel, the legendary Chicago writer, summed up that mind-set best when he said, "I think they're more endearing in defeat than in victory. I like their loser-like quality."

That's what we were up against.

• • •

I had no delusions of grandeur when I got to Chicago. But as someone who liked a good challenge, I relished the chance to try and rebuild an organization. Teams win games, but organizations establish the framework for success. And while the Cubs may have been a vener-able organization, they certainly weren't a successful one.

It was hardly a coincidence that the Cubs' record for single-season attendance to that point had come in 1969, the year the team played inspired baseball until they blew a nine-game lead and lost the divi-sion to the Mets in the final weeks of the season.

It's simple: when you win, you put people in seats. And because the Cubs didn't win a lot in the 1970s and early 1980s, they didn't draw well. Fewer people watched games at Wrigley Field in 1980 than at the outset of the Great Depression in 1930. Among the reasons for that was the team's difficulty selling season tickets.

I leveled with Cubs fans about their misplaced love of failure, a phenomenon further perpetuated by the 1969 team. I did a call-in radio show in Chicago that gave me a chance to interact with fans. And by that I mean it gave me a chance to set fans straight on some things.

"The '69 team that you loved so much *lost*," I told them. "They were losers. Why did they lose? Because Wrigley Field didn't have lights. The team got tired from coming off the road late at night and then reporting to the ballpark early for day games. That sapped their stamina."

The 1969 team and day baseball were both sacred to Cubs fans. But there I was on the airwaves disparaging both. That led to a lot of pissing contests with callers to the show, especially after we got off to another losing start in 1982.

I've always had a loud mouth and yakked too much, but I didn't do the show just to make people angry at me. I felt it was a way to reach a section of the fan base that knew the game and could give me feedback on how we were doing. I guess it all made for good radio. A lot of the callers were your typical talk show types who just wanted to harangue me. Well, I'm not harangue-able. My advocacy for lights at

Wrigley Field, which started slow and built over the next few years, was evidence of my willingness to mix it up with the locals.

The new general manager and the stubborn old fans agreed on one point: Wrigley Field was a wonderful place to watch a game. So many Chicagoans had childhood memories of taking the train to Wrigley with their parents or grandparents. Now, they were parents or grandparents themselves who were passing on the same tradition.

A love of the Friendly Confines and the game itself is a perfectly good reason to come out to the ballpark. But I felt we had to move beyond that by bringing back pride to the organization.

The Cubs weren't cursed. They just had come to accept losing.

14

ON A VISIT TO OUR SPRING training facilities in Mesa, Arizona, shortly after we joined the Cubs, Lee Elia and I saw firsthand the Cubs organization's lack of pride.

Before the trip, we informed our minor league coordinators that we were coming to check out our prospects in the Fall Instructional League. That's what general managers and managers do to acquaint themselves with their organization. To us, that was a given. But in the Cubs' world, it apparently was a revolutionary concept.

When Lee and I landed at the Phoenix airport, no one came to meet us. We took a taxi to the team hotel, but there weren't any signs identifying it as such. In Clearwater, Florida, where the Phillies train, we hit fans over the head with reminders of our presence. It helped locals establish a connection to the team.

Lee and I threw our bags in our rooms and went out to HoHoKam Park to get a glimpse of our Instructional League team. Again, no signs identified the park as the spring training and Instructional League home of the Chicago Cubs. Not only that, but there wasn't anybody at the park.

We reasoned that Instructional Leagues don't wake up as early as some of us and waited for some activity to commence. After a while, I turned to Lee and said, "You think we're in the right goddamn stadium? Shit, shouldn't someone be out there throwing the ball or checking out the field?"

We sat there for two hours before anybody showed up. And when our staff finally arrived, no one came up to introduce themselves to the new manager and general manager. I had come from a Phillies organization that cared about its people and tried to make every new employee feel welcome. I interpreted the silent treatment we got that day as my staff saying, "So you're the new guy, big fucking deal! We're the old Chicago Cubs."

Well, that attitude had to change.

• • •

I had started to overhaul the front office and the team. Next up was the broadcast booth.

Harry Caray, who had worked White Sox games for the past decade, was on the outs with management for his support of broadcast partner Jimmy Piersall, who had been suspended by the organization for calling the wives of White Sox players "horny broads." Harry said he'd quit if Jimmy got fired for his comment.

White Sox manager Tony La Russa and his coaches hated Piersall, but they didn't think much of Harry, either. They were sick and tired of Harry ripping the team at every turn. When the White Sox announced they were moving their games to a pay-TV service, Harry declared himself a free agent.

Our own legendary play-by-play man, Jack Brickhouse, was retiring, and the brass wanted a big name to fill Jack's shoes. Jim Dowdle, the Tribune Company's executive vice president for media, asked me what I thought about Harry coming aboard as the Cubs' play-by-play man on Tribune-owned WGN.

I said I didn't like Harry's tendency to get personal on the air. "I know he's a great announcer and brings a lot to the table with his personality," I told Dowdle, "but the White Sox want to run him out of town. What's he going to do when he comes over here?"

The Cubs weren't good enough to win, and I wasn't sure I wanted to give Harry a platform to skewer the team. Still, I agreed to meet with Harry and Dowdle at some clandestine Chicago club to hash out the situation.

Over drinks, I looked Harry in the eye and told him I respected him as a broadcaster. "But I know your reputation for telling it like it is, and I can't have you burying my guys like you did the White Sox," I said. "We're a few years away from making any noise. If you beat up our guys, no one is going to want to come and play here."

I invoked an incident with Garry Maddox as an example. "Harry, if a guy loses a ball in the sun because he's not wearing sunglasses, I don't have a problem with you ripping him. Hell, I'll do it myself. But I can't have you ripping families or the way a guy goes about his business off the field. That's not acceptable to me."

Harry gave me the assurances I wanted to hear, so I gave his hiring my blessing.

My only other concern was how Harry's presence would impact Cubs broadcaster Milo Hamilton, who had been groomed to replace Brickhouse. With Harry in the booth, he'd be playing second fiddle again. On top of that, Harry and Milo had worked together in St. Louis in the 1950s and didn't particularly like each other. They ended up coexisting in Chicago for two years before old grudges from their St. Louis days spilled over into on-air squabbles. Milo was fired after the 1984 season. With my blessings and support, he joined the broadcast team in Houston, where he remained until retiring after the 2012 season. Milo, like Harry and Jack, is in the Hall of Fame.

We made the right decision with Harry. He brought a lot of life to the broadcast booth and became an inseparable part of the Cubs brand in the 1980s.

Sylvia and I got to know Harry and his wife, Dutchie, pretty well. On our first dinner out with them, Harry plopped down next to Sylvia at the restaurant bar and got morose about having to pay alimony to two ex-wives. This turned into a general rant against women. We had yet to be seated for dinner, and Harry was already on his fifth or sixth drink.

Harry turned to Sylvia and asked with great scorn, "What did *you* ever do?"

I'm not sure if the question was directed at Sylvia or all females. But Sylvia didn't back down. "What the fuck did *you* ever do?" she responded.

I could be wrong, but I think the rebuttal sobered Harry up pretty quickly. A few days later, Harry was on his way to the broadcast booth at Wrigley Field when he saw Sylvia. He walked over to her, held up her arm, and said, "The winner!"

As a broadcaster, he didn't let me down. He didn't hurl personal insults at players. In fact, he established himself as the Cubs' biggest fan. To this day, people associate Harry Caray with his joyful on-air call, "Cubs win! Cubs win!" And his performances of "Take Me Out to the Ballgame" during the seventh-inning stretch at Wrigley Field inspired a much-loved tradition.

• • •

In 1982, Lee Elia and I convinced most of the team to report early for spring training. Lack of talent was going to be an issue all season. I didn't want lack of preparation to compound our problems.

Our retooled lineup featured Ryne Sandberg, Larry Bowa, and Keith Moreland. It remained to be seen if the addition of those players would translate into wins.

No matter how long you've been associated with the game, the excitement of Opening Day never gets old. In most years, it announces the arrival of spring. But in my first season in Chicago, it signified the continuation of winter.

The night before our home opener against the Mets, several inches of snow fell in Chicago. As the snow accumulated, I called in some outside workers to help our grounds crew get the park ready for the next day's game. God bless those guys! They worked their tails off, shoveling every single aisle and cleaning off all the seats. By morning, the sun was out, but the temperature was below freezing. The crews continued working right up until game time.

It wasn't the best weather for baseball, but nearly 27,000 fans showed up to watch us beat the Mets 5–0 behind a strong outing by 39-year-old Ferguson Jenkins. After the game, I brought the grounds crew workers a couple of cases of beer to thank them for their hard work. In contrast to my disheartening experience at the Instructional League, our home opener showed we might yet develop the kind of can-do spirit that makes organizations successful.

It was time to celebrate.

Yosh Kawano, our clubhouse manager, was a Cubs institution, a cantankerous old devil but a man who was very effective at his job. Somewhere in the sales contract between the Wrigley family and the Tribune Company was fine print stipulating that Yosh had a lifetime contract with the team. It had long been tradition for Yosh to take the manager and general manager to dinner on Opening Day. John Vukovich and my secretary, Arlene, who was also Yosh's girlfriend, came along.

We had a wonderful meal in a semi-private room at an Italian restaurant. After we finished eating, we started drinking pretty good—Black Russians for me and wine for the rest of the table.

Yosh, Arlene, and I were yakking it up when we heard a commotion coming from the bar area. When I went to check it out, I saw a guy pushed up against the wall with two other guys about to beat the hell out of him.

The two other guys were Elia and Vukovich! Apparently the guy pinned to the wall had made some negative comments about the Phillies *and* the Cubs.

Lee was an emotional guy, but he never flew off the handle just for the hell of it. The restaurant fight happened because somebody took a shot at his former and current employers. Lee, like me, oozed passion for his work and took insults about his team personally. Vuke was the same way.

Here's how Lee reflects on that particular incident and the bonds between him, Vuke, and me: "None of us were going into the Hall of Fame as players. We got to where we got in the business because we worked and competed and cared about what we were doing. Our teams became like families. And it wasn't tolerated if someone said anything about our family. There we were at Yosh's party, having a good time, not looking for trouble, but somebody opened his mouth, and that created a little bit of a situation."

• • •

The win over the Mets in the home opener brought our season record to 2–1. It was the only time all year we had a winning mark. By the end of July, we were 25 games under .500, and if not for a strong finish, we might have suffered the ignominy of a 100-loss season in 1982.

Not surprisingly, we again finished near the bottom of the league in attendance.

Our best pitcher in 1982 was Jenkins, who led the team with 14 wins and a 3.15 ERA. A bright spot offensively was Sandberg, who came to the plate 687 times in his first full season in the major leagues. He hit .271, stole 32 bases, and played a capable third base. His rookie year confirmed what we already knew: Ryno was going to be a major contributor to the team for many years.

Our on-the-field product was a work in progress. But the behind-the-scenes culture at Wrigley Field remained a problem.

I've always felt that employees make a baseball organization what it is. They should feel like they are part of a family. I experienced that in Philadelphia and wanted to duplicate that atmosphere in Chicago. That wasn't an easy sell. During my first season with the Cubs, I learned something about day baseball. It turns employees into 9-to-5 people, as opposed to 24-hour people. Here's what I mean by that: when a team plays only day games, employees arrive at the ballpark around 9:00 AM, do a little work, take a break to watch the game, and then go home.

There were plenty of days I wanted to have meetings after games, but I'd walk through the hallways and see empty office after empty office. Even when our staff was present, I observed lot of people running around but not doing anything in particular.

I wanted hard-working and dedicated employees. Anyone simply going through the motions was better off someplace else.

After the 1982 season, I cleaned house.

In what became known as "Bloody Monday" at Wrigley Field, I fired our promotions director, ticket director, traveling secretary, director of publications, public relations secretary, clubhouse attendant, group sales manager, head of security, and several office assistants. I also got rid of a guy who liked to tell people his job was organizing staff birthday parties.

A *Chicago Tribune* columnist named John Husar called it the "biggest front office purge in Chicago sports history."

It was a bloodbath, and it wasn't fun. But I had to send a message that the 9-to-5 way of doing business was a relic of the past. In his column, Husar compared me to a caveman: "Early man made room at the table by shoving out the weak and the old. Those who couldn't hunt were left to be hunted. Well, some of these (people fired by the Cubs) were fair hunters but poor office politicians."

That was nonsense. My message was clear: the Wrigley family wasn't around anymore to take care of everyone. You had to work to earn your keep.

After the purge, we eventually doubled the size of the front office. The increase in quantity and quality made us a better organization.

• • •

I even had to give Cubs legend Ernie Banks his walking papers in 1982.

This was sensitive stuff, because Ernie is so revered in Chicago, and rightfully so. I loved Ernie as a player and as a person. Heck, I thought so highly of him that I made sure we retired his number soon after I got to Chicago. He is Mr. Cub, after all.

Ernie is the nicest guy you'll ever meet. But his niceness caused me some headaches.

Ernie represented the Cubs as a goodwill ambassador, appearing at various events in the community, where he'd say a few words and pose for pictures. Everywhere Ernie went, people approached him to request his attendance at an event.

"Hey, Ernie, great to see you. We're having such and such a function at 1:00 PM on Saturday. Can you make it?"

Ernie would reply, "Oh yeah, sure, I'll be there."

Later that same day, someone would say, "Hey, Ernie, we're having a Little League thing on Friday. Can you come and throw out the first pitch?"

And Ernie would respond, "Yeah, yeah, I'll be there."

The problem was he said yes to everybody, but he hardly showed up for anything. Then my office dealt with the fallout. We'd get calls from people cursing us out for promising Ernie Banks and not delivering him. Of course, it had been Ernie doing the promising, not us.

I scheduled a meeting with Ernie's agent to address the situation. I told him we very much wanted Ernie to represent the organization, but we couldn't have him agreeing to appear at events and then not showing up.

"We'll get a gal to handle all his stuff for him," I told Ernie's agent. "She'll keep his calendar and call him to make sure he's available to attend an event. And on the day of the event, she'll make sure he gets there."

That idea worked fine for a while. We paid Ernie a few dollars as an official employee and made sure he followed through on his commitments. But another problem arose. For every event his assistant booked for him, he committed to three or four others without our knowledge. We continued to catch hell from jilted members of the community when Ernie was a no-show.

I met with his agent again.

"Look," I said, "we're going to do this one more time, and one more time only. You have to tell Ernie to pass along any information he gets about appearances to his gal, and she'll take care of it."

It still didn't work.

At that point, I decided we wouldn't accept any more phone calls requesting Ernie's presence at events. And we wouldn't take responsibility for any arrangements he made on his own. I made sure Ernie knew he was welcome at the ballpark any time he wanted. Like I said, Ernie is one of the nicest people you'll ever run across. But, goddamn, he just couldn't say no.

I don't think Ernie held that whole episode against me, which is good, because I have the utmost respect for his baseball career. I also had enough thorns in my side as it was.

15

BILL BUCKNER WAS AN ACCOMPLISHED baseball player, but his selfish attitude never sat well with me. Lee Elia didn't like him, either, which is probably why hc and Buckncr got into a scuffle during a game at San Diego in 1982. On paper, Bill had a fine season in 1982, hitting .306 and exceeding previous career highs with 15 home runs and 105 RBIs. But he wasn't my kind of ballplayer.

Buck bitched about everything. If we let the grass at Wrigley Field grow because we wanted to give our infielders an edge out in the field, Buckner complained that the tall grass cost him hits. When we expanded the bleacher area in center field so we could sell a few more tickets, Buckner whined that the people in the seats obstructed his view of pitches. Everything we did, Buckner cried about.

He also constantly expressed his wish to be traded.

Buck was happy to put his numbers up, but he was never truly content. And he most definitely never embraced the idea of baseball as a team sport.

Maybe it was all the losing he had experienced as the longest-tenured position player on the Cubs. When you lose that much, it becomes ingrained in your thought process. I also think it creates a player who is more interested in his own statistics than his team's won-lost record.

Moving forward, that wasn't the kind of guy I wanted on my team.

I fully intended to trade Buckner after the 1982 season. And I knew I wouldn't have a problem finding a taker, because other general managers didn't know the Buckner I did.

As I shopped him around, I looked to the free agent market for a player to replace him at first base.

It didn't take long to zero in on Steve Garvey, an eight-time All-Star with the Dodgers, who hit the free agent market after Los Angeles declined to give him a five-year contract. Garvey had already made it known the Cubs were one of five teams he wanted to play for. The others were the Giants, the Padres, the Astros, and the Yankees. I felt I could make a compelling case that we were the best fit for him.

At the 1982 winter meetings in Honolulu, I delivered my pitch to Garvey and his agent, Jerry Kapstein. The Cubs were headed in the right direction, I told them, and Garvey could play a major role in bringing playoff baseball to the north side of Chicago. I also touted the city itself, arguing it was an ideal place for Garvey and his magnetic personality.

Gordon Goldsberry, our director of scouting and player development, helped me woo Garvey. During breaks in negotiations, Gordie and I huddled in my suite at the Sheraton Waikiki and took notes on a blackboard. We penciled in what we hoped would be our new infield: Ryne Sandberg at third, Larry Bowa at shortstop, and Garvey at first.

A five-year deal for Garvey was going to cost us about $7 million, not much by today's standards, but a lot at the time. The cost was secondary, however. I knew Garvey would help improve our club. That's all that mattered. The Tribune Company had given me carte blanche to make all baseball decisions, and I was going to exercise that power.

• • •

A few days into the winter meetings, news broke that Garvey had narrowed his list to two teams: the Cubs and the Padres. I knew we had an excellent shot at landing him, because Garvey seemed to like the spotlight that came with playing in a large market.

Kapstein, Garvey, and I talked again, and this time we agreed in principle to a deal. I then turned around and made a handshake agreement with Paul Owens of the Phillies on a trade involving Buckner. Maybe Pope would have better luck with Buck than I did.

Late that evening, Gordie and I met with Tribune liaison Andy McKenna, who had come with us to Hawaii. We showed Andy the blackboard with all our notes. Andy studied the board, which included players' names, dollar figures, and assorted scribblings.

Finally, he spoke.

"Dallas, we can't make the deals right now."

What? I couldn't have possibly heard that correctly.

"Andy, I shook hands on it. We're making those deals, and I'm going to announce it first thing in the morning."

"Well, before you do that, I have to get a hold of Stan Cook," Andy replied.

"Then go ahead and get a hold of Stan Cook, but we're moving ahead!" I bellowed.

About an hour later, Andy called my suite to let me know he was having trouble reaching the Tribune chairman. "He's on the Concorde coming back from Paris," Andy said. "Until he gets back, I won't be able to talk to him."

It didn't occur to me to ask why the goddamn Concorde wasn't equipped with phones.

"Andy, we made the deal," I hissed. "We shook hands on it, and we're going to announce it."

"But Dallas, I can't let you do that…"

"Okay, you've got till 10:00 in the morning to get a hold of Stan Cook, because that's when I'm making the announcement."

Cook's flight on the Concorde must have been the longest in aviation history, because when Andy called me early the next morning, he sounded absolutely frantic: "Dallas, we can't go through with it. I still can't get a hold of Stan. He's still not home."

I couldn't believe what was happening. The whole story about not being able to reach Cook sounded like a ruse. The fact was that the Tribune Company didn't want us to spend that kind of money on Garvey.

"Do you remember what you guys told me when you hired me?" I screamed at McKenna. "I was authorized to make all baseball decisions. *All* baseball decisions, Andy!"

"I just can't accept responsibility for this," McKenna groveled. "I just can't let you do it."

I was really pissed. And hurt. The Padres had an equally attractive offer for Garvey on the table, and he and his agent took it, rather than waiting for us to make up our minds.

Without Garvey on our team, I had to kill the deal for Buckner. Talk about being embarrassed! I had to go to Pope and say, "They're not going to let me make this deal until my boss gets off the Concorde."

Gordie and I were beside ourselves. When the winter meetings ended, we went to Molokai with our wives and got very drunk. Lying on the beach, wallowing in our own unhappiness and drink, I became defiant. "Fuck 'em!" I said. "I'm going to do something. I don't know what I'm going to do, but I'm going to do something!"

• • •

It was hard to take. The Tribune Company broke its word to me, we didn't get Garvey, and maybe worst of all, Bill Buckner was still in a Cubs uniform.

At least the whole story never hit the papers. If that had happened, I'm not sure I would have been able to show my face at the winter meetings ever again. I guess the writers were too busy reporting on trades that actually got consummated in Hawaii. Undaunted by not acquiring Buckner, Pope made a major splash by trading five players to the Indians for outfielder Von Hayes.

When I got back to Chicago, I demanded a meeting with Stan Cook. "We have some things we need to discuss," I told McKenna. The next day, Gordie and I took a private elevator to Cook's office in the Tribune Tower.

"You told us we had carte blanche to make baseball decisions," I said to Cook. "Well, this was a key baseball decision for this organization, and you went against your word by not allowing us to make it. That's not acceptable. It embarrassed us and it embarrassed this organization."

I was ready to continue on in this vein, but Cook cut me off: "Dallas, we're sorry this happened. It was an unfortunate thing. I'll make sure it doesn't happen again."

I had no choice but to take him at his word. I decided to test the waters by going after another player I felt could help the Cubs become a winner.

The Dodgers were also shopping Ron Cey, one of the best third basemen in the game. I shared my plan with Gordie: "Let's go after Cey. If we get him, we'll move Sandberg to second base."

A few weeks later, we acquired Cey in exchange for two minor leaguers. One of the first people I contacted after making the trade was Larry Bowa. "Bow, I trust you," I told my shortstop. "You have to help Sandberg make the transition to second base."

I would have much preferred Garvey at first instead of Buckner, but I couldn't complain about how the rest of the infield was shaping up.

To further help Sandberg, I hired my old friend, Ruben Amaro Sr., as an infield instructor. I hoped Ruben would join me in Chicago when I first got hired, but he chose to keep his Phillies job that allowed him to split time between the United States and Latin America. When I asked him again to come to Chicago, much to my delight, he said yes.

• • •

We lost six consecutive games to start the 1983 season, giving up seven runs to our opponents in three of the losses and eight runs in another. Our defense and relief pitching were terrible.

It was only April, but boos started ringing loudly through Wrigley Field.

I tried to keep my cool amid a growing chorus of criticism that I was full of shit and had no plan for turning the Cubs' fortunes around. On my radio show and in the newspapers, I reminded everyone that I never promised overnight success.

Lee Elia, who shared my temperament but not my patience, also got beat up in the press. He let his emotions bottle up until he famously blew a gasket after a tough loss to the Dodgers at Wrigley Field.

The loss on April 29, 1983, dropped us to 5–14. Lee could see it was going to be a long, frustrating season. In front of an assemblage of reporters, one of whom recorded the outburst for posterity, he made his feelings known.

"I'll tell you one fucking thing, I hope we get fucking hotter than shit, just to stuff it up them 3,000 fucking people who show up every fucking day, because if they're the real Chicago fucking fans, they can kiss my fucking ass right downtown!" Lee raged.

That was a pretty memorable sound bite. But Lee wasn't nearly finished yet.

"Those motherfuckers don't even work. That's why they're out at the fucking game! They ought to go out and get a fucking job and find out what it's like to go out and earn a fucking living! Eighty-five percent of the fucking world is working. The other 15 percent come out here!"

He went on to call Wrigley Field "a fucking playground for the cocksuckers," a colorful phrase but not exactly in keeping with how we wanted to market our stadium. At least Lee finished on a hopeful note, expressing confidence that the Cubs would hit a groove and start playing better baseball.

Lee didn't know he was being taped. After he calmed down, I don't think he even remembered half the things he said. But before leaving the ballpark, he realized he needed to call me.

"I was a little tough with the media today," Lee explained.

By that time, I already knew, because, with heavy bleeping, the recording was on the local news.

"I'd like you to come up to my office," I told him.

"Dal, I'll see you tomorrow, okay? I need to get the hell out of here. I'm going to go watch my daughter play softball."

"No, Lee, you need to come up here right now. If you don't, I'm going to remove you from your job."

That got his attention.

When he saw the news report, I could tell he was shocked by his own words.

I decided to back him, however, because I still thought he was the best man to manage the Cubs. Plus, I knew a thing or two about going berserk in a baseball clubhouse. We weathered that storm, but Lee never quite lived down that incident.

It was another dust-up with the press later in the season that ultimately forced my hand.

Lee was off by himself after another loss, this time trying to keep his emotions confined within the four walls of his office. When he saw a WGN cameraman coming up the steps, he shouted, "No TV!" But the guy kept coming. That set Lee off. "Goddamn it, I said no TV!" he repeated. He then pushed the guy, who took a tumble down the steps, causing the camera to crash to the ground. The Tribune

Company, which has owned WGN for years, didn't take too kindly to the assault on its equipment.

I really appreciated that Lee tried to bring pride and character to the Cubs. But the restaurant incident, the tantrum directed at the fans, and the attack on the cameraman did him in.

Three strikes and you're out. It's always been that way in baseball. The team's poor play obviously didn't help his cause.

With our record at 54–69, I let Lee go in August 1983. It was the most difficult personnel decision I ever made in my career. Lee was one of my best friends, after all.

Looking back, it might have been premature. We played well during certain stretches of the season and had started to put a competitive team together. As a first-time manager, Lee had yet to learn how to deal with all the attention directed toward him. He probably would have gotten better at that over time.

Lee was a great baseball guy. It's just that when his fuse was lit, it went off big-time. That probably hindered his career. After managing the Cubs, he became skipper of the Phillies for parts of two seasons in the late 1980s. But that was his last managing job. He and I remained close, and when George Steinbrenner hired me to lead the Yankees in 1989, I brought Lee on as a coach.

Lee never held his firing against me. Looking back on his time with the Cubs, he says, "It was the first time I managed a major league ballclub, and I didn't have enough experience with the media to understand that you had to conduct yourself in a certain way. I'll always feel bad about how things played out there. The main reason I feel bad is because I let my buddy down."

• • •

Charlie Fox, a veteran baseball guy I had with me in the front office, went down to the field and saw our fifth-place season to completion.

I tried to stay positive. Though we showed no improvement from 1982, I liked a lot of what I saw, especially from our offense. Ron Cey hit 24 home runs and knocked in 90 runs. Sandberg further established himself as a star in the making. Bowa responded to my early-season appeal to take Ryno under his wing and help him master his new position. Thanks to Bowa's leadership, Ruben's coaching, and Sandberg's raw talent, Ryno won a Gold Glove in his first year at second base.

While we were struggling to win games, the Phillies won another pennant in 1983, the year Pat Corrales got fired as manager with the team in first place. Pope came down from the front office to lead the team to the World Series, where they lost to Baltimore. I was proud of Pope and in no way measured myself against what was happening in Philadelphia. I was on a new adventure and determined to move past my choppy first two years in Chicago.

The White Sox were also riding high, fresh off a 99-win season and a division title. At an off-season banquet, White Sox manager Tony La Russa wondered aloud why his team wasn't getting the credit he felt it deserved. "I don't know why you're giving the Cubs so much attention," he told the assembled reporters. "We're the team that just won a division." That was Tony's way of jabbing, but he had a valid point. In good times and bad—mostly bad—the Cubs were the team that captured the imagination of the city.

It was fun to think how excited people would get if we actually started winning.

16

AFTER TWO YEARS IN CHICAGO, I certainly wasn't feeling a great sense of accomplishment. At the same time, I didn't feel any real pressure, either. I had faith in my ability to make the Cubs successful.

Though the major league club had struggled to win games during my tenure, I could point to the scouting and drafting of future Cubs as areas where we excelled from the very beginning. That was thanks to farm director Gordon Goldsberry. Before I arrived, the Cubs relied heavily on the Major League Baseball Scouting Bureau, a centralized office through which scouts provided reports to every franchise. It was a way of scouting on the cheap, and my farm director and I were dead set against it. We wanted our own scouts to produce reports that didn't become communal property.

My time in Philadelphia taught me the importance of identifying and developing young prospects. The Phillies wouldn't have won the 1980 World Series without the players who were first spotted and signed by our organization's scouts in the 1960s and 1970s.

The Cubs had a severe lack of homegrown talent. Pitcher Lee Smith and outfielder Mel Hall were two of the few players on the major league roster in 1983 who came up through the system. I could only do so much to build the team through trades and free agent signings. At some point, we needed to develop talent from within.

Scouting is all about projection. I can send my wife out to a high school game, and without too much difficulty, she'll point out the best player on the field. Raw ability is easy to spot. The more difficult task is projecting how a talented player will grow and develop at the professional level. To do that, scouts have to try and get inside a player's head and heart.

Vedie Himsl, who preceded Gordon Goldsberry as Cubs farm director, believed in the scouting bureau. We worked to convince him that sharing information with other teams wasn't the best way to land players. To his credit, he showed a willingness to try things our way.

I put Vedie in charge of our scouting department. He and Gordie ended up working well together. I'm not sure Vedie ever really bought into our program, but he had no choice if he wanted to keep his job. In the end, he became more of Gordie's assistant than a true scout.

Our lousy record dating back several seasons had the benefit of giving us a pick at or near the top in each year's amateur draft. That was the reason behind the draft, after all—to help the have-nots compete with the haves. In 1982, we made a high school kid from Brooklyn named Shawon Dunston the first overall pick of the draft. Shawon became a productive member of the Cubs for many years. Only two of the top five picks that year made much of an impact in the major leagues. The other was Dwight Gooden, who went fifth overall to the Mets.

In June 1984, Gordie took pitchers Greg Maddux and Jamie Moyer in the second and sixth rounds, respectively. He also drafted catcher Damon Berryhill and outfielder Dwight Smith that year. In 1985, he selected outfielder Rafael Palmeiro in the first round, and in what proved to be a real coup, he got Mark Grace in the 24th round.

• • •

The drafts helped make our future appear brighter, but in the here and now, I had several crucial decisions to make.

The hiring of a new manager was at the top of the list. Charlie Fox returned to his role as a scout and adviser, and I set out to find someone who could help turn us into winners. I considered a lot of different guys before ultimately settling on my counterpart in the 1980 World Series, Jim Frey. Our pitching coach, Billy Connors, who had held the same position in Kansas City under Frey, gave us positive feedback about Jimmy. After getting several other upbeat reports about Jimmy's ability to handle and teach players, I decided he was the right guy for the job. An added bonus of hiring him was that he brought Don Zimmer with him as a coach. I loved Don. He was a helluva baseball guy.

Early in my tenure in Chicago, the Cubs got the nickname "Phillies West." My first manager came with me from Philadelphia, as did a couple of coaches, a bunch of executives, and a handful of players.

The distinct Philadelphia flavor in our clubhouse and front office was a matter of curiosity for most baseball fans, but it remained a sore point for Cubs supporters who wondered why the organization had become so reliant on a division rival for talent and ideas.

I wasn't trying to trample on tradition by bringing in outsiders. I just happened to know the Phillies had a lot of gifted people.

On the heels of two losing seasons, I guess I could have decided to stop importing from Philadelphia.

But I didn't.

After we lost 18 of our first 21 spring training games, I scrambled to make sure 1984 wouldn't be a repeat of every season since 1972, the last time the Cubs finished above .500.

Bill Buckner was still our best trade chip. I badly wanted to move him, for the reasons previously stated, but also because he didn't figure into our plans in 1984. We had decided to switch Leon Durham from the outfield to his natural position at first base. That meant Buckner would go to the bench. It also left us with a hole in left field.

That situation prompted a phone call to Philadelphia. I knew the Phillies didn't care much for young outfielder Bobby Dernier, because I had put in a waiver claim for him before the Phillies pulled him back. Now I wanted to acquire him by trade.

I had helped bring Bobby up through the Phillies organization. At Triple-A Oklahoma City in 1981, he and Ryne Sandberg were a dynamic one-two punch at the top of the lineup, stealing more than a hundred bases between them and playing hit-and-run at all the right times. I was confident they could replicate that performance in Chicago.

We quickly worked out a deal that sent utility player Mike Diaz and pitcher Bill Campbell to the Phillies for Bobby, left fielder Gary Matthews, and pitcher Porfi Altamirano.

Getting Sarge was a bonus. I loved everything about the guy.

That deal for Bobby and Sarge went a long way toward assuring we would play better defense and score runs in 1984. I'm not sure how well we would have fared without them.

• • •

In Durham, Matthews, Sandberg, Ron Cey, Jody Davis, and Keith Moreland, we had a lineup full of guys capable of knocking in runs. The challenge was going to be keeping our opponents from outscoring us.

In 1983, we were the only National League club with a team ERA over 4.00. If we didn't rectify that problem, we would continue to go nowhere. A starting rotation of Chuck Rainey, Steve Trout, Fergie Jenkins, Dick Ruthven, and Dickie Noles just wasn't going to cut it. Of those guys, only Trout and Ruthven would have been a top-four starter for most teams. And Trout was a question mark. After coming over from the White Sox, Trout, a Chicago native, won 10 games for us in 1983. He had a decent arm and good stuff, but he had a loose-cannon personality. He'd arrive at the ballpark from his Indiana home with a dazed look and his hair all over the place.

Our off-season acquisition of Scott Sanderson, a serviceable start-ing pitcher with the Expos, was a step in the right direction. But it hardly solved our problem.

If I was pulling a little harder for Dickie Noles and Fergie to stay in the rotation, it was because I had a special connection to both.

To me, Dickie was "Pie,' a nickname he got from Pete Rose for the pie-eating grin on his face when Philadelphia fans gave him an ovation during a 1979 game that turned out to be his first major league victory. Pete was good at giving nicknames. He also came up with "Sarge" in honor of Matthews' take-charge attitude on the field.

I brought Dickie up through the Phillies organization, always hoping his talent would help him conquer his inner demons. We knew from the get-go that Dickie was a wild kid. Wes Livengood, a Phillies scout, went to a North Carolina jail where Dickie had spent the night for fighting to present him with his first professional con-tract. He later admitted he consumed alcohol every day of his life between the ages of 16 and 26.

His drinking got him into a lot of jams, some more significant than others. After a heavy night of boozing while playing winter ball in Venezuela, Dickie started tossing furniture out the window of his sixth-floor apartment. As with many of his alcohol binges, Dickie didn't remember a thing about the incident. Only when Venezuelan authorities came to kick him out of the country the next day did he learn what happened.

Whenever I suspected another player of having a drinking prob-lem, I'd check and see if he was hanging around Dickie. Birds of a feather flock together, and Dickie was a thirsty bird.

Dickie drank to excess, but he also loved to play baseball and worked his ass off at the ballpark. You don't give up on a guy like that.

That's why I traded for him when I got to Chicago.

The change of scenery didn't help Dickie.

In April 1983, Lee Elia and I took some local sportswriters to dinner during a road trip in Cincinnati. During the meal, I got a call at the restaurant from our traveling secretary.

"Dickie's in jail," he told me.

"Jail?" I repeated. "What for?"

I didn't wait for the answer, because I already knew the answer.

At the police station, Connors and John Vukovich were waiting on us. The sergeant on duty told us Dickie got drunk and beat the shit out of a Cincinnati cop.

Enough was enough. After we bailed Dickie out of jail, I told him not to bother showing up for the game the next day.

"You're going directly from here to rehab," I told him.

"No, no, Dallas, I'll be all right," he protested.

"Dickie, you just decked a cop and don't even remember doing it! Either you get some goddamn help, or I'll make sure you never play an inning of baseball again. You have a chance to be a good man. But you need to go get yourself straightened out."

Faced with banishment from the Cubs, Dickie could have appealed to the players union for guidance. But he chose to follow my orders and get himself dried out. He checked into a 30-day rehab program and took the first steps toward beating his addiction. Later that year, he was sentenced to 16 days in jail for his assault on the police officer.

He had a disappointing 1983 season, but more importantly, he took steps toward becoming a productive human being.

Dickie remained with us for the first half of the '84 season, albeit relegated to the bullpen. Then he became crosswise with Frey and demanded a trade. He felt Jimmy never fully forgave him for the high-and-tight pitch he threw to George Brett in the 1980 World Series. Maybe that was it, or maybe Jimmy just didn't trust him. Dickie wanted to go to a team that would put him in its starting rotation. He thought he needed a fresh start someplace else, so I honored his wish by trading him to the Rangers.

• • •

Fergie Jenkins was another guy who didn't end up fitting into our plans in 1984. That disappointed me, because I really liked Fergie, who represented a link to my past as a player.

During my third year pitching for Philadelphia, Fergie signed with the Phillies organization. We crossed paths at Triple-A Arkansas in 1965, the year he made his major league debut as a September call-up.

Phillies manager Gene Mauch, who had a problem handling pitchers, couldn't stand Fergie for some reason. Thanks to Gene's lobbying, the Phillies traded him to the Cubs in 1966. That turned out to be a huge mistake. Fergie's career took off in Chicago, where he became a Cy Young–caliber pitcher year in and year out. He went on to win a ton of games for Chicago, Texas, and Boston.

I brought Fergie back to the Cubs in 1982, partly because he was closing in on 300 career wins. It would have been sweet for him to reach that milestone with the Cubs.

He pitched fairly well his first season back in Chicago. At the age of 38, he won 14 games and posted a 3.15 ERA. But his win total slipped to six in 1983. By the end of the season, he had 284 career wins.

In spring training in 1984, I could see he didn't want to go through the grind anymore. The running, the workouts, and the side throwing sessions had started to feel like work for him. We needed to make changes to our pitching staff, so I decided to release Fergie.

He and I have remained close, and as far as I know, he feels no animosity about how his career ended. Enshrinement in the Hall of Fame tends to heal most wounds.

• • •

Despite the addition of Sanderson, we went into the '84 season with a starting pitching rotation nowhere near strong enough to keep us competitive. For that reason, many baseball writers picked us to finish last in the National League East. Based on our past performance, nobody was going to quibble with that prediction.

But thanks in part to three wins apiece by Trout and Sanderson, we finished April tied for first place in the National League East.

Our unexpected level of play continued into May, and at the end of that month, much to the pleasure of both parties, we finally unloaded Bill Buckner, whose bad legs concerned me as much as his troubling personality. The timing of the trade was perfect. The Red Sox coveted Buckner and had enough depth in their pitching rotation to be able to offer us former 20-game winner Dennis Eckersley in return. Eck was coming off a terrible 1983 season in Boston, but I felt he still had several good years left in his arm.

Our scouts, especially Charlie Fox, did a quality job putting together reports on Eck. He had pinpoint control and was adept at keeping the ball in the ballpark. On the flip side, we knew he had been drinking a little too heavily and that the Red Sox were disenchanted with his work ethic. Before making the deal, I grilled Eck and his agent on whether he could give us the effort we needed.

To Eck's credit, he was a pro from the day I first met him.

For what it's worth, Buckner harbored a grudge against me and the Cubs.

During the 1986 World Series, a few days before he became infamous for letting a ball squirt through his legs with the Red Sox on the verge of a championship, Buckner reflected on his trade to Boston. He said I did him a favor by shipping him off to Boston, which had been his preferred destination. "But I didn't ask for Boston," he told Jerome Holtzman of the *Chicago Tribune*. "Maybe it was a good thing.

If I had said I wanted to go to Boston, Dallas might have sent me the other way."

Nah, Billy Buck, I just wanted you out of Chicago.

I don't wish failure upon anyone. That's not my style. But there was something fitting about a guy who exemplified selfishness committing an error that royally screwed up his team and his own legacy.

• • •

Through the first three months of the '84 season, the National League East race was a tight one between the Cubs, the Mets, and the Phillies. We played consistent baseball, not going on long winning streaks but avoiding drawn-out slumps. By winning more series than we lost, we stayed in the mix.

Sanderson and Ruthven, who held down the fifth spot in our rotation, went down in late May with injuries. Suddenly we were even thinner in the pitching department.

My eyes lit up when Cleveland general manager Phil Seghi approached me in mid-June to gauge my interest in Rick Sutcliffe. After leading the American League in ERA in 1982 and winning 17 games in 1983, Sut was just 4–5 with a 5.15 ERA. But I had a hunch he was just going through a rough spell. I felt his talent level and competitive nature would make him a valuable addition to our club.

He wasn't going to come cheap, however. In return, Cleveland wanted outfielders Mel Hall and Joe Carter. Hall had placed third in the Rookie of the Year voting the previous season. He was a reckless guy off the field, but I liked him as a ballplayer. Carter, the second overall pick in the 1981 draft, was tearing up the minor leagues.

When I arrived in Chicago, I promised the beginning of a new—and winning—tradition. Back then, I was the new general manager looking to trade veterans for prospects. Now, with a playoff run looking plausible, I felt comfortable gambling on a player who might help us get over the top.

A paperwork glitch almost scuttled the deal, but once we got that straightened out, Sut was ours. He came to the Cubs along with reliever George Frazier and catcher Ron Hassey. In addition to Hall and Carter, we sent pitchers Don Schulze and Darryl Banks to Cleveland.

It was a steep price to pay for a pitcher not considered among the game's elite, but again, I had a feeling Sut would emerge as the ace we needed.

I told reporters at the time, "We don't like giving up promising players, especially a player such as Mel Hall. But we need a first-class pitcher, and if we are going to win, our players, not just management, have to grab the brass ring."

As it turned out, Carter, not Hall, became the superstar. Carter was a 30-30 guy with Cleveland and later helped lead the Toronto Blue Jays to two straight championships. Hall had some pretty decent years with the Indians and the Yankees but is now serving a long prison sentence for rape.

In addition to bringing us Sut, the trade helped defuse Keith Moreland's anger at Frey for platooning him with Hall. In our pursuit of a top-flight pitcher, Keith thought for sure he would be dangled as trade bait. I couldn't easily tell Jimmy how to fill out his lineup card, but I could decide who to offer to other teams. I thought highly of Keith and believed we'd be more likely to make a pennant run with him on the team. When Hall got traded, Keith was poised to reclaim right field for himself. I told him, "Okay, big boy, you got the job. Now stop bitching and moaning and go out and play."

Like a lot of guys that year, he stepped up to the challenge.

• • •

Shortly after that trade, the Phillies rolled us in a four-game series at Wrigley Field. The sweep dropped us to third place and vaulted Philadelphia into first. As the Phillies left town, manager Paul Owens assured the baseball world that his team had every intention of repeating as division champions. Pope's proclamation hinted at something many were surely thinking after Philadelphia handed our tails to us: Like clockwork, another June swoon awaited the Cubs.

I was as concerned as anybody about the Cubs' tendency over the years to fall into a rut in the middle of the season. While with the Phillies, I saw it firsthand in 1977 when the Cubs held onto first place through July but suddenly ran out of steam, allowing us to catch and pass them.

I agreed with the conventional wisdom that all the day games took a toll on the team.

Knowing Wrigley Field wouldn't have lights any time in the near future, I came up with the idea of 3:05 PM start times for games taking place on days after the team returned from a road trip.

I thought an extra couple hours of rest between night and day games would help our players. And in my opinion, it did. But the later start times also presented challenges. As these games entered the later innings, shadows crept across home plate, making it difficult for batters to pick up incoming pitches. It was a tough go at times, but I never questioned the choice. Day baseball is a wonderful thing—until fatigue starts costing you games.

I didn't hear too much grumbling from my own players about the 3:05 games (Buckner was gone, after all), but a former player of mine, Mike Schmidt, ripped me for making his job a little harder.

"I guess it's Dallas Green's decision, but there's no concern for players and players' performance," Schmidt told the *Chicago Tribune*. "When a team plays a 3:05 game, they're pretty sure that if the sun's out, by the fifth, sixth, seventh, eighth, or ninth inning, they're not going to be able to see the ball when it gets to home plate."

Quite honestly, I never really worried about anything Schmitty said. He had long been his own worst enemy. And I could have cared less about other teams' bitching about the 3:05 start times. I did it to help the Cubs, not them.

I guess I couldn't blame Schmitty too much for not wanting to hit in the late innings at Wrigley Field if the Cubs had a lead. That meant hitters likely had to face our closer, Lee Smith. I hate the word *dominant*, because I think it's overused. It ranks up there with *small ball* on my list of least preferred terms. But Lee was as close to dominant as you can get a lot of the time. In 1983, his first year as a full-time closer, he led the league with 29 saves and gave up just 19 earned runs in more than a hundred innings.

The shadows definitely worked to Lee's advantage. His 95 mile-per-hour fastball was difficult to hit at any time of the day, but in the fading late-afternoon sunlight, it was next to impossible. Lee would rear back and throw that lively fastball or a tricky slider. Halfway to the plate, it would momentarily disappear before emerging from the shadows. Hitters had precious little time to decide whether to swing or not.

My only criticism of Lee was that he didn't throw inside. I'd say, "Lee, do me a favor and bust them in every once in a while just to let them know you're there. Pitch them in, jam them, make their fingers hurt." He had a hell of a time with that. He liked to pitch away.

Lee didn't have a stellar year, by his standards, in 1984, but his presence at the back end of our bullpen meant a lot to us. Like Tug McGraw in 1980, he had the head, heart, and belly to close games.

• • •

What can I say about Ryne Sandberg? Well, for starters, I can say I'm glad he didn't listen to his mother and accept the college football scholarship he was offered out of high school. If he had, my time in Chicago likely would have been drastically different.

The letter of intent Ryno signed with Washington State turned him from a hot baseball prospect into an afterthought in the 1978 major league draft. No team wanted to squander a pick on a player it couldn't sign. As Phillies farm director, I knew how much our scouts loved Ryno. But why waste a pick?

"What the hell," I said when I saw him still on the draft board at the start of the 20th round. "Let's take a chance and hope the kid changes his mind about college."

A few days later, Bill Harper, our scout for the Northwest region, and his supervisor, Moose Johnson, visited with Ryno and his parents in Spokane, Washington. Bill, whose grandson, Bryce, became a pretty good player himself with the Washington Nationals, must have given the Sandberg family one hell of a sales pitch. He and Moose walked out of the house with a signed contract.

Over the next couple of years, I watched Ryno's rapid development in the minor leagues. As GM of the Cubs, I insisted the Phillies include Ryno in the 1982 Larry Bowa trade. That ended up being the single best decision I ever made as a general manager.

Ryno's first two seasons in Chicago confirmed he had a bright future in the majors. He adjusted quickly to major league pitching and put up respectable offensive numbers.

But I don't think any of us were prepared for what happened in 1984.

Recognizing Ryno had some pop in his bat, Jimmy Frey talked to him in spring training about how to utilize his power. "Especially when you're ahead in the count, look for a ball in the middle of the plate and try to drive it, even if it means hitting foul balls down the third-base line," Jimmy told him.

It was simple advice, but Ryno hadn't heard it before. Back then, a slick-fielding infielder who stole 30-plus bases and hit .270 was a pretty damn good player. That was Ryno before 1984. The talk with Jimmy helped him add a new dimension to his game.

From that time on, whenever he fell behind in the count, he tried to make solid contact. But when he got ahead, he showed off a nice power stroke. In 1984, he hit 19 home runs, more than he hit in the previous two seasons combined. He also hit a league-leading 19 triples. By adding power to his game, he became the rare five-tool second baseman.

• • •

A nationally televised game on June 23, 1984, against the Cardinals marked Ryno's emergence as a superstar and ours as a contender for the division crown.

The game showed no signs of being remarkable early on.

St. Louis jumped all over Steve Trout, scoring six runs in the second inning to take a 7–1 lead. In years past, the Cubs would have folded tent. And despite the home team's ineptitude, the fans at Wrigley Field would have enjoyed a nice summer afternoon anyway.

On that day, however, the team fought back, and the fans learned just how enjoyable winning baseball can be.

A two-run single by Sandberg in the bottom of the sixth capped a five-run inning that cut the Cardinals' lead to 9–8. An inning later, Whitey Herzog brought in Bruce Sutter to try and quell our comeback.

Remember what I said about Lee Smith being dominant at times? Well, Sutter, a former Cub, also could be described that way. He had led the league in saves in 1984, the fifth time in six years he captured the NL saves title. And up to that point in the '84 season, his split-finger fastball had been almost unhittable. Despite routinely pitching multiple innings in relief, his ERA was just a shade over 1.00.

Sutter got the final out of the seventh and breezed through the eighth. Strong relief work by our Tim Stoddard and George Frazier kept it a one-run game going into the bottom of the ninth.

Ryno stepped to the plate to lead off the inning against Sutter, against whom he was 2-for-11 in his career to that point. That's a stat that confuses me. Did it mean Sutter owned him? Or did it mean Ryno was due for a hit? It turned out to be the latter. Ryno followed Jimmy's advice and put a compact swing on a Sutter split-finger fastball. The ball jumped off his bat and into the air, eventually landing in the left-field bleachers for a game-tying home run. The crowd went bananas. And so did the Cubs front office, watching the game from our ballpark suite.

The thrill was short-lived, however. Lee Smith coughed up a couple of runs in the top of the 10th to put us back in a hole. Willie McGee finished off his cycle with a double that gave the Cardinals the lead.

Sutter retook the mound in the bottom of the 10th. One comeback against him was improbable, but two in the same game? That seemed next to impossible.

We started the inning with two ground outs. Down two runs with two outs and nobody on base, it looked as bleak as it gets. From my seat near the press box, I could hear NBC broadcasters Bob Costas and Tony Kubek preparing to sign off by thanking their crew and announcing that night's prime-time lineup.

Sutter ran the count full to Bobby Dernier, taking us down to our last strike. Bobby hung tough and drew a walk.

With a runner on first, Ryno came to the plate again.

The rest is history, I guess.

He smacked another homer to left to tie the game at 11–11. The hit completed his 5-for-6 day at the plate. After the home run, I ran over within earshot of Costas and Kubek and shouted, "You guys better take all those thank-yous back! We're still playing!"

We won the game in the 11th on an RBI single by Dave Owen.

After the game, Herzog said Sandberg was the best baseball player he'd ever seen.

It was just unbelievable storybook stuff. That game defined Sandberg going forward. And it defined the Cubs in 1984 as anything but pushovers.

We avoided a swoon in June and every other month. In fact, we had a winning record every month of the '84 season.

17

AFTER RYNE SANDBERG'S CAREER-MAKING game at Wrigley Field against St. Louis, we really got on a roll. We moved into first place in the National League East for good on August 1 and ended up winning the division by 6½ games. Over the last three months of the season, we went 54–31.

Rick Sutcliffe was as good a pitcher in the second half of the 1984 season as you'll ever see. He won 16 games and lost only one after we traded for him. Seven of those victories came in games following a Cubs loss. On September 7 at Shea Stadium, the second-place Mets trounced us 10–0 on a one-hitter by Dwight Gooden, who struck out 11. It was the kind of win that can propel a team to a late-season run. But Sut took the mound the next day and kept the Mets from inching any closer. He threw a four-hit, complete-game shutout, striking out 12 while walking none.

Dennis Eckersley and Steve Trout also chipped in with double-digit win totals.

The Dernier-Sandberg combination at the top of the lineup lived up to my expectations. A *Chicago Tribune* article pointed out we were 25–6 in 1984 when those two players combined for three or more hits in a game. In addition, both won Gold Gloves.

Bobby and Ryno got on base, and the guys hitting behind them made sure they crossed the plate. In the process of scoring the most runs in the National League, we had six guys with 80 or more RBIs. Three of the six were ex-Phillies, but no one was complaining anymore about the Phillies-heavy influence in our lineup. As Bobby said later in the season, "The important thing is not where guys come from, but whether or not they're good players. All the guys that came over here from other clubs qualify."

Longer-tenured Cubs like Leon Durham and Jody Davis also had fine years.

In short, it was a team effort that got the Cubs to the playoffs for the first time since 1945.

· · ·

Thinking back on everything that fell into place that season, I remember the euphoria of Cubs fans as we marched toward a division title. Many had never experienced a pennant race before. From the "Sandberg Game" onward, Wrigley Field became an incredible place to watch a baseball game. And the excitement wasn't confined to the ballpark. You could hear the buzz about the Cubs all around town, especially in the Wrigleyville neighborhood.

It had been 39 years since the Cubs won any kind of title, and my theory about success being a boom for business proved correct. In our case, winning put asses in seats. For the first time in Cubs history, 2 million fans walked through the Wrigley Field turnstiles. We had the second-best attendance numbers in the National League in 1984. Since then, Cubs yearly attendance has dipped below 2 million in a non-strike year only once. There's no doubt in my mind that the '84 season had a lasting impact on Cubs baseball.

They called it a miracle season, but there were actually concrete reasons behind it. Some attributed our success to the Tribune Company loosening the purse strings and allowing me to acquire first-rate players. Others, including Jimmy Frey, opined that I deserved most of the credit for smart personnel decisions. When we clinched the division in

'84, only three players—Leon Durham, Jody Davis, and Lee Smith—had been with the Cubs longer than I had.

As we prepared for the National League Championship Series against San Diego, rumors swirled that I was looking to get back to Philadelphia. A year after reaching the World Series, the Phillies played .500 ball in 1984. After almost 30 years with the Phillies, Paul Owens, the team's manager and former general manager, was headed for a smaller role in the organization.

Since the 1970s, Pope and I had discussed the idea of me succeeding him as general manager. But that plan hinged on Pope voluntarily retiring and me still being in the Phillies organization when that day came. Neither was the case by 1984. Another factor was Phillies owner Bill Giles, who had a more hands-on role in running the team than his predecessor, Ruly Carpenter. Giles liked to make baseball decisions on his own, and a lot of people questioned how well he and I would work together.

When reporters asked me at the end of the '84 season about my thoughts on returning to Philadelphia, I told them the truth: "First of all, they haven't asked me back, and I haven't asked to go back. The rumors have persisted, I guess, because I haven't really killed them, except to say that I'm a guy that honors my contract, and I've got two more years on my contract. I had a goal I set for myself here, and the goal, of course, was to win for the Cubs, and I think we're going to accomplish that goal. After that, we'll see what happens."

But first, we had to accomplish that goal.

• • •

The joy of a division title was tempered somewhat by Major League Baseball's threat to keep postseason games from being scheduled during the day. Commissioner Bowie Kuhn was concerned that afternoon playoff games would hurt television revenue.

"The Cubs' involvement in the divisional race has built excitement, and that's great for their fans," Kuhn said. "But we have an obligation beyond the local fans. For the future, baseball must promptly find a clear-cut solution to the lights situation."

Translation: the Cubs would be deprived of home playoff games if Wrigley Field didn't get lights.

I was a realist. I loved the charms and tradition of daytime baseball. At the same time, I felt that night games at Wrigley were an inevitability. The commissioner's warning further convinced me of that. But Wrigleyville residents and the politicians who represented them needed to be brought around to that way of thinking. That wouldn't happen without some prodding.

At the end of August, Kuhn came up with a short-term "solution" he hoped would satisfy everyone. In 1984, the National League was in line for home-field advantage in the World Series, which meant its representative would host the first two, and if necessary, the last two games of the series. Kuhn said that would still be the case—unless the Cubs were representing the National League. If that happened, home-field advantage would go to the American League team, reducing the number of day games by one while allowing the Chicago games to be played on the weekend when more people across the country would be home to watch games on television.

Kuhn said he thought it was a fair decision and the only way to avoid having to offer NBC a rebate for loss of ad revenue.

I didn't like Kuhn's ruling one bit, but I managed to focus on the positive—sort of. "I guess the neighborhood got what they wanted then, didn't they?" I said when reporters asked me about the decision. Our team president, Jim Finks, took a rosier view of the situation, saying the Cubs had an obligation to the rest of the league to compromise.

That was nonsense.

Of course, it was all hypothetical for the time being. We needed to reach the World Series first. Still, I realized this was the beginning of an effort by Major League Baseball to penalize the Cubs for not playing night baseball.

• • •

Our opponent in the National League Championship Series had a Cinderella story of its own. The Padres had just won their first division title, posting a winning record for only the second time in the franchise's 16-year history. They were a solid team, but I felt we had an edge in talent and experience. The Cubs hadn't played postseason baseball in decades, but 10 of our players had appeared in the playoffs with other teams. In the best-of-five NLCS, we got the first two games at home before going to San Diego for as many as three more games. I expected an added lift from the fans at Wrigley Field. Their enthusiasm was part of the reason we were 22 games over .500 at home during the season.

The playoffs represented a huge moment for the Cubs organization, and I wanted to include everyone in the celebration—even infamous farm animals.

Among those invited to attend Game 1 were Sam Sianis, owner of the Billy Goat Tavern, and his pet goat. This was our tongue-in-cheek way of reminding people of a key piece of Cubs lore. Back in 1945, William Sianis, the founder of the tavern and Sam's uncle, had supposedly put a curse on the Cubs after he and his goat were denied admittance to a World Series game.

The goat idea and others like it were the brainchild of our marketing team of Bing and Patty Hampton, whose creativity took us to new places. They thought up the gimmicks—all I had to was approve them. Bing and Patty came up with the idea of ballgirls at Wrigley Field. That was a big hit—until one of the gals posed nude in *Playboy*.

That kind of exposure didn't sit well with the staid old Tribune boys, so she was let go. But the rest of the ballgirls stayed.

A more serious piece of business during the World Series concerned Mr. Cub. Ernie Banks' failure to show up for public appearances had forced me to sever official ties with him. With the Cubs in the playoffs, I saw a perfect opportunity to show Ernie he would always be a cherished part of the Cubs family. On the eve of the NLCS, I announced Ernie would be in uniform as an honorary member of the team for the series opener.

• • •

Wrigley Field was the place to be on October 2, 1984—except for major league umpires, who had gone on strike to protest not getting a pay bump for postseason games. New commissioner Peter Ueberroth, who had taken over for Bowie Kuhn the day before, refused to negotiate, delegating that task to the league presidents. That meant the NLCS opened with college umpires from the Big Ten Conference. I wouldn't have blamed them for being nervous. I'm sure the last thing the fill-in umps wanted was any kind of controversy that might affect the outcome of the game.

Fortunately for them, Game 1 had no drama or suspense. And while it featured a 20 mile-per-hour wind blowing out of Wrigley Field, only one team took advantage of that.

Behind two home runs by Gary Matthews and seven shutout innings from Rick Sutcliffe, we crushed the Padres 13–0. Sut, who also homered in the game, won his 15th straight decision. He allowed only two hits, a bunt single and a bloop single, to a Padres lineup that included Tony Gwynn, Steve Garvey, and Graig Nettles.

As our lead grew throughout the afternoon, Wrigley turned into a giant outdoor party.

Ernie thoroughly enjoyed every moment of our win. "So this is how the playoffs feel?" he said with a wide grin on his face.

After the game, Nettles tried to downplay the drubbing: "They hit the holes. Our best shots were right at 'em."

I don't know how you save face after a 13–0 loss, but give Nettles credit for at least trying.

Riding the wave of a blowout victory, we came back the next day and jumped out to a 3–0 lead in the third inning. Game 2 wasn't another laugher, but thanks to a strong outing by sinkerballer Steve Trout and an outstanding defensive play by first baseman Leon Durham, the Padres couldn't dig themselves out of the early hole. In the top of the ninth, Lee Smith induced a fly out from Terry Kennedy with a runner on base to preserve a 4–2 win.

In baseball, you rarely hear about postseason mismatches. That's because anything can happen in a playoff series pitting two quality teams against each other. To win in the postseason, you have to get hot at the right time. As I learned with the Phillies in 1980, events unfold quickly in October.

I experienced that again in 1984. In the span of 24 hours, the Cubs had gotten to the brink of the World Series. We didn't feel like anything could stop us now.

One win in San Diego. That was all we needed.

• • •

Before Game 3, Jimmy Frey cautioned that the series wasn't over yet. "Losing three in a row would be embarrassing," he said. "We still need 27 more outs before we can call ourselves National League champions. The breaks can turn in a hurry. When the dam opens, it's tough to close it."

Ideally, the first postseason game ever played in San Diego would also be the last of the 1984 NLCS. We'd sweep the Padres and move on to play the Tigers, who won three straight games against the Royals in the ALCS.

As I saw it, even the worst possible scenario looked pretty appealing for us. If we happened to lose two games in a row to set up a winner-take-all Game 5 at Jack Murphy Stadium, we'd have Sutcliffe on the mound for the decisive game. I hoped it wouldn't come to that, but if it did, I liked our chances.

We had a 1–0 lead in Game 3 before the Padres got to Dennis Eckersley in the fifth and sixth innings. San Diego coasted from there to a 7–1 win.

Game 4 could have gone either way. The seesaw battle ended in the bottom of the ninth when Steve Garvey, the player I tried to bring to the Cubs before the 1983 season, hit a tie-breaking two-run homer off Lee Smith.

The dam had opened. And the Padres were suddenly a very energized ballclub.

So many times during the season, Sutcliffe had stepped up for us when we needed a win. His dominant performance in Game 1 only added to his air of invincibility. With the possible exception of Steve Carlton in his prime, there wasn't a pitcher I would have more preferred on the mound with the series and the hopes of the Cubs organization on the line.

• • •

Instead of Chicago writers penning articles about Dallas Green and his Phillies fixation, Philadelphia columnists were banging out copy about America's new favorite team, the Chicago Cubs.

During the NLCS, Ray Didinger of the *Philadelphia Daily News* wrote, "The Cubs aren't a baseball team anymore, they're a cult. You could stick up a bank tomorrow and get away with it if you were wearing a Cubs hat. The cop would hold the door open and say, 'How bout that Ryne Sandberg?'"

The eyes of the nation were really on us now. If we won Game 5, we'd be hailed as conquering heroes, even though the World Series had yet to be played. If we lost, words like *choke* and *cursed* would get thrown around for years to come.

Early in the game, it looked like we'd be celebrated, not scorned.

Leon Durham's two-run homer in the first inning staked us to a 2–0 lead. Jody Davis' solo shot in the second made it 3–0, and Padres manager Dick Williams removed starter Eric Show from the game after a single by Sutcliffe later that inning.

Suddenly, all we needed from Sut was an average outing. But the word *average* wasn't in Sut's personal vocabulary that season. He was in total control through the first five innings, surrendering just two hits, both infield singles. He gave up two runs in the sixth, but even that felt like a minor victory considering he had loaded the bases with nobody out.

It would've been a relief to put the game away by scoring a few insurance runs off the Padres bullpen. Instead, we went hitless against Andy Hawkins, Dave Dravecky, and Craig Lefferts in the 5⅔ innings after Show left.

We clung to a 3–2 lead when the worst inning of my baseball career took place.

Carmelo Martinez, a former Cub I traded away after the '83 season, led off the seventh with a four-pitch walk and advanced to second base on a sacrifice bunt.

To avoid facing Gwynn and Garvey, Sut needed to retire the next two batters. He took a step in that direction when he got Tim Flannery to hit a ground ball right to Durham, who was a very capable first baseman. His .994 fielding percentage during the '84 season ranked among the highest in the league. He had helped us win Game 2 by making an outstanding play in the field.

Flannery's grounder went right through Durham's legs for an error that allowed Martinez to score the tying run.

The momentum in the series shifted back to the Padres.

With Trout warming in the bullpen, Jimmy decided to stick with Sut, who hadn't even reached the 80-pitch mark yet.

After the error, Sut couldn't get anyone out. Alan Wiggins singled, Gwynn doubled, and Garvey singled to score three more runs. Trout came in to get the last two outs of the inning.

Trailing 6–3, we couldn't get back in the game against San Diego closer Goose Gossage.

Heartbreak.

I had a hard time finding the words to express my disappointment.

"We had them by the throat, but we let them get away," I said after the game. "I think the emotion swung their way when we left Chicago. I think they became electrified and played more confidently and more aggressively."

To this day, a lot of Cubs fans blame Durham for the Game 5 loss. Many forget that his two-run home run in the first inning accounted for two of our three runs in the game. Sut's loss of effectiveness in the seventh is also overlooked, except by those who feel Trout should have come in the game earlier. That's classic second-guessing. Sut had been so effective for us all year, and I would have been reluctant to take him out, too. Some critics argued we might have won the series if we had skipped Sanderson's start and pitched Sutcliffe in Game 4, leaving Trout to pitch a possible Game 5.

Would that have changed the outcome of the series? We'll never know.

• • •

I cried like a baby on the flight from San Diego to Chicago.

Only two other experiences in my baseball life came close to matching the disappointment of the '84 NLCS: the Phillies squandering the pennant in 1964, and the Phillies losing in the NLCS to the Dodgers in 1977.

But what happened to the Cubs still holds a special and painful place in my heart and mind.

We fought like hell to build that team and make it competitive, and it hurt like a son of a bitch to fall just short of the World Series. There was no question in my mind that we had the best team in the National League that year.

It took me a long time to get over that hurt. I didn't watch on television as the Padres lost to the Tigers. I sat at my suburban Chicago home and stayed away from baseball for a while.

It hit the players hard, too.

Steve Trout had a very personal reason for wanting to pitch against Detroit for all the marbles. Back in 1945, when the Tigers beat the Cubs in the World Series, his father, Dizzy, threw a complete game that helped Detroit win the title in seven games.

Keith Moreland, who now broadcasts Cubs games on WGN radio, says he still hasn't gotten over the loss: "It was like someone ripped your heart out. You get your heart back at some point but with a piece of it missing."

Gary Matthews echoes that sentiment. Sarge quickly became a fan favorite in his first season with the Cubs. The fans recognized his zest for the game, and he fully embraced the idea that we were ushering in a new era for the Cubs. He brought his drill sergeant attitude and offensive prowess to the park every day.

After a two-homer game in the series opener, he went 1-for-11 the rest of the way. He says he began pressing too hard for a hit and ended up swinging at bad pitches. "You win or lose as a team," he said. I couldn't agree more. And it's that way of thinking that made me want to have Sarge on the team in the first place. Sarge still dwells on that Game 5 loss: "It's hard to explain the haunting feeling you have when you know you should have accomplished something you didn't."

We racked up a lot of individual accolades that year: Ryno was National League MVP, Sut won the Cy Young, Jimmy got Manager of the Year, and I was selected as *The Sporting News* Executive of the Year.

And the Cubs were division champions—but nothing more.

I did a lot of moping that off-season. I had been in baseball long enough to know losing was part of the game, but that didn't make it any easier to deal with. It took a while for me to kick my self-pity in the ass and get back to work again.

And there was a lot of work to do before the 1985 season started. The creation of a postseason-caliber team had come at a cost. The acquisitions of Sutcliffe, Eckersley, Matthews, and Cey added a lot of money to the books. And our top three starting pitchers were all free agents.

My goal was to keep us moving forward.

18

THE PHILLIES NEVER CONTACTED ME about becoming their new general manager. I was loyal to the Cubs, but I didn't make a secret of the fact that I had deep affection for the Phillies. Early in my tenure, I probably sounded like a man pining for his lost love whenever I talked about "the Phillies way" of running an organization. I was a Phillies player, farm director, and manager. And it had always been my ambition to add general manager to the list.

I guess if I had been more diplomatic, I might have gotten a call from Giles. When asked my opinion about the Phillies' struggles in 1984, I suggested poor trades were the culprit. Instead of Gary Matthews and Bobby Dernier, who helped the Cubs immensely in '84, the Phillies had two underachievers in the outfield, Von Hayes and Glenn Wilson. I also felt Philadelphia's minor league system, once my pride and joy, had started to deteriorate.

I was content to remain in Chicago, where the Cubs' future was still very much in my hands.

During my first three off-seasons in Chicago, I pursued trades and signings that could help turn around a struggling team. Times had changed. After the 1984 season, I set out to retain our current players. I felt we had a good chance to continue winning with the team that got us to the National League Championship Series.

My top priority was holding onto the entire top end of our pitching rotation. Rick Sutcliffe, Dennis Eckersley, and Steve Trout all were eligible for free agency. In the span of three weeks in November and December 1984, we re-signed all of them: Eckersley for three years and Trout and Sutcliffe for five. Sut's deal cost us $9.5 million over the life of the contract. That's peanuts today, but very few players were making that kind of money back then.

I knew Sut's services would be coveted by a number of other teams. The Padres, the Royals, and the Braves all put in comparable bids for him, but his sense of loyalty to the Cubs prevailed in the end. He felt he had more to accomplish in a Cubs uniform. If we hadn't re-signed him, that would have meant we gave up Joe Carter and Mel Hall, two promising young outfielders, just to rent Sut for half a season.

As I said at the time, "We made a commitment to the city of Chicago and our ballclub to get our people back."

To ensure further continuity on the field, I also extended manager Jim Frey's contract through the 1987 season.

I handed out rewards for meritorious performance, and I also received one myself from the Tribune Company. After Jim Finks resigned as Cubs president in December 1984, I took on his responsibilities. A few months later, Andy McKenna stepped down as the liaison between me and the company. My bosses were taking off the training wheels. In announcing the changes, John Madigan, the company's executive vice president, said my growth as a businessman and success at putting the organization on the right track had earned me more autonomy.

I didn't make any major personnel moves that off-season, but I did take a gamble on a marginally talented kid whose passion for the game and will to succeed ranked up there with any player I had ever seen. I figured I'd give him a shot, if for no other reason than to help him get baseball out of his system. That he happened to be my son John was secondary, believe it or not.

If I hadn't signed John, he would have convinced someone else to. He had taken part in a College World Series at the University of Arizona and won a junior college national championship. The kid could definitely play. I just didn't know if he had major league potential, and I hated the thought of him being a career minor leaguer.

As long as he was in my organization, I knew he would be trained right and that I could keep an eye on him.

John reported to our rookie team in Wytheville, Virginia. From that point on, he wasn't Dallas Green's son. He was just another pitcher chasing a dream.

• • •

A couple of things happen when your team puts together a successful season. First, other organizations start taking you seriously. That was a big deal, considering how negatively the Cubs had been viewed for so many years. The second result of winning is increased buzz surrounding your team. I saw that before the 1985 season even opened when, for the first time, the Cubs started selling out spring training games in Mesa, Arizona.

A lot of people had scoffed at the marketing strategy we adopted when I first got to Chicago. But the slogan "Building a New Tradition" didn't seem so dumb anymore.

We had the talent to repeat as division champs, but recent history frowned on our chances. No National League East team had won consecutive titles since the Phillies in 1976, 1977, and 1978. Since then, every team except the Mets had taken a turn as king of the hill.

As far as I could tell, we had no glaring weaknesses. The only real question mark was whether Larry Bowa would remain our starting shortstop. He had provided valuable leadership in 1984, but at age 39, he had ceded playing time to Tom Veryzer and Dave Owen. Neither of them was our shortstop of the future. That distinction belonged to Shawon Dunston, the first overall pick of the 1982 draft. Shawon's steady progress in the minors convinced us he was about ready for the big leagues. But "about ready" and "ready" were two different things. I didn't want to rush him.

• • •

Unlike other general managers, I had more to deal with than just baseball operations. The lights issue at Wrigley Field started feeling like a part-time job.

Before the season, an Illinois judge upheld city and state laws that banned night games from ever being played at Wrigley Field. This was a disappointment, because I knew Major League Baseball would seek retribution by taking home playoff games away from us.

The judge ruled that 37,000 visitors roaming their streets at night would subject the neighborhood around Wrigley to a public nuisance. He asserted the ban on lights didn't impact our bottom line or ability to win games.

I don't recall ever showing the judge our books, so I'm not sure how he came to those conclusions. The sole basis for his argument was our division title, which in his opinion proved we could accomplish our goal by playing exclusively day baseball. I thought our goal was winning a World Series. Then again, I was just president and general manager of the team.

I guess the judge was out of town when new commissioner Peter Ueberroth told us future postseason games might be played "elsewhere than at Wrigley Field, perhaps not even in Chicago." The only downside to starting the 1985 season 35–19 and selling out almost every home game was that that the damn judge probably felt further vindicated.

At that point, a third of the way into the season, we led the National League East by four games. Our record put us on pace for 105 wins.

Then the June swoon we had avoided the season before hit us doubly hard.

What a difference a year can make. On the one-year anniversary of the Sandberg Game, we got shut out in St. Louis on just two hits. Another defeat a couple of days later against the Mets gave us a 13-game losing streak, which tied a franchise record. The skid included a pair of three-game sweeps on successive weekends by the Cardinals, who were establishing themselves as the class of our division.

After such a hot start, we soon found ourselves in fourth place.

Injuries were at least partly to blame for our downfall. Matthews and Dernier had played vitally important roles in 1984. Matthews' knee surgery and Dernier's foot problems caused both to miss games during the streak. Even more damaging, all of our starting pitchers lost time due to injuries in the first half of the '85 season.

We never recovered from that awful stretch in June. The Cardinals held onto first place for most of the season and ended up with 101 wins. We finished 77–84 and in fourth place.

• • •

During a difficult summer, I opened my mouth and turned a lights controversy into a full-blown stadium controversy.

I felt Cubs fans needed to confront reality. If the residents of Wrigleyville didn't budge on their opposition to night games, the Tribune Company would consider replacing Wrigley Field with a new stadium in the northwest suburbs.

"I don't get a sense of any cooperation with the neighborhood," I told a local radio station. "We're dead here."

The possibility of leaving Wrigley wasn't a secret. We had already shared the plan with the Illinois state legislature. Now I was taking the news directly to the fans. Suddenly, all of the good will I accumulated in 1984 went out the window. I was a bad guy with a big mouth again.

Some neighborhood denizens banded together to form a group called Citizens United for Baseball in Sunshine. That was an acronym, or so I was told. They were never going to be confused with the Dallas Green Fan Club.

Given the choice of putting up lights in Wrigley or abandoning the stadium altogether, I felt Cubs fans, even those in Wrigleyville, might start to see things my way. Apparently the Tribune Company didn't want me publicly announcing its thought process. A couple of days after letting the cat out of the bag, I was sent out before the media to try and put it back in.

"We are trying to work out our problems and stay and work in peace with the Wrigley Field community and the people of Chicago," I told reporters.

We had struck out in the courts, the legislature, the court of public opinion, and with Chicago aldermen. Other than some buddies at Murphy's Bleachers, a bar that wouldn't have minded nighttime patronage at their Sheffield Avenue address, we had few allies.

I asked some aldermen to set up a town meeting in Wrigleyville, so that I could take my point of view to the people in an interactive, face-to-face setting.

A couple hundred people showed up to hear me give my old speech about how the beloved 1969 team faded in the final weeks of the season because of the wear and tear of so many day games. I talked about how TV was taking over the game and that the Cubs would lose playoff games if Wrigley didn't get lights.

I loved day baseball, I told them. It's what made Wrigley Field special. But Major League Baseball was trying to impose its will upon us. Under the circumstances, a limited slate of night games seemed the only reasonable option.

"We have to live like everybody else in the game of baseball, or we're not going to be able to win championships," I told them.

Soon I was drowned out by booing, screaming, and hollering.

"They're going to piss on my lawn!"

"The dogs will bark all night!"

"Lights will be a pain in the ass!"

I put up with the heckling for a few minutes. Then I restated my point, a bit more firmly this time.

"I've told you what I think is necessary to build a championship team, and we'll do everything we can for the neighborhood. But I'm tired of only hearing about what's negative about lights. The positives are very simple. If you want a championship baseball team in Chicago, you better put lights in there."

Okay, it was a little more profane than that, but that was the gist of it.

The leader of the neighborhood group, Nancy Kaszak, told reporters that our disappointing season had clouded my judgment.

"One of the things I like about Dallas is that he always speaks from his gut, and I think like the rest of Chicago, he's just upset about the losses," she said.

For Nancy's information, I was perfectly capable of being upset at more than one thing at a time.

• • •

A lot of people in Chicago wanted to wring my neck. But at least I had a pretty amicable relationship with the local media. I think the writers liked my bluntness and the opportunity to verbally mix it up with me. I got along particularly well with *Chicago Tribune* columnist Jerome Holtzman. Jerry and I had one important thing in common: we both could be antagonizing as hell. He knew I wouldn't lie to him, and I knew he'd research the hell out of a story before having it published. He understood the ins and outs of the lights situation and did a thorough job representing all sides in his column. Jerry also got in the occasional jab at me. When asked by a reader in 1985 whether I should make a trade for a "take-charge guy," Jerry responded, "Dallas has already made a half-dozen deals for take-charge guys, and, from the looks of things, they're taking charge of fourth place." A sentence like that made me feel like I was back in Philadelphia.

Twenty-five years after leaving Chicago, I still get calls from reporters there. Usually it's for a story or just to yak about baseball. But our personal bond also prompted a lot of them to drop me a line when my granddaughter was killed in Tucson, Arizona, in 2011.

I may have had trouble convincing some people that I had the right vision for the team, but at least I felt Chicago's baseball writers gave me a fair shake.

• • •

As Jerry pointed out in his column, many of our players had down years in 1985. Our fourth-place finish was doubly disappointing coming on the heels of a division-winning season and a promising start in '85.

We had looked forward to having Sutcliffe for a full season, but a pulled hamstring meant he wound up starting just as many games in 1985 as he did in a partial season with us in 1984, posting only half as many wins. Eckersley was the only pitcher on our staff to reach double-digit victories. And only two players, Ryne Sandberg and Keith Moreland, reached the 80-RBI mark, compared to six players in '84.

It was a rough season in many ways. In August, a story broke linking Eckersley and Steve Trout to cocaine use earlier in the 1980s, before either joined the Cubs. We had heard rumors that Eck and Trout had dabbled in drugs when we traded for them. I was confident they were now clean.

The issue of drugs in baseball weighed on my mind, however. I didn't think it was a rampant problem, but I still supported mandatory drug testing for all players. I felt it was the only way to prove that drugs hadn't in fact taken over the game—at least not yet.

For the time being, I had more pressing problems to deal with. Keeping the team intact in '85 didn't work out.

In August, when it became apparent we wouldn't compete for another division crown, I released Bowa, who was in a seesaw battle with Dunston for the starting shortstop job. It was a tough decision. Bowa and I had waged some highly publicized battles in Philadelphia, but my respect for his work ethic and passion prompted me to bring him to Chicago. He was an undrafted free agent out of high school in 1965 who became a starting major league shortstop for 16 seasons. In the course of his career, he collected more than 2,000 hits and won a pair of Gold Gloves. I could only hope that Dunston would have as impressive a career.

The release of Bowa signified larger changes for the team.

"Every effort will be made to bring in new blood to increase the competitive spirit," I said after a six-hour meeting with manager Jimmy Frey and our coaches and scouts during the final week of the season.

Dunston represented a significant part of my hopes for the on-field future of the team. I just wished there had been more promising news about a major off-the-field matter.

As the season drew to a close, the Illinois Supreme Court unanimously upheld the ban on night games at Wrigley Field. In addition to trying to help the team win again, I also had to deal with the prospect of the Cubs moving out of Wrigley.

And to think just a year earlier we were celebrating a division championship and the dawning of a joyous and successful new era on the north side of Chicago.

• • •

A down season forced me to get tough. I issued an ultimatum to all Cubs players eligible for free agency: if you put yourself on the open market, we're done with you. That convinced Gary Matthews, Scott Sanderson, and Chris Speier to bypass free agency and re-sign with us.

I then traded for Manny Trillo, one of my favorite players from my Phillies days. I managed Manny at Class-A and again in Philadelphia. He wasn't a vocal guy, but he went about his business in a professional way. In the twilight of his career, Manny wasn't going to have a major impact on our team, but his versatility as an infielder would allow Jimmy to give third baseman Ron Cey and second baseman Ryne Sandberg an occasional day off.

The only other significant addition to the roster was Jerry Mumphrey, a veteran outfielder who made the 1984 All-Star team with the Astros. We picked him up in exchange for a young outfielder named Billy Hatcher. They were similar players, but I hoped Mumphrey's experience would help us more in the short term.

Some people expected us to go after Kirk Gibson, the best available free agent that off-season. Gibson had helped lead Detroit to a World Series title in 1984 and put up even better numbers in '85. Rumors of our interest in Gibson persisted until I spoke up and quashed the speculation. "We've told Kirk's agent that we were going to the winter meetings with the hopes of making a couple of trades, and we made the deals," I said. "We told his agent we weren't interested in other people's free agents."

The second part of that quote got the attention of Marvin Miller and the players union.

A month after Gibson re-signed with the Tigers for almost twice his previous salary, the players union threatened to file a grievance alleging owners were acting in collusion to prevent free agents from signing deals with anyone but their current teams.

It is true that major league teams had become acutely aware of the escalating costs of free agency. And we took steps to try and keep those costs down. We didn't call it collusion, because there was no overt conspiring to keep player salaries at a certain level. As baseball commissioner Peter Ueberroth correctly noted, we were simply using common sense. And that meant sharing information with each other, a well-established practice among player agents. The opportunity to see other teams' ledger books was a real wake-up call. As I told the *Chicago Sun-Times* in 1986, "It was like the first chance to get to see somebody else's checkbook. We looked [at the books] and said, 'Ugh.'"

As a result, we general managers made a gentleman's agreement not to pursue other teams' free agents. That practice eventually landed us in court.

I had developed serious concerns about lucrative, long-term free agent deals.

"The facts are there," I said at the time. "After a guy signs a multi-year, guaranteed contract, the next year he breaks down. Well, that's scary. Especially when you're not talking about nickel-and-dime guys. You're talking millions of dollars. You can't come out of that decently."

Before the 1986 season, major league teams shrunk rosters from 25 to 24 players, a move allowed by our contract with the union. That only increased tension with Marvin and his gang.

One thing was certain. The hostility between management and the union wasn't going away.

• • •

I believed we could make waves again in the National League East. We still had the core of players who won a division title in 1984, and they all had another year of seasoning under their belts.

Much would be said later about how I let the team grow old, but that was another example of second-guessing. Age shouldn't have been an issue in 1986. Our oldest starting pitcher, Eckersley, was only 31. And five of our everyday position players were in their twenties.

To help recapture the intangibles that had turned us into winners two seasons earlier, I hired former Cubs great Billy Williams as our hitting coach. I figured it had to be a positive influence for our guys to have a legend like Billy around the clubhouse. I also invited former Gold Glove outfielder Jimmy Piersall to work with our guys during spring training.

Jimmy and I had a history. Back in 1963, he showed me up by running the bases backward after taking me deep for his 100th major league home run. At the time, I was pissed off by his antics. I stalked him as he rounded the bases, swearing up a storm. But I came to like Jimmy. More importantly, he had been one helluva defensive outfielder. I knew he could teach our guys a thing or two.

The tough love carried over into spring training. I set weight limits for players, most notably Rick Sutcliffe. I asked Sut to shed 20 pounds. He complied and reported to camp complaining that his clothes didn't fit him anymore.

As good as we had been in 1984, it wasn't 1984 anymore. In press interviews, I took aim at Ron Cey, Bobby Dernier, Gary Matthews, and Jody Davis, hoping to light a spark under them.

I also spoke candidly about Jimmy Frey. "In 1984, Jimmy was a great manager," I told reporters. "In 1985, he was a lousy manager. We won in '84. We lost in '85. That's what managing is all about, I guess."

I was mostly referring to the public perception that a manager is only as good as his team's record. It's always been that way, and it always will be. If our team hadn't been so banged up in 1985, we might have made another playoff run. To lay the blame on Jimmy was unfair. I was simply stating he had a chance in 1986 to show he could help make us winners again.

The press jumped all over my comment and repeatedly asked Jimmy to respond. When we got off to a lousy start, losing eight of our first 10, the Chicago sports pages were suddenly filled with stories about impending managerial changes in the Windy City. Tony

La Russa was about to lose his job with the White Sox, and according to the articles, Jimmy was next.

• • •

We learned in May that if we won the division in 1986, our home playoff games would be played in Busch Stadium, the National League East ballpark (with lights) located closest to Chicago, not to mention the home field of our fiercest rival.

When asked to comment on Major League Baseball's decision, all I could really muster was a "told ya so." Nobody in the Cubs front office got too worked up about the news. It had a definite silver lining, in fact. We knew it gave us leverage to renew discussions about getting lights at Wrigley Field. "Chicago doesn't do anything until it's a crisis," I said.

By the time of the announcement on May 19, when we were already 10½ games out, it was evident these hypothetical playoff games wouldn't take place, not in 1986 anyway. On June 12, we were 17 games behind the division-leading Mets.

Jimmy hadn't recaptured the magic of 1984. It was time for him to go.

After the firing, third-base coach Don Zimmer came to me and said he could work with whomever succeeded Jimmy as manager. But I concluded that he and Jimmy, who had been high school classmates in Cincinnati, were tighter than he and I were. I felt it might be disruptive to keep Donnie around, so I let him go, too. I regretted that decision almost immediately. On his way out the door, Donnie told reporters, "I don't think God could have come down and made this team win."

First-base coach John Vukovich managed the next two games. I had the utmost faith that Vuke could do any job in baseball, but I felt we needed an experienced guy from outside the organization to manage the club.

The guy I wanted was former Yankees third-base coach Gene Michael, who had managed that team for parts of two seasons in the early '80s. As a courtesy, I contacted Yankees owner George Steinbrenner to let him know about my interest in Stick. George gave me his blessings and told me Stick was my kind of guy.

Zim was right. We were 11 games under .500 when I fired Jimmy, and by the end of the season, we were 20 games under .500. We finished 37 games behind the Mets, a team that went on to win the World Series.

Our team ERA in '86 was worst in the league, which more than negated the fact that we led the league in home runs. After the season, I fired pitching coach Billy Connors and replaced him with Herm Starrette, who filled that position for me in Philadelphia in 1980.

At this point, I was willing to trade anyone on the team except Sandberg and Dunston. We needed a shake-up, but I didn't view the future as bleak. Before long, we'd have the services of some talented players coming up through our farm system.

I maintained hope, but I would soon find out that losing seasons in 1985 and 1986 spelled major trouble for me and the Cubs.

19

I'll admit I was growing impatient.

Just a few months after hiring Gene Michael as manager, I announced he needed to start winning games if he hoped to keep his job. It was a common-sense remark that I figured Gene would let roll off his back. I knew he wanted to win as badly as any of us. I just wondered how committed he was to managing the team.

You'd think a guy who served as manager and general manager of the George Steinbrenner–run New York Yankees would have thick skin. But my remark apparently bothered Gene a lot, leading him to request a meeting with me.

On the day of the meeting, I had an interview scheduled with Ray Sons of the *Chicago Sun-Times*. As Gene and his hurt feelings waited in the reception area of my office, I finished up my conversation with the reporter. In reply to a question about Stick, I said, "When somebody asks me a question, I answer as honestly as I can. Do I have to sit here and tell you I'm happy with everything? That's bullshit. If Gene Michael can't understand that, Gene Michael should get fired."

With gasoline thrown on the flames, my secretary let Gene know I was ready to see him.

He told me he was caught off guard by my initial comments, which he regarded as a threat.

I looked Stick in the eye and laid my cards on the table.

"Gene, I get a sense you don't want to manage," I said. "It's like you're not even watching the game in the dugout. You stand there and make little notes in notebooks, but I don't see you running the game like an aggressive baseball guy should. I see you acting more like a general manager. If you don't want to manage, I'll buy out the rest of your contract. I don't want you to be unhappy, but I do want to see you applying yourself to managing this team."

Gene assured me he still wanted to manage. The notes, he said, were to remind him of certain players' tendencies. Having taken over the team in the middle of the previous season, he said he had spent a lot of time evaluating and observing. Now he was ready to manage.

I wasn't thrilled with the idea of making another managerial change, so I gave Stick an opportunity to stay on.

• • •

I had to look in the mirror, too. As president and general manager, I was as responsible for the team's struggles as anyone. And I needed help.

I hired longtime Phillies scout Hugh Alexander as my special adviser. Hughie was smart, hard-working, and above all, loyal. I looked forward to hearing his thoughts on the direction of the team. It also wouldn't hurt to have him around in case I ever had to fend off a revolution. The Tribune Company gave me public assurances that my job was safe, but you can never be sure where you stand when your fate is in the hands of men in starched suits, especially ones who don't know a helluva lot about baseball.

Speaking of starched suits, Jim Dowdle, the Tribune's media guy, asked me during the off-season whether I had a problem with the company adding Jim Frey to the Cubs' radio broadcast team. When I fired him as manager, Jimmy still had 18 months left on his contract. I figured the company was just trying to get its money's worth from Jimmy.

I told Dowdle to go ahead and make the hire. I added that I thought Jimmy spouted just the right amount of bullshit to be a good broadcaster. It seemed harmless enough to let him call the games on WGN Radio.

Only later did I view his hiring in a different light.

I didn't worry about Jimmy trying to exact any revenge on me over the airwaves. The only opinion of me that mattered was that of the Tribune Company. And if you went by what was said in the newspaper, they still thought highly of me. Tribune chairman Stan Cook and executive vice president John Madigan both said they had faith in my ability to get us back on a winning track.

I had a pretty good idea of what was wrong. I just needed time to fix it.

• • •

In my first five years with the Cubs, I tried to build the team through the draft, strategic trades, and the re-signing of players I believed would be long-term contributors to the team.

The latter strategy backfired on me in a big way.

After the 1984 season, I gave multiyear deals to Rick Sutcliffe, Steve Trout, and Dennis Eckersley, the starting pitchers who most contributed to our division title. In 1984, Sutcliffe went 16–1 for us after coming over from the Indians. In 1986, Sutcliffe, Eckersley, and Trout won 16 games *combined* while posting some of the worst ERAs in the league. That, more than anything, explained our struggles.

I could have tried to bolster the rotation through a trade, but that likely would have cost us a top prospect like Mark Grace or Rafael Palmeiro. We weren't close enough to being competitive to mortgage our future like that. And our minor league kids were still a year or two away from making an impact in the majors.

In the current climate of limited free agent movement, signing a big name didn't seem to be in the cards, either.

But that's what ended up happening when the best player on the market came to us and begged to be signed.

• • •

Andre Dawson had established himself as one of the best outfielders in the game during his 11 seasons in Montreal. But his knees and relationship with the Expos had both deteriorated. He didn't want to play anymore for general manager Murray Cook or on the hard turf at Olympic Stadium. He publicly chose Wrigley Field as his preferred destination because he had always hit well there and liked the idea of playing on a grass field.

Every GM knew Andre's agent, Dick Moss, had been an attorney for the players union before becoming an agent. I knew him even better, because he represented some current Cubs. Dick was smart and knew how to exploit a situation to benefit his clients. Dick and his union pals strongly believed teams were colluding to prevent free agents from signing high-dollar contracts. By making it known the Expos weren't willing to give Andre much of a raise, Dick was trying to entice us into bidding.

I defused speculation that we would make an offer to Andre by citing the financial burden of already having several players with multi-year deals on our payroll. I also pointed to the large number of young outfielders on our 40-man roster. When pressed again on the possibility of signing Andre, I laid it out in even simpler terms: "Can one guy, even with the skills of an Andre Dawson, turn us around and mean 90 or 95 wins instead of 70? I don't think so."

But a simple "no" never deterred Dick Moss. I flat-out told him on the phone that we didn't have the money to sign Andre. Dick ran to the papers and accused Peter Ueberroth of using his clout as commissioner to prevent the signing. That statement bugged the hell out of me. I publicly stated that Andre would be better off hiring a new agent.

Dick still didn't go away. He and Andre showed up unannounced at our spring training complex in Mesa to talk further. If they had called ahead, they would have learned I was at an owners meeting in Palm Springs, California. But as Andre himself said later, the point of the visit wasn't necessarily to meet with me. It was to get the media to spread the word that Andre Dawson was adamant about playing for the Cubs.

Angels owner Gene Autry flew me back to Arizona on his private plane, and that's when I encountered the circus Dick had created.

I again called Dick out in the press. "I find it rather strange that we come to spring training [where an agent] wants to put on a dog-and-pony show at my expense in my complex using my press," I said.

Dick had accomplished his goal, however. At this point, I had no choice but to take the meeting. After two losing seasons, the Chicago media was warming up to the idea of having a player of Andre's caliber in a Cubs uniform.

At the meeting, Dick and Andre presented me with a blank contract with their signatures already on it. All I had to do, they told me, was fill in the numbers and sign it myself.

Dick Moss had outdone himself.

With Andre willing to take *any amount of money* to play for us, I was backed into a corner. If I refused to put in a bid, the union would bitch and moan about collusion.

The Expos' final offer to Andre was $2 million over two years. I took a day and played around with some numbers before presenting him with a one-year deal for $500,000 plus performance bonuses.

If he had turned it down, I would have torn up the contract and hoped Dick finally took a hike. But he accepted. Suddenly and unexpectedly, we had one of the best outfielders in the game on our roster.

It remained to be seen how many games we'd win with Andre on the team.

• • •

It pleased the Tribune Company that we had Dawson at a cut-rate price for the upcoming season. Our $15 million payroll the season before, the third-highest in the league, was less pleasing.

The high price of losing led to new marching orders. The Tribune Company wanted me to cut spending.

Before the start of the 1987 season, I started dumping salary. First, I traded third baseman Ron Cey to the Oakland A's for infielder Luis Quinones. A couple of months later, Eckersley joined him in California, where he transitioned to the bullpen and became a dominant closer and Hall of Famer.

It didn't surprise me that Eck did so well out of the bullpen. But it hurt me, because I had approached him about making the switch for us. Lee Smith was our closer, but I saw Eck as a guy who could pitch multiple innings late in a game. He had precise command and he had heart, two of the most important qualities of a good reliever.

Eck protested the idea, believing he still had productive years left as a starter. Tony La Russa obviously felt the same as I did. He talked Eck into closing games, and it worked out well for the A's. Eck was almost unhittable for a while and helped Oakland win a World Series in 1989. In 1992, he won the AL Cy Young and MVP awards.

Steve Trout was another guy I knew I had to deal away. The five-year contract he got after winning 13 games in 1984 had turned into a bad investment. He didn't reach double-digit wins in either '85 or '86.

With Trout on the disabled list at the start of the '87 season, I questioned whether I could even find a team interested in him. Fortunately, my manager, without even knowing it, helped facilitate a deal.

It was common knowledge that George Steinbrenner liked to have spies, or at least guys he liked and trusted, in as many major league clubhouses as possible. The Yankees were in desperate need of a fifth starting pitcher in 1987, and I believe Gene Michael kept him apprised of Trout's availability and performance.

Stick provided the scouting report, and Trout took care of the rest. It had been two years since he threw a complete-game shutout, but in back-to-back starts against the Padres and the Dodgers before the All-Star break, he pitched two in a row. Suddenly he looked like a world-beater. Seeing an opportunity to sell him high, I immediately got on the phone with the Yankees.

I made the trade in the middle of a game without Stick's knowledge. Afterward, Stick told reporters he was disappointed I hadn't consulted him. "Gene doesn't consult me when he wants to bunt," I shot back. "Why should I consult him about a trade?"

I might have added that Steinbrenner just as easily could have told him about the trade.

It was a helluva deal for the Tribune Company, one that cut about $5 million from the payroll.

I knew Trout wouldn't last a day in New York. He was a good kid but kind of an airhead. That's not an auspicious combination when pitching in the pressure cooker of the Bronx. In return for Trout, we got Bob Tewskbury and two minor league pitchers. We thought Tewksbury had potential, but what we most liked about him was he came cheap.

I heard Trout's first couple of pitches in New York went to the backstop. He didn't win a game for the Yankees. And Tewksbury didn't win a game for us. Trout got traded by the Yankees after the season. Tewksbury lasted a little longer with the Cubs before signing with the Cardinals as a free agent.

• • •

Some veterans got traded. Others got benched. Now that we were in full rebuilding mode, it was time to give the young players in our organization a chance to show what they had.

In 1987, Dave Martinez took over center field from Bobby Dernier, who went back to the Phillies after the season. Rafael Palmeiro got a lot of playing time in left field, both before and after I traded Gary

Matthews to Seattle. And Greg Maddux, Jamie Moyer, and Les Lancaster, all 25 years old or younger, joined our starting rotation.

Leon Durham, Jody Davis, and Keith Moreland also faced uncertain futures in Chicago.

With all the comings and goings, I knew we were in for a long season.

But 1987 turned out to be a great year—for Andre Dawson, who had the best season of his career. He hit 49 home runs, knocked in 137 runs, and won the National League MVP Award.

We still finished in last place.

By early September, Stick saw the writing on the wall and submitted his resignation. Frank Lucchesi, a part-time Cubs coach with whom I had a long history in the Phillies organization, finished out the season as interim manager.

I'm sure Stick felt I too often communicated my thoughts about him through the media. But he turned the tables on me by announcing his departure on a radio show. "It's nice he told somebody," I said when I heard the news. "I would think he would have wanted to talk to me about it first." The press prodded Stick to criticize me on his way out the door. But to his credit, he held his tongue. After he left us, he went back to his real baseball home in the Bronx.

This time around, I planned to take my time before hiring a new skipper. The stakes were too high to rush the decision. I had burned through three managers in six seasons, and I think the Tribune Company was bothered by what it perceived as organizational instability.

I thought about interviewing Billy Williams, whose number we retired in 1987. I not only had the utmost respect for Billy's knowledge of the game, but I also felt it would send the right message in the wake of Dodgers executive Al Campanis' remarks earlier that season about African Americans not possessing the right tools to be managers.

When the time was right, I intended to talk with Billy.

But first, I had to deal with the fallout of our last-place finish.

As the season drew to a close, the finger pointing began. I apologized to Cubs fans for the team's poor performance, telling the *Chicago Tribune*, "The reason I have to apologize is because we quit with a capital Q. Q-U-I-T. There is no other explanation for it." Jody Davis didn't appreciate my comments and fired back that I hadn't done anything for the team. I'm not sure Jody did much for the team after 1984, but that's beside the point. Ultimately the Tribune Company, not Jody, would decide whether I was worth keeping.

20

DURING MY YEARS IN PHILADELPHIA, those of us in the front office discussed any and all problems openly. There was usually a lot of yelling, screaming, and cussing, but in the end, we found a way to settle matters and move on. Phillies general manager Paul Owens created that kind of atmosphere, and we all thrived in it.

The Tribune Company didn't operate that way. With the Phillies, everything was free and loose. With the Cubs, everything was inhibited and corporate.

I wasn't looking forward to meeting with my superiors after the 1987 season. They had come to consider themselves real baseball guys. John Madigan, a Tribune executive rising through the company's ranks, started attending the annual slate of baseball meetings. He had learned the lingo and had started questioning player personnel decisions. It irritated the hell out of me, but I took it in stride. As long as he didn't get in my way, he was free to go where he wanted. The company also appointed Don Grenesko to serve as its liaison to the Cubs, a position it had deemed superfluous after the successful 1984 season.

I felt like I was being watched.

That doesn't mean I considered myself beyond reproach. Looking back, I realize I made some mistakes with the Cubs. I was premature in firing Lee Elia during the 1983 season. Lee's temper had caused us some public relations problems, but he wasn't the first skipper to let his emotions get the better of him. Given time, I think he would have become a helluva manager. I also think I too quickly fired Jim Frey during the 1986 season. Relieving Don Zimmer of his coaching duties at the same time was definitely an error on my part.

By the time we lost yet another manager in 1987, I think the Tribune Company was starting to have its doubts about me. Rather than offering up a list of possible successors to Gene Michael, I decided on a bolder course of action.

"I don't know if you'll like this idea or not," I told Madigan, "and I don't know if I really want to do it, but since I don't trust anybody but myself, suppose I go down on the field and manage?"

Hell, it had worked before in Philadelphia, and I saw no reason why it couldn't be effective in Chicago, too. I proposed that Gordon Goldsberry and John Cox, two of my most trusted advisers, take over my current duties if I became manager.

Madigan seemed generally enthused with the idea. He was a newspaper guy, after all, and he recognized the steady stream of headlines my return to managing would generate. I thought we had a deal. But then Madigan put a fly in the ointment by suggesting Grenesko succeed me as general manager.

That was completely unacceptable to me. If I was down on the field, I didn't want to have to worry about a non-baseball guy upstairs pulling off deals and making other major decisions.

"No, no, no," I protested. "We've worked too long and hard to get where we are. We can turn this thing around. Gordie and Coxey know me and know what this organization is all about. I can't trust anybody else to do the job."

It was like talking to a brick wall. For them, it was Grenesko or nobody. I scrambled to come up with an alternate plan.

I had two years left on my contract and wanted to continue working to improve the team. I was confident the Tribune Company would give me breathing room to do my job again once we started winning games. And that was going to happen soon. In the meantime, if they wanted Grenesko to get hands-on experience in a major league front office, I was willing to play along.

"Okay, here's what we can do," I told Madigan. "I'll make John Vukovich manager, and I'll train anybody you want to be the next general manager. That way, if you ever get tired of me, that person can take over."

I've never been worried about getting fired. Whenever I took a job, I worked like the devil to accomplish my goals, but not out of fear of getting a pink slip. I just got more personal satisfaction out of doing my work well. I wouldn't have worried about Grenesko taking my job as general manager. I knew I could outwork him or any other company guy. I was a baseball lifer—they weren't. If the Tribune Company ultimately felt Grenesko or someone else could do the job better than me, then so be it.

I met with Tribune CEO Stan Cook to make a case for how much we'd accomplished in a relatively short time. I told him the team was about to get a positive jolt from all the young talent in our system. Not only that, but we'd also continue making money for the company. Attendance remained high despite a couple of losing seasons. The Cubs were a thriving business.

Cook seemed receptive to my proposal. But I guess you can leave a room thinking everything's rosy only to find out there are meetings taking place behind your back.

• • •

The Tribune Company decided it was already tired of me.

I didn't get a definitive answer to my proposal, so I told Madigan I'd interpret that as a "yes." The next step was to announce Vuke's hiring as manager. If need be, we could call another press conference if the Tribune officials decided they wanted me to have a general manager trainee.

In late October, Vuke flew in from his New Jersey home. The next morning, PR guy Ned Colletti, Vuke, and I got together at Wrigley Field to go over the details of the announcement. I would praise Vuke's leadership skills and joke that, like me, he hadn't been much of a ballplayer, but that his exceptional knowledge of the game would make him a successful manager. Ned helped us figure out where to stand and how many questions Vuke would take.

As we were going over these details, a flustered John Madigan rushed in the room.

"Dallas, we gotta talk!" he said.

I assumed he was going to tell me the Tribune Company had decided that Grenesko would work with me in the front office. That meant Grenesko probably wanted to say a few words at the press conference.

But Madigan's news was a lot bigger than that.

He told me our working relationship was over. If I didn't resign as general manager, I would be fired.

I could have taken that as my cue to use the press conference as an opportunity to blast the Tribune Company for its backhandedness. But what would have been the point? I had tried to work out a plan that would benefit the Cubs, but they thought they had a better plan.

A little while later, I stood at a podium in front of dozens of reporters who were expecting to hear confirmation of Vuke's hiring. Instead, I told them the real purpose of the press conference was to announce my resignation. Rather than trying to explain the reasons the Cubs and I were parting ways, I chose instead to repeat what Madigan had just told me about "philosophical differences" between us.

"I'm outta here," Vuke had said as soon as I told him what was happening. He listened to the press conference on the way to O'Hare, where he boarded a flight back to Philadelphia. He was hired by the

Phillies as a coach later that fall. He remained with the Phillies until he died of brain cancer in 2007.

My phone started ringing the moment I went back to my soon-to-be former office. Every writer wanted to know more about the philosophical differences. Over the next week, I showed uncharacteristic restraint by declining to elaborate. What was done was done. And with two years left on my Cubs contract, I didn't feel it would be in my family's best interests for me to attack the Tribune Company.

Madigan, on the other hand, chose to talk about it. But instead of explaining the series of events that led to my departure, he simply said I resigned rather than accept a reduced role in the organization. He also announced he would personally fill the newly created job of director of baseball operations. The general manager position would be eliminated, he said.

Someone must have told Madigan a baseball team needed a general manager, because about a month after my "resignation," everything came full circle. Madigan hired Jimmy Frey, who I had fired, as general manager. Jimmy then hired Don Zimmer as manager.

I was happy for Donnie. If the Cubs continued to struggle, I doubted it would be his fault. He and I are still tight. Jimmy and I haven't spoken since I fired him as manager. That's just the way baseball is sometimes.

• • •

When Keith Moreland heard the news of my resignation, he and his wife put their house in Chicago up for sale. It was a wise move. A couple of months later, the Cubs traded him to San Diego.

It was fitting, I guess, that my last trade as GM of the Cubs involved Dickie Noles. The two of us had a long and eventful history. In the span of a decade, I drafted him, managed him, traded for him, traded him, signed him as free agent, and traded him again.

In the last move, I sent Dickie to the Tigers in September 1987 for a player to be named later. Dickie registered two saves that helped Detroit win the American League East. Then the situation got weird. We couldn't reach an agreement with the Tigers on what player we'd get in return for Dickie, so he came back to the Cubs after the season. In essence, we had loaned Dickie to the Tigers for the last couple weeks of the season.

Commissioner Peter Ueberroth's office opened an investigation into whether there was "premeditated intent" for Dickie to be the player to be named later. A week after my resignation, the commissioner's office ruled we had acted appropriately.

As another "Dallas Green guy," Dickie wasn't long for Chicago anyway. He signed as a free agent with the Baltimore Orioles before the 1988 season.

While Dickie's career didn't turn out the way he or I thought it would, at least he cleaned up his act. He's been sober ever since the night in 1983 when I bailed him out of a Cincinnati jail for scuffling with a police officer. Dickie now works for the Phillies as an employee assistance professional who counsels young players on the dangers of drugs and alcohol.

Dickie got traded for himself. He also traded in his old self for a new one.

• • •

Four words sum up my time in Chicago: we won too quickly.

Between 1982 and 1984, we went from an also-ran to a contender. But it took a lot longer than two years to fix the problems in our farm system. That gave us little choice but to re-sign the veterans who brought us a division title in 1984.

If the Cubs had won the division, say, in 1986, the situation would have been different. By that time, Greg Maddux, Jamie Moyer, Dave Martinez, and Rafael Palmeiro were on the team. And Mark Grace, Jerome Walton, and Dwight Smith were about to join them. That good, young core of players would have given us leverage to pick and choose which veterans to keep. The end result would have been a much lower payroll and a team built for success over the long term.

That's not the way it happened, obviously. After 1984, we became expensive losers. But with all the young talent ready to make a splash, I left the team in pretty good condition.

The season after I stepped down, the Cubs played their first night game at Wrigley Field. Despite the history of the moment and my role in helping make it possible, I never considered attending the game. When I left Chicago, I left Chicago for good. There was no reason to go back, other than to visit our son Doug, who graduated high school there and went on to attend the University of Illinois. I spent 1988 with Sylvia on our Pennsylvania farm. I tended to our animals, read a lot, and generally recharged my batteries. I knew I'd eventually get back into baseball in some capacity, but I was willing to wait for the right opportunity to come along.

Due largely to Ryne Sandberg and his young teammates, the Cubs won a division title two years after my departure. Jimmy Frey didn't have to do much to improve the team. By and large, it was my guys who won the division. And it was my guys who lost to the Giants in the National League Championship Series.

That was the beginning of the end for the Cubs. Jimmy wasn't cut out to be a general manager. Under his leadership, the team went into a tailspin after the 1989 season. The Tribune Company replaced him with Larry Himes in 1991. Under Himes, the Cubs continued to struggle.

With the Cubs, it's all a vicious cycle, I guess. After some good years in the early 2000s, the Cubs cleaned house again before the 2012 season, hoping another new regime might finally get them to the promised land.

I had really hoped to get them there first.

The next team I went to practically lived in the promised land, though it had been in exile for more than a decade when I got there. It just so happened that team had an owner who liked to shoot his mouth off as much as I did.

21

George Steinbrenner and I went way back.

When I pitched for Triple-A Buffalo in 1960, George came to town a lot to check the operations at his family's shipping company. He was close friends with Max Margolis, the owner of the Royal Arms, a tavern located below the $8-a-week apartment I shared with teammate Bobby Wine. George would pop in on weekends while Bobby and I were having dinner. Sometimes we'd stick around and have a few drinks with him. He seemed intrigued by our baseball careers. "I'm gonna buy a team someday," he informed us. We thought that was just talk. At the time, George's sports experience was limited to playing a season at halfback for Williams College and serving as an assistant football coach at Northwestern and Purdue.

But wouldn't you know it, George followed through on his promise by purchasing the Yankees in 1973. I guess George had a lot of affection for his time in Buffalo. He immediately hired Margolis to run the restaurant at Yankee Stadium. And whenever he ran into Bobby, he'd reminisce about the nights at the Royal Arms.

While I was GM of the Cubs, George and I developed a mutual respect for each other, probably because we were both no-bullshit kind of guys. George told me he liked how I went about business in 1980 with the Phillies. He also admired that I was helping make the Cubs relevant again. He'd rib my Tribune bosses at owners meetings by saying, "I should have hired Dallas before you did. Maybe I'll still have that chance."

That was just George's style. He never violated baseball's tampering rules, nor did he ever let me know I'd be a front-runner for any job openings with the Yankees.

In 1988, George ousted Lou Piniella as manager for the second time in less than a year. That's when I got a call from Yankees general manager Bob Quinn, who was the son of former Phillies GM John Quinn. Bob asked if I'd be interested in field managing again. Without getting into the details of my failed plan to manage the Cubs in 1988, I told Bob I was open to the idea. Before the conversation ended, he offered me the job. A few days later, I signed a two-year contract. The opportunity was too attractive to pass up. It gave me a chance to associate myself with one of the most storied franchises in all of sports.

Sylvia and I rented a house about 10 miles from Yankee Stadium in Saddle Brook, New Jersey. Two-year contract or not, I'd be working for George. We decided to enter into a month-to-month lease agreement with the landlord.

On the day of my hiring, I told reporters I knew what I was getting into. "Any management situation is liable to explode," I said. "I know it's part of the game. I'm not afraid to cross any bridge that comes to me."

George had hired and fired a parade of managers since buying the team. You didn't have to be a math whiz to figure out how often he changed his mind about someone. In 16 years, he had ordered 16 managerial changes.

I came in under a different set of circumstances, however. I was only the second manager hired from outside the Yankees organization. And I was the first George permitted to hire his own coaching staff. To me, that was acknowledgment from the top that the team needed an infusion of new blood.

The staff I assembled included four former major league managers: Lee Elia, Pat Corrales, Frank Howard, and Charlie Fox, as well as two other solid baseball guys, Billy Connors and John Stearns.

The Yankees were accustomed to winning titles. That must have made the 1980s a frustrating time for George. After winning back-to-back championships in 1977 and 1978, the Yankees had entered a historic dry spell. Since the 1910s, the team had never gone an entire decade without winning at least one World Series. When I came on board, that streak was in jeopardy of coming to an end. The Yankees were coming off an 85–76 season, a decent record for most teams but the worst mark in six years for the Yankees.

The moment I took the job in New York, my friends in Philadelphia started making bets on when George would kick me to the curb. Former Phillies owner Bob Carpenter told me as much when I ran into him at a University of Delaware football game. I got a hearty laugh out of that. I hoped I would be the son of a bitch who convinced George to fade into the background.

• • •

Before taking the Yankees job, I had spent only one month of my 33-year baseball career in the American League. That month came in the spring of 1965 when I pitched six games for the Washington Senators.

Still, I understood that Yankee Stadium was hallowed ground.

I recognized that the first time I attended a game there in 1956. After my second year of pro ball, a couple of friends and I decided it would be fun to try and get tickets for a postseason game in the Bronx.

Kenny Mahan, Bill Kelly, and I ended up securing bleacher seats for Game 5 of the World Series between the Yankees and the Brooklyn Dodgers. We took the train up from Wilmington and arrived at the stadium hours before game time. We were among the first people in the bleachers when the gates opened. It was a thrill to see Jackie

Robinson, Gil Hodges, and Duke Snider trot out onto the field for pregame warm-ups. When they left, Mickey Mantle, Yogi Berra, and Enos Slaughter took their place.

It was a great day already, and the game hadn't even started.

With the series tied at two games apiece, Sal Maglie and Don Larsen each carried shutouts into the fourth inning. Then the Yankees got on the board when Mantle hit a Maglie pitch into the stands. The Yankees scored again in the sixth to take a 2–0 lead.

The Dodgers couldn't get to Larsen.

In the seventh inning, I looked up at the scoreboard and noticed Brooklyn had nothing. No runs, no hits, no walks, no base runners.

I wasn't rooting for either team, but at that point, I started to cheer for history. And Don Larsen delivered it, throwing the only perfect game to date in a World Series game.

I didn't view managing the Yankees as just another baseball job. They were a special franchise. I learned that on the day Berra jumped into Larsen's arms to celebrate the perfect game. I was excited to wear the same pinstripes as Ruth, DiMaggio, Gehrig, and all the other Yankees legends.

I knew full well, however, that tradition doesn't win pennants. Ballplayers do.

• • •

My problems in the Bronx started before the season did.

I would have put a starting outfield of Dave Winfield, Rickey Henderson, and Claudell Washington up against anyone in the majors.

Unfortunately, that lineup never materialized.

George promised he would retain Washington, who was a free agent, but he allowed the Angels to outbid him. At least we still had Winfield and Henderson—or so I thought.

Early in spring training, Winfield left the field with back spasms. A few weeks later, he underwent surgery to remove a herniated disc. He didn't play a game all season.

That still left us with Henderson, the best leadoff hitter in the game. But I soon learned that when Rickey was dissatisfied, he hardly played like it.

Starting in spring training, Rickey caused me headaches. He arrived late for camp in protest of George's refusal to renegotiate his contract following a season in which he hit .305 and stole 93 bases. When asked my thoughts on Rickey's tardiness, I stated in no uncertain terms that I, not Rickey, was leading the Yankees. The New York press ate it up and braced itself for a Dallas Green meltdown when Rickey finally showed his face at camp.

A few days later, I saw Rickey stroll into our spring training complex. I immediately invited him into my office for a little chat.

"Nice to see you, Rickey," I told him. "Now that you're here, I want to make sure you understand that, from now on, you show up on time and play your ass off. We'll need you this season."

That was it. There was no yelling or screaming. But the newspapers still had a field day writing about the behind-closed-doors showdown between Rickey and his new manager. They didn't know what transpired, so they used their imagination.

Did my words get through to Rickey? Not a chance.

He pouted during spring training, though he was occasionally generous enough to show off his talent by request. Elia had never seen Rickey in person but knew he had led the American League in steals eight out of the past nine years. An injury in 1987 was the only thing that prevented that from being nine out of nine. Before a spring training game, Elia told Corrales he wanted to see Rickey steal a base. Corrales, who seemed to get through to Rickey better than anybody on my staff, relayed the message to him. During the game against the

Mets, Rickey reached base against Dwight Gooden and took off for second on the next pitch. He went in standing up. And that was the first and only base Rickey swiped all spring.

Rickey promised to be a laugh a minute all season.

At least George and I only butted heads once during spring training. It was over an older Mexican pitcher George wanted to release after a rough outing. Because we had a round of cuts scheduled in a couple of days, I didn't see the urgency of letting him go before then. It would only serve to embarrass him and possibly strain our relations with the Mexican league. But George sent Bob Quinn down to tell me to do it right away. I said I wouldn't. Then Syd Thrift, who had just been hired as the team's vice president of baseball operations, paid me a visit to reiterate that George wanted the guy gone immediately. I told Syd that if George felt so strongly about it, he could come down and take care of it himself.

The guy got cut that night. And he got the news personally from the owner.

• • •

Already without Winfield in body and Henderson in spirit, I also had to make do with the loss of starting shortstop Rafael Santana because of a bone chip in his elbow.

When you lose two big bats and a slick-fielding middle infielder and have doubts about the attitude of your star left fielder, the last thing you can afford is a thin starting pitching rotation. A few months before the season, the team traded Rick Rhoden, whose streak of seven consecutive double-digit-win seasons made him one of the most consistent pitchers in the majors. Longtime Yankee Ron Guidry had elbow surgery in spring training and retired before making it back.

Steinbrenner and Quinn didn't consult me before trading Rhoden to the Astros for three minor leaguers. I didn't make a stink about it, though. After all, I was the guy who once said general managers shouldn't tell managers when to bunt, and managers shouldn't tell general managers when to make trades. Then again, George was notorious for blurring those lines.

We picked up starting pitchers Dave LaPoint and Andy Hawkins, but that still left us a couple of arms short of a full rotation. That's when George offered a contract to 45-year-old Tommy John, who was just 14 wins shy of 300. He had gutted out nine wins for the Yankees in 1988, but I doubted he could keep it up much longer at his age. George wanted him on the club, and I honestly didn't see any better options, so Tommy entered the season in our starting rotation. Not only that, he was our Opening Day starter. And he earned a victory that day.

It remained our only win for quite a while.

We started the season 1–7 and were outscored 57–15 during the seven-game losing streak. We got trounced almost every night.

The season was still young, but the verbal fireworks were about to begin.

"I'm getting sick and tired of watching it, sick and tired of seeing pitchers not get people out and seeing us get one, two, three hits," I screamed after an 8–0 loss to the Blue Jays in which we got just one hit. "If there was a bright spot, we'd look for it, but I don't see too many."

Only in New York could the media question a manager's job stability eight games into his first season with the club. But that came with the territory. Philadelphia and Chicago each had two major newspapers. The greater New York area had five: *The New York Times*, *Daily News*, *New York Post*, *Newsday*, and the *Star-Ledger*. And each tried to one-up the competition on a daily basis.

Some of the scribes reached George in Tampa, where he was looking after his sick mother, and asked him whether I should be worried about my job.

Even George wasn't ready to throw me under the bus quite yet. "Dallas Green will continue to manage this team this year, no matter what," he told the *Times*. "I'm committed to him, and he knows it. I know that some people will say that's usually the kiss of death from me, but it isn't."

• • •

Despite his soothing words in the press, George was clearly rattled by our slow start.

It wasn't long before he started taking jabs at my coaches. He blamed first-base coach Pat Corrales for Rickey Henderson's dramatic decline in stolen bases, and he chastised third-base coach Lee Elia for not scoring more guys from second base on singles. This was George being George. It wasn't as if Pat could steal the bases for a clearly unmotivated Rickey. And Lee couldn't make guys like Ken Phelps and Steve Balboni fast enough to round the bases more quickly. I'd guess Rickey, if he felt like it, probably could have run from home to second faster than either of those guys could have run to first. My coaches were among the best teachers in the game, and it made me angry to hear them unfairly criticized.

When Don Mattingly struggled at the plate early in the season, George went after our hitting coach, Frank Howard.

Slumps are part of the game. Even career .300 hitters like Donnie went through rough patches. A month into the '89 season, he was hitting just .200, but I had no doubt he would soon regain his form. But George felt we had a crisis on our hands. He told me he wanted Lou Piniella, my predecessor as manager, to come down from the Yankees broadcast booth to work with Donnie on his swing. I had a problem with that. Lou was a good hitting coach, but he wasn't *our* hitting coach. Hondo was.

"We're on top of it," I told George. "If you want Hondo and Lou to compare notes, that's fine with me. But I want Hondo to be the one who works with Donnie."

"No, I want Lou to come down," he repeated.

With the season just a month old, I wasn't yet at the point where I felt I would gain anything by openly defying George.

I went to Hondo and explained what was going on. To his credit, he didn't get territorial.

"Bring him down, D," Hondo said. "If it helps Donnie, that's great. If not, it was worth a try."

I didn't take it nearly as well as Hondo. The whole situation kind of frosted me. I sensed the nitpicking against me and my coaches was just beginning.

Lou worked with Donnie, who brought his average back up to a respectable level. I guess we'll never know whether that was the result of a professional hitter's adjustments or a meddling owner's intervention.

You would think George's deep involvement in the daily operations of the ballclub would have negated the need for a general manager. You'd be wrong. Late in spring training, George decided he needed *two* GMs. Bob Quinn, the GM who hired me, carried the official title, but Syd Thrift shared the duties of the job.

I didn't have a real problem with this unusual arrangement. Syd and I got along well, and Bob and I had known each other since I was the Phillies' assistant farm director and he was GM of our Double-A team. Syd and Bob were knowledgeable baseball guys, but George all but neutered them. Rather than devising and implementing strategies, they simply did what George wanted. And that kept them plenty busy.

At the end of the day, it was George who ran the show. A shocking revelation, I know.

• • •

By the time George traded a disgruntled Rickey Henderson to the A's, my honeymoon with the Yankees was long over. When he left the Bronx, Rickey was hitting just .247 and on pace for a career low in stolen bases. Rickey didn't get his new contract from the Yankees, so he took his poutiness out on the field with him.

In return for Rickey, Oakland sent us two relief pitchers and out-fielder Luis Polonia. Before long, those relievers, Eric Plunk and Greg Cadaret, joined the starting rotation. And Polonia and Mel Hall, neither of whom was with us at the start of spring training, were sharing time in left field.

Depleted by injuries and limited in talent, it looked like we might still salvage the season. In mid-July, we were a game over .500 and in second place behind the Orioles.

Several guys stepped up to help our patchwork team stay competitive.

Deion Sanders, who made his major league debut at the end of May, infused energy and excitement into the clubhouse. At second base, Steve Sax, in his first year with the Yankees, went out and had an All-Star season, more than filling the shoes of the departed Willie Randolph. And Alvaro Espinoza, the fill-in at shortstop for Santana, gave us a workmanlike effort every day.

Arguably our best pitcher was closer Dave Righetti, who busted his ass and saved a lot of games. Lee Guetterman was also effective out of the bullpen. Unfortunately, the rest of our relief corps cost us a lot of games. Our starting pitching wasn't much better. Andy Hawkins ended up leading the team in wins and losses, with 15 apiece. No other pitcher on our staff won more than six.

At the end of July, we lost nine of 10 games and fell all the way to sixth place in the American League East. Despite that slide, we were still only 7½ games out of first.

George intimated that changes might soon take place, but he insisted my job was safe. He blamed injuries and underperforming players for the disappointing season. The situation required patience, he told reporters.

• • •

There has always been a misconception that George and I were constantly at each other's throats during my time with the Yankees. The truth is George rarely picked up the phone and called me. He occasionally asked to sit down with me and my coaches, but he ended up canceling those meetings more often than not. Other than the dispute over how to handle Mattingly's slump, we co-existed pretty well. He didn't ask me to fill out the lineup card a certain way or demand that I play anybody. He did, however, issue edicts from time to time, like when he pissed off the team by banning beer on the team's charter flights. That came after Rickey Henderson told the media that several members of the previous year's team drank to excess.

All in all, George and I had a functional relationship—until we didn't anymore.

I've never been one to run from a fight, whether it's with a player, owner, manager, or general manager. And I found myself in a hell of a fight after George second-guessed my coaches and me one too many times. It came during an August series against the Minnesota Twins. George complained about the defensive positioning of our outfielders and my choice of a pinch hitter in the ninth inning of a game. He also wondered aloud if we were getting the most out of our players.

I wasn't going to let George get away with that.

"The statement that 'Manager George' made about game situations is a very logical second-guess," I told a couple dozen reporters who were about to dazzle their editors with the best back-page story of the baseball season. "And hindsight always being 20-20, that's why managers get gray…It's easy [for George] to view it from above."

I felt I expressed my feelings well. But most of what I said was immediately forgotten. Everyone seized on two words: Manager George.

The last Yankees manager to stand up to George like that was Gene Michael, who literally dared George to fire him in 1982. George obliged.

I wasn't daring George to let me go. I just didn't appreciate his penchant for telling veteran baseball guys how to do their jobs.

And he didn't appreciate that I called him out for it.

George tried to laugh off the comment. "It was a cute remark," he told reporters. "He's a cute guy."

He thought I was a cute guy? That was a first.

George also reminded everyone of his background in coaching. I guess carrying a clipboard on a college football sideline for a couple of years had taught him to recognize when outfielders were playing too deep.

As George and I went back and forth in the press, Piniella jumped in the fray by suggesting I move center fielder Roberto Kelly up in the batting order.

Everyone was suddenly a critic. But George once again affirmed I was his guy.

His loyalty to me was a mile wide and a centimeter deep. I knew I wasn't going to be in the Bronx much longer.

• • •

Less than two weeks after my third vote of confidence from George, I got fired.

I knew something was brewing when I heard George, who rarely traveled with the team, had tagged along on a road trip to Detroit. We had just gotten swept in Milwaukee to fall 10 games under .500 for the first time all season. Nobody was in a particularly good mood.

In the first game of the series at Tiger Stadium, Righetti helped me go out a winner by recording a five-out save.

Early the next morning, George summoned me to his hotel suite.

"Dallas, I wanna make some changes," he told me. "I'm going to replace the coaching staff."

He was going to fire my coaches but spare me? I didn't buy it.

"Look, George, I'm going to make this easy for you," I replied. "You're using my coaching staff to get back at me. I hired the coaching staff. I think they're excellent baseball guys. If you're going to fire them, you might as well fire me."

I didn't have to do any arm twisting. I later found out my replacement, Bucky Dent, had already arrived in Detroit.

The meeting with George didn't last more than a few minutes. I didn't like his decision to let me and my coaches go, but I accepted it.

For one last time, we both told our stories in the press. I explained that loyalty to my coaches precluded any chance of me staying if they all got fired. George countered by saying I had intentionally provoked him with the "Manager George" comment because I knew I couldn't turn the Yankees into a winning team.

After I was fired, I went back to speak to George. It was to ask him for a favor. Hondo was going through a divorce at the time and having a rough go financially. Elia, Corrales, Fox, and I could afford to be unemployed for a while, but I hoped George could find a place in the organization for Hondo.

George had his flaws, but at the end of the day, he was a decent man. He called in all the coaches except Hondo and told them they were gone. Then he called in Frank and asked him to replace Bucky Dent as manager of Triple-A Columbus.

Hondo's reply to George impressed the hell out of me: "Thanks, George, but I came in with the big boy, and I'm leaving with the big boy."

That was an incredible display of loyalty and friendship.

• • •

Whoever had August 18 was the winner of Mr. Carpenter's pool.

My time with the Yankees ended almost as soon as it began. Under Dent, the team finished the year 18–22. After another slow start in 1990, Bucky got the axe, too. That made 18 managerial changes in 17 years for the Yankees.

Looking back on my months as Yankees skipper, I'm disappointed I wasn't given more time to produce positive results. We didn't have a really talented baseball team in 1989, but I would have liked to stick around long enough to manage under better circumstances. It's frustrating when you don't have an opportunity to do the job you're hired to do. Of course, it's difficult to function in any job where your boss is seeking to control you.

I guess we were doomed from the beginning by my big mouth and George's lack of patience.

After leaving Yankee Stadium for the last time, I never spoke to George again. It wasn't a conscious decision on my part. We just never had a reason to talk. I never went back to Yankee Stadium again, either, not for an old timers' game, the last game at the old stadium, or the first game at the new stadium.

Maybe events would have turned out differently if I had taken the Yankees job a year later. In July 1990, Major League Baseball commissioner Fay Vincent came down hard on George for hiring a gambler to dig up dirt on Dave Winfield. Vincent banned George from any involvement in the day-to-day operation of the Yankees. The ban was lifted a couple of years later, but even after regaining the ability to push his agenda, George chose to take a backseat in running the team.

The old George insinuated himself too much into situations others were better equipped to handle, but I still admired and respected his overall intentions. Unlike a lot of owners, he wanted to win, and he put his money where his mouth was.

I don't regret having taken the Yankees job. I enjoyed wearing the pinstripes and managing in the House That Ruth Built. Those days hold a special place in my memory.

22

I WASN'T THE ONLY MEMBER of the Green family to go from the Cubs to the Yankees before the 1989 season. My son John had pitched reasonably well in the Cubs system for four years, and while I still questioned whether he had enough talent to reach the majors, I knew he could hold his own at the minor league level.

I asked George Bradley, the Yankees vice president of player development, if he had room for John down on the farm. I didn't apply any pressure and wasn't asking for any favors. I just gave him my honest assessment of John's abilities. Bradley had enough faith in my judgment to make a trade for John.

John was with me at spring training before reporting to Single-A Fort Lauderdale. At 25, he was one of the oldest players on the team. But that didn't bother him. He knew from having grown up with me as a father that promotions came to those who earned them. John posted a 3.40 ERA in 21 relief appearances in the Florida State League, enough to earn a call-up later in the season to Double-A Albany-Colonie. He pitched even better for that club, where he played for manager Buck Showalter and helped the team win the Eastern League championship.

My son outlasted me in the Yankees organization. In 1990, he got a shot at Triple-A after Opening Day major league rosters temporarily expanded to 27 players due to a recent labor stoppage. That

caused a domino effect in the minor leagues that allowed for his promotion. He pitched in two games for the Columbus Clippers. Then
he was told to return to Double-A. Rather than accepting the demotion, he decided to retire. He wanted to go out on his own terms.

John returned to the University of Arizona to finish his studies.
His degree in geological engineering guaranteed him a comfortable
living after baseball. But John had baseball in his blood. While working full-time for an engineering firm in Tucson, he squeezed in some
unpaid, part-time scouting for the Orioles. His smarts and experience
as a pro player equipped him well for that job. Gordon Goldsberry,
my farm director in Chicago who had since moved on to Baltimore,
eventually hired him as a paid scout. John has worked in that capacity ever since, most recently with the Dodgers.

• • •

I heard through the grapevine that baseball commissioner Bart
Giamatti chewed out George Steinbrenner for letting me go. When
I was in Chicago and Bart was the president of the National League,
we became good friends. He valued my opinion on the issues of the
day and appointed me to several committees, including one that studied the state of umpiring in the game.

He and I came from very different backgrounds. Bart was a writer,
a philosopher, and a Yale man. I was a career baseball guy. What we
shared was a deep love for the game. I'm confident Bart would have
established himself as one of the best commissioners ever had he not
died of a heart attack about a year into his tenure.

Bart wasn't the only high-ranking baseball official in my corner.

Following my dismissal from the Yankees, National League pres-
ident Bill White, a former Phillies teammate of mine, called to see if
I'd be interested in replacing Pete Rose as manager of the Cincinnati
Reds. He was willing to put in a good word for me with team owner
Marge Schott. Bill thought Cincinnati would benefit from having a

strong manager who could help keep Marge in check. He also believed the Reds needed a big-name skipper to succeed Rose, whom Bart had permanently banned from baseball in 1989 for betting on games.

"I'd really like you to take the job, Dallas," Bill told me in the winter of 1989.

I wanted no part of it.

"Goddamn, Bill, I just got fired by one ogre," I told him. "Now you want me to go into another ogre's den? I don't think I can do that. I don't want to go from the frying pan into the fire."

"Well, I tried," Bill said, laughing. "You think Piniella would be interested?"

Lou was braver—or more masochistic—than I. He went into the ogre's den, and it paid off for him. The Reds won a World Series in his first season on the job. Of course, he also had to deal with all of Marge's nonsense, which eventually forced her to sell the team.

• • •

According to the newspapers, the Braves were on the verge of hiring me to succeed Bobby Cox as general manager. I was never even contacted about the job, which ended up going to John Schuerholz. I was still cashing Steinbrenner's checks, so I took it easy for a while on my new farm in Conowingo, Maryland, which was about half an hour from our property in West Grove, Pennsylvania. Sylvia and I also traveled around the region, visiting Civil War battle sites in Pennsylvania and Virginia. We both are huge admirers of Abraham Lincoln. Sylvia wrote a college research paper on him, and I've read loads of books about his presidency. From my standpoint, he was the ultimate leader, a man willing to fight for his convictions.

I knew baseball would beckon me back. It always did.

In 1991, at the age of 56, I was back in New York after joining the Mets front office as a scout. That surprised a lot of baseball writers. "Why would Dallas Green, still in the prime of his career, accept a lowly scouting job after holding such high-profile positions in Philadelphia, Chicago, and New York?" they wondered. It didn't compute with them that I took the job because I loved scouting and player development. Soon, I read news reports describing me as the Mets' "manager-in-waiting."

That bothered me. It wasn't in my nature to take a job just because I was waiting for someone else to lose his job. I've always hated people who do that.

Bud Harrelson was the Mets manager, and I never lobbied for his job.

As a Mets scout, I enjoyed attending their front office meetings and talking about the finer points of the game. It was an ideal situation for me. I lived on my farm and scouted future Mets opponents when they played in Philadelphia. I went to the ballpark at night, wrote up my reports in the morning, and enjoyed working in the fresh air of the farm during the day.

When Harrelson got fired with a week left in the 1991 season, Mets general manager Frank Cashen never approached me about the vacancy. Frank and I knew each other well from my days as GM of the Cubs. He and his wife were friends with Sylvia and me. But Frank knew I enjoyed my work as a scout.

Frank stepped down as GM before the Mets hired a new manager. His successor, Al Harazin, hired former Indians and White Sox manager Jeff Torborg to a four-year deal. Jeff inherited a team loaded with veteran talent.

The writers concluded I had been jilted and wasn't long for the Mets. They had me penciled in as an executive with one of the expansion teams in Colorado or Florida. Those reports were completely false.

Under Torborg, the Mets were expected to compete for a postseason berth. With all the high-priced players on the roster, it came as a shock when they struggled to a fifth-place finish in 1992.

After they got off to a terrible start in 1993, my phone rang.

It was Harazin.

"We need an aggressive leader to run this team," he told me.

To that point, only Casey Stengel and Yogi Berra had managed both the Mets and the Yankees. I was about to join that list.

• • •

In 1962, the expansion Mets, managed by Stengel, lost 120 games. I witnessed their futility firsthand. On an August day at the Polo Grounds that season, I pitched 10⅓ innings of one-run ball in a game won by the Phillies in 15 innings. That outing against the Mets, the longest of my major league career, trimmed a lot of points off my ERA.

In 1986, the Mets won a franchise-high 108 games en route to a World Series title. With the Yankees in a funk that lasted longer than a decade, the center of the baseball universe started to shift from the Bronx to Queens.

Somehow, the Mets I managed in 1993 had more in common with the '62 club than the '86 team.

Since finishing 91–71 in 1990, the team had gone into a rapid decline. Despite having the highest payroll in baseball in 1992, they finished 18 games under .500. And a 13–25 start to the '93 season suggested the team was still in free fall.

We weren't just also-rans, we were *very expensive* also-rans.

I took on the challenge of managing the Mets for the same reason I had taken all of my other jobs. I liked to try and fix troubled teams.

Even though I came from within the organization, I confess I didn't know much about the major league Mets. As a scout, I spent all my time watching other teams play. But it didn't take a lot of observation and analysis to figure out why they had struggled to win games under Torborg.

"Another manager has gone down, because the players didn't perform up to their capabilities," I said at my introductory press conference. "I'm here to win games regardless of whose feelings get hurt."

That was a variation of my message in 1979 when I replaced Danny Ozark in Philadelphia. Like Ozark, Torborg had a reputation for being a players' manager. He didn't like to offend or criticize anyone. Yet his guys still complained about him. One of their beefs was that he announced starting lineups on his pregame radio show before posting them in the clubhouse.

On paper, the '93 Mets looked nowhere near as dreadful as their record indicated. The team included Eddie Murray at first base, Bobby Bonilla and Vince Coleman in the outfield, longtime Met Howard Johnson at third, and newly acquired Tony Fernandez at shortstop. The starting rotation included two key members of the '86 World Series team, Dwight Gooden and Sid Fernandez. It also featured two-time Cy Young Award winner Bret Saberhagen and capable closer John Franco for late-inning save situations.

In reality, the team was god-awful.

We showed no improvement in my first months on the job. At the All-Star break, the Mets had the worst record in the majors, even though two expansion teams were introduced that season. Harazin's short tenure as GM had already ended. Co-owners Fred Wilpon and Nelson Doubleday replaced him with Joe McIlvaine, the Mets' director of baseball operations when they won the World Series in '86.

• • •

It's easy to identify why Harazin failed. By the time he took over in the fall of 1991, Keith Hernandez, Darryl Strawberry, Gary Carter, Ron Darling, and much of the backbone of the great Mets teams of the late 1980s were gone. In an attempt to keep the team afloat, Harazin stocked the roster with expensive veterans acquired in trades and free agency. He just wasn't a very skilled talent evaluator.

He also had tough luck; even moves that seemed beyond reproach backfired on him. Before the '93 season, he acquired Tony Fernandez, one of the best all-around shortstops in the game, in a trade with San

Diego. He hardly gave up anything in return, because the Padres were simply looking to shed salary.

Fernandez's career with the Mets lasted 173 at-bats. He hit just .225, and I dropped him from second to eighth in the batting order. On June 11, with our record at 19–38, Harazin traded Fernandez to the Blue Jays, where he hit .306 the rest of the season and helped Toronto win a World Series.

By the halfway point of the '93 season, Franco admitted the team had grown used to losing. Gooden said the game was no fun at all anymore.

They were speaking for the whole team. In the clubhouse and out on the field, I saw no fire, emotion, or sign that anybody gave a damn. The only bit of energy came from young second baseman Jeff Kent's frequent temper tantrums. Kent, who came to us in a trade for pitcher David Cone, was in his first season as a full-time player in the majors. He was an enigma. Unlike most of his teammates, he demonstrated a clear will to succeed. But when things didn't go his way, he tended to go a little berserk. After a strikeout or pop out, he'd hurl his bat or helmet in the dugout or get into a shouting match with himself. He said he was motivated by a fear of failure. At least that meant he cared. He hit .270 with 21 home runs and 80 RBIs in 1993. He also committed 22 errors in the field, which translated into 22 outbursts in the dugout between innings.

It's difficult to stop a team on a downward spiral.

And in 1993, the signs of our ineptitude were everywhere. That made our games difficult for me to watch. As I said after one particularly sloppy effort, "I can't live with a lack of work. We played like kindergarten people."

And to make matters worse, we acted like kindergarten people, too.

• • •

I had always thought highly of Bret Saberhagen's ability and felt his stuff was still sharp enough to make him an ace in our rotation. Once I got to know him, however, I observed how little time he spent working at his craft. Since becoming a Met, he had put off-the-field pleasures and clubhouse antics ahead of baseball. While out with a knee injury in 1993, Sabes did further damage to his body while tooling around on a jet ski at his house in Long Island. He didn't pitch again that season.

He endangered his own health in the boating accident. But his other screwup that season put other people in harm's way. After a game against Florida, he decided it would be funny to spray bleach on a group of reporters conducting interviews in the clubhouse. That earned him a five-day suspension at the start of the '94 season.

Among my challenges in New York was making sure Sabes got his priorities back in order.

Saberhagen's incidents weren't the only off-the-field distraction in 1993.

Bobby Bonilla almost got into a fistfight with Bob Klapisch, a journalist who wrote a book about the '92 team titled *The Worst Team Money Could Buy*. Bobby, who may or may not have actually read the book, got in Klapisch's face early in the season and threatened to knock his teeth out. The equipment of a nearby television crew ended up taking the brunt of Bobby's anger.

Later that April, Vince Coleman struck Gooden on the shoulder while making a practice swing with a golf club. The accident caused Dwight to be scratched from his scheduled start that night.

There was certainly a lot of competition in 1993 for Stupidest Act of the Year by a New York Met. But Coleman clinched the prize in July with an unbelievably dumb—and criminal—act in the parking lot at Dodger Stadium.

After a game, Coleman set off what at first was thought to be a large firecracker. The blast injured three people, including a two-year-old girl walking with her parents. Investigators later concluded the explosive device was similar to a quarter-stick of dynamite.

I couldn't for the life of me figure out what Coleman was thinking. It was harmless fun when our pitchers set off small firecrackers in the bullpen after the performance of the national anthem, but Coleman's behavior showed terrible judgment.

Worst of all was that my players refused to take responsibility for their actions. For months, Saberhagen denied being the culprit in the bleach incident. And Coleman at first lied about setting off the explosive device.

I had to wonder what these guys saw when they looked in the mirror.

• • •

We needed someone, anyone, to step up and be a team leader in 1993.

I held out hope that Eddie Murray could at least serve as a role model, if not an outspoken leader. He was a future Hall of Famer, and at 37 years old, still putting up numbers in line with his career averages. With the Mets in 1992, he hit his 400th career home run.

Eddie had a powerful bat but not much of a personality. In his book, Klapisch described interviewing him as "only slightly less painful than a tax audit."

You don't have to be on friendly terms with the media to be a team leader, however. You don't even have to say much at all. A disapproving look or a shake of the head from a veteran is sometimes enough to send a message to a younger teammate. But the best way to lead is by example.

I respected Eddie, but I realized I hadn't done anything with the Mets to earn his respect back. His actions over the summer let me know he had no interest in a leadership role. Managers don't have to force leaders to participate in pregame warm-ups, like I had to do with Eddie. He went out and did his job well that season, knocking in 100 RBIs for the first time in eight years. Away from the field, he wasn't a positive or negative influence. He was just…there.

The few carryovers from the much-celebrated '86 World Series team also didn't take charge. Third baseman Howard Johnson's career was on a downward slide. His All-Star season in 1991, in which he led the National League in home runs and RBIs, seemed like a distant memory. With his low average and lack of power production, I viewed him as a liability. I told reporters his days at Shea Stadium were numbered if he didn't start playing better. But Howard felt entitled to playing time based on his past contributions to the team. He responded by accusing me of not knowing him as a player or a human being. But I knew what I saw. And what I saw, I didn't like.

Then there was Doc Gooden, who had become a World Series champion, 100-game winner, and national celebrity before the age of 25. He was still riding the coattails of those accomplishments. But the 28-year-old Doc that I got to know had fallen far from grace. He went 12–15 in 1993 as he battled mounting personal problems that would fully emerge in the coming years.

• • •

No one was more affected by the Mets' inability to win ballgames in 1992 and 1993 than pitcher Anthony Young. On July 24, 1993, his loss to the Dodgers dropped his season record to 0–13. Adding the 14 consecutive losses he suffered at the end of the '92 season, Young extended his major league record losing streak to 27 games.

When Anthony broke the record, the media turned out in such large numbers that we had to stage a postgame press conference in my office. Interest in his losing streak had grown throughout the summer. After one loss, I commented that I hadn't seen as many media members in a major league clubhouse since I won the World Series with the Phillies. Late-night television hosts even got in on the act, cracking jokes about Anthony, who became a poster child for our team's poor play.

Anthony was a talented young pitcher. I wouldn't have kept using him as a starter and reliever if I didn't think he gave us a chance to win. There were a variety of reasons he struggled to get a victory. Dumb luck played a role. So did the fact that he was pitching for a team that didn't bail out its pitchers with timely hits in the late innings. Part of it had to do with Anthony himself. Having spent his first full season in the majors in 1992, he was still finding his way in the big leagues, and the pressure to make the right pitch at the right time increased each time he notched another loss. I respected how he went out and battled every time.

When Anthony finally broke the streak with a win against the Marlins on July 28, we cracked open champagne bottles and celebrated. He finished the season with a 1–16 record and a not-so-shabby 3.77 ERA. His difficulties garnered all the attention, but his wasn't the only lowly won-lost record on the team in 1993. Frank Tanana went 7–15, Eric Hillman went 2–9, Pete Schourek went 5–12, and Mike Maddux went 3–8.

We traded Anthony to the Cubs before the 1994 season. He never finished a season with a winning record and had his career cut short by an arm injury. Before he retired, Young ripped me for being too critical of players. I had heard that a lot during my career, but I didn't expect it from a guy I tried my best to support during a historically unsuccessful time in his career.

• • •

I even got caught up in the feeding frenzy of negative attention directed at the Mets.

It stemmed from my attempt at a joke when a reporter asked me how I cope with losses.

"I just beat the hell out of Sylvia and kick the dog and whatever else I've got to do to get it out," I responded.

I was trying to capture the essence of how difficult it was for me to deal with defeat day after day. Sylvia was a great baseball gal. She knew losing made me pouty as hell. The idea that I would actually do any harm to her or my dog was comical. At least I thought it was.

The backlash didn't come right away. I guess the leaders of the National Organization for Women weren't avid readers of the sports pages, or maybe it just took them time to figure out they were insulted. But a couple of weeks after my comment, someone in the Mets public relations office reached out to Sylvia.

"You're going to get a call from *The New York Times*," he said. "Some groups are planning to protest us for what Dallas said about beating you and kicking the dog."

Sylvia got contacted by more than one reporter. She tried to calm the storm while at the same time making it clear I didn't have a future in comedy.

"I had to laugh, because I know Dallas," she said. "I knew he was trying to be funny, and it wasn't funny."

The media jumped all over the story. The *New York Post* ran a cartoon of me walking into a house and kicking a dog. Sylvia was in the background with her arm in a sling.

NOW held its demonstration outside Madison Square Garden. They accused me of sending a message that domestic violence was a laughing matter.

In 1972, when Sylvia and I fought for my daughter Kim's right to play Little League baseball, NOW and other women's rights groups stood solidly in our corner. Twenty years later, I was a villain in their eyes. Sylvia got fed up with all the negative attention directed at me.

On the day of the protest, I told reporters, "I can't have beat her too bad—we've been married 36 years now."

Make that 55 years now.

• • •

Considering all I had to deal with in 1993, I thought I exercised a lot of self-control—toward my players, of course. It was a difficult group to relate to.

Bonilla may not have read Klapisch's book, but I did. The 1992 team gave him plenty of material to support his premise. But if he had waited a year, he might have had an even better story about the worst team money could buy.

The only silver lining to the '93 season was that we won our last six games, giving up a total of just seven runs in the process. The streak included Sid Fernandez's last win for the Mets. It brought our season record to 59–103, the team's worst mark since 1965. The expansion Florida Marlins and Colorado Rockies won more games than we did in '93, though we managed to go 15–10 head to head against them. Under my stewardship, the Mets were 46–78.

We finished 38 games behind the Phillies, who reached the World Series before losing to the Blue Jays. I really respected that Philadelphia team. They were a bunch of blue-collar guys who liked to have a good time but put winning baseball games above all else. Their idea of fun was having a few beers, singing some songs, and agitating a lot. Their success on the field earned them the freedom to do what they wanted away from it. In that sense, they were like the '86 Mets team that won the World Series.

My team, meanwhile, sprayed bleach, set off explosives, *and* played terrible baseball.

We had a leadership void. We had a talent void. And I couldn't wait for Joe McIlvaine to dismantle the team.

23

If I had been managing the Yankees in 1993, I probably would have been out of a job, even with two years still left on my contract. But Mets ownership realized it would take time to fix the problems I inherited. Unlike George Steinbrenner, Mets co-owners Nelson Doubleday and Fred Wilpon seemed to value patience.

It was impossible to pretend that the 1993 season was anything but a complete and utter embarrassment for the organization. The team's stunning lack of discipline on and off the field gnawed at me the entire off-season. I couldn't believe players would perform—and behave—in such a manner. Going into spring training, I vowed to make my first full season with the Mets a completely different experience. A middle-of-the-pack finish in the National League East was within reach. But more importantly, I wanted to restore pride to an organization whose reputation had taken a severe hit.

I had never been in this type of situation before. When the Phillies hired me for the final month of the 1979 season, I got immediate results. And the team's high level of play carried over to the following season and postseason. The Mets were playing lousy baseball when I took over the team, and they showed no improvement after my arrival.

No manager could have won with the 1993 Mets. As I told the *Daily News*, "I was supposed to ride in here on a horse like John Wayne and beat the heck out of guys and make them play great baseball. There has to be a realization you can only do so much as manager with the material that you have."

I didn't beat my wife, dog, *or* my players, by the way. And I still couldn't ride a horse.

If we couldn't win with our veterans, I hoped to look to the future by giving young players like catcher Todd Hundley, outfielder Jeromy Burnitz, and pitcher Bobby Jones a chance to prove themselves. But unlike in Philadelphia, where I knew the farm system like the back of my hand, I didn't have a lot of firsthand knowledge about these guys.

I had a lot to learn about my team before I could hope for better results.

• • •

My coaches and I were in this together. My closeness with my staff in Philadelphia helped get us through some rough patches, and I wanted to build similar kinship in New York. Bobby Wine in Philadelphia and Frank Howard in the Bronx were the only coaches on my staff with whom I had worked before.

During an off day in spring training at Port St. Lucie, I got the coaches and their wives together for a little boat ride off Florida's Treasure Coast. The idea was to build camaraderie. A local doctor offered us his yacht for the excursion. We packed up some picnic baskets and a cooler of beer and headed off to the dock. When we arrived, the doctor was there, but his boat wasn't. Apparently he had forgotten he promised the yacht to someone else that day.

Determined not to cancel the trip, I rented a pontoon boat that seemed big enough to accommodate all our passengers: Sylvia and I, Greg Pavlick, Bobby and Fran Wine, Mike and Jan Cubbage, Frank Howard, and Tom McCraw. I passed on renting a driver, because Pavlick, my pitching coach, insisted he could captain the vessel.

After pushing the boat out through some mud, we loaded it up with the food and drink and climbed aboard. Most of us huddled around the cooler in the front of the boat. It was a windy spring day, and the water was choppy. When we reached the middle of the channel, another more powerful boat cruised by us. Suddenly the seas got even rougher.

Instead of bringing the boat to a stop, Pavlick chose to accelerate into the wake of the larger boat. We started taking on water—lots of it. Potato chips and sandwiches started floating all around us. Fran Wine yelled, "Holy hell, we're going down!" She proceeded to toss her camera overboard.

McCraw and Cubbage couldn't swim—and we neglected to locate the life preservers before setting sail.

Most of the water was collecting in the front of the boat, weighing it down so that Pavlick couldn't maneuver us out of trouble.

"Throw the cooler overboard!" Jan Cubbage yelled.

Hondo and Wino, who were still in the front of the boat, put their arms around the cooler and held on for dear life. There was no way they were going to make such a sacrifice.

Finally, Pavlick figured out what he needed to do. He backed off, the boat steadied, and we continued our journey. Fran's camera was the only casualty.

The entire Mets coaching staff almost bit it that day. But I think we grew closer. We had saved our ship. But could we save the 1994 season?

• • •

Every April offers teams a fresh start. That cliché applied even more in '94, the first year of Major League Baseball's latest round of divisional realignment. Instead of two divisions in each league, there were now three. And in addition to each division winner, a wild-card team from each league would qualify for a postseason berth.

With the Braves now in the National League East, that extra playoff spot sounded pretty good to everyone else in the division. The

Braves had dominated the NL West in 1993, going 104–58 before getting knocked off by the Phillies in the National League Championship Series. It was Atlanta's third division title in a row.

In Greg Maddux, Tom Glavine, and John Smoltz, they most certainly had one of the best pitching rotations in baseball history.

Maddux, who I drafted in Chicago, was at the peak of his career in 1994. He had won the previous two Cy Young Awards and was about to win another two in a row. Every time I saw Greg pitch, I thought to myself, *How the hell could the Cubs have let this guy go?* But Cubs GM Larry Himes couldn't re-sign Maddux after the 1992 season. That was obviously a huge mistake.

When I had Greg in the minors, I took immediate notice of how well he commanded his pitches. Command is what pitching's all about. A lot of guys can throw fastballs in the upper 90s, but if they can't put their pitches where they want them, they can't win. I've never been awed by great arms, because I've seen too many guys with great arms who couldn't pitch. Greg could always throw strikes at will, but he became a great pitcher when he also learned how to locate pitches in a way that exploited a hitter's weaknesses. That's the difference between control and command.

The Braves would go on to win 11 consecutive NL East titles. From a manager's standpoint, I viewed Bobby Cox as a driving force behind the team's success. He was one of my all-time favorite managers. Critics point out that for all those division titles, Coxey won just one World Series. I'd counter that by saying there were a lot of years when he got more out of his team than most managers would have.

• • •

I would have liked to start from scratch in 1994, with a whole new roster of Mets players ready to commit themselves to my program. That's not how baseball works, however, so we had to make do with cutting ties with as many problem players as possible.

We traded Vince Coleman and his fireworks collection to the Royals for outfielder Kevin McReynolds, a former Met. We let Eddie Murray sign as a free agent with the Indians. And we also didn't make an effort to re-sign a disenchanted Howard Johnson, who landed in Colorado.

When you're coming off a 103-loss season, very little about your team is carved in stone. Few everyday jobs were guaranteed, and I was open to any and all possible changes.

We had question marks all over the diamond. A couple of weeks before the start of the season, I still didn't know who'd be starting at catcher, first base, or shortstop. I hadn't decided who would hit lead-off or fill the back end of the pitching rotation. And other than John Franco, our bullpen situation was completely unsettled.

Todd Hundley beat out Kelly Stinnett for the starting catcher's job. We acquired first baseman David Segui in a trade with the Orioles. And Jose Vizcaino, a shortstop and leadoff hitter, came over from the Cubs in exchange for Anthony Young.

But on Opening Day, middle relief and the third and fourth spots in our rotation were still up in the air.

If we sputtered again in '94, it wasn't going to be due to lack of preparation. I put the players through a rigorous spring training program intended to get them in shape and reinforce the importance of fundamentals.

We started the season with three consecutive wins. Despite the small sample size, I sensed the team was more engaged mentally than it had been the year before. We were hardly world-beaters, however, and still quite capable of playing ugly baseball. Four errors in our home-opening loss to the Cubs proved that.

We remained competitive, which is all I could really ask for. A three-game sweep of the Reds in late May put us just a few games out of first place in the NL East. In June, however, we evoked memories of the season before with a 9–18 record that dropped us as many as 10 games under .500.

After a couple of losses in June, I threatened to demote everyone to Triple-A if we didn't start playing better. "Some of you think you can sit on your fat asses and not do anything!" I screamed. "I'll get rid of you, if you don't want to grind it out once in a while. You're not a bad ballclub, but if you let the other team come after you, they will every fucking time! We did that the whole fucking series here! You sat on your fat asses, and if you want to sit on your fat asses, you're going to be on the way to Norfolk!"

Unlike in 1993, I had hope this team could actually be moved by my words.

• • •

I think Bret Saberhagen got my message.

In his first two years with the Mets, Sabes had battled injuries and won just 10 games.

But he still had it in him to be a top-flight pitcher. He just needed to exercise a little common sense, cut out the bullshit, and work at his craft.

Before the 1994 season, general manager Joe McIlvaine called out Bret on his shenanigans. "You can be a child all you want," Joe said. "But there is a level of behavior that is expected by the public and by your employer. Bret lost a lot of fans last year by not living up to that level."

The best way for Bret to win back those fans was to pitch well.

I felt Bret's struggles were partly due to an overreliance on his fastball. I encouraged him to mix up his pitch selection by occasionally using a changeup as his "out pitch."

Sabes stepped up to the challenge by pitching better than he had in years. His 10–4 record in the first half of the '94 season earned him a trip to the All-Star Game. He went on to win all four of his decisions after the All-Star break.

Sabes and Bobby Jones, who went a combined 26–11, made my job a lot easier in 1994. By pitching deep into most games, they saved me from having to depend too much on our shaky bullpen.

Those two gave our rotation a real boost. Dwight Gooden did not.

In 1994, we witnessed the self-destruction of Doc. After he failed two drug tests, Major League Baseball suspended him for 60 days in June. Upon his release from the Betty Ford Center in Southern California, he failed two more tests.

"Doc has fallen by the wayside by his own choice—put that into perspective," I told reporters after his first two positive drug tests. "The organization is hurt. Baseball is hurt, because he's a big name. But his wife and kids have to be devastated. The kids are at an age where they understand what's going on. I feel compassion for the family."

Doc was due to become a free agent after the season, and I saw no point in trying to re-sign him. He had failed *four* drug tests, after all. Even if he straightened himself out, I believed his arm and shoulder problems would prevent him from ever again being a successful pitcher.

Doc, in his 11th season with the team, meant a lot to the franchise. Our fans still loved him for his brilliance in the 1980s. His teammates gravitated toward him. Even our clubhouse attendants adored him, probably because he was the best tipper on the team.

But I found it difficult to give him a pass. If he had looked in the mirror, he would have seen his own worst enemy staring back at him. Doc was suspended for the entire 1995 season. In 1996, the Yankees decided to take a chance on him.

After we cut ties with him, our clubhouse guys wore a patch on their sleeves to honor him. I thought that was garbage.

• • •

I've worked in a lot of big cities, but I'm not a city kid. Sylvia and I grew up in modest homes in the suburbs of Wilmington, Delaware.

Later in life, we purchased sprawling farms in Pennsylvania and Maryland.

Living in a congested housing development in Queens during the season was a big adjustment for us. But we enjoyed our time there. The neighborhood was close to Shea Stadium and LaGuardia Airport, which made it very convenient. And whenever Sylvia needed a little taste of nature, she'd head over to the New York Botanical Garden.

I didn't venture out into the city too often while I managed the Mets. If Sylvia was out of town, bullpen coach Steve Swisher and I would sometimes go out for a few beers. But for the most part, you weren't going to see the manager of the New York Mets wandering around Times Square. Sylvia and I really enjoyed the mom-and-pop restaurants in Queens and going to the movies and Broadway shows.

My life in the summertime revolved around baseball. It was comforting to know that the joys of farm life awaited after every season.

But thanks to Swisher, I was able to indulge my agrarian side at Shea Stadium, too.

Swish, a West Virginia guy, maintained a garden with tomatoes, beans, carrots, and a bunch of other vegetables out in the home bullpen. Before games, I'd find an excuse to go out there and talk to him. The real purpose of my visits, however, was to give him gardening tips.

Based on the amount of shade in the bullpen, I encouraged him to plant lettuce, which requires less direct sunlight. I also helped him get the right moisture level in his soil.

It likely surprised some fans to see me on my hands and knees working the land before Mets home games.

• • •

Though we made strides, we couldn't pull it together on the field in 1994.

Pete Smith, a pitcher who came to us in an off-season trade with Atlanta, was a bust. Muscled out of the terrific Braves rotation, McIlvaine thought he would thrive in a situation where he knew he would get the ball every five days. He miscalculated. Battling tendinitis and a dead arm, Smith went 4–10 with a 5.55 ERA in 1994. He became so ineffective that I dropped him from the rotation in July.

The biggest disappointment of the season was Jeromy Burnitz, the team's first-round pick in 1990, whom we all expected to help ignite the offense.

Jeromy's problem was very simple: he thought he had enough talent to just go out and play the game. He didn't like working, and that frustrated the hell out of me. His defense and base running were lousy. And his hitting wasn't great, either. In about 400 at-bats over two seasons with us, he hit just .241 with 16 homes runs, 53 RBIs, and 111 strikeouts. Jeromy and I had a lot of screaming sessions during his brief time with the Mets. We ended up trading him in November to the Indians in return for some pitching help. He went on to hit 315 home runs during a 14-year career, but I think he could have been a star if he had been willing to work harder.

To a lot of people's surprise, the Expos, the youngest team in the National League with the second-lowest payroll in the majors, held a slim lead over the Braves in the National League East going into the All-Star break.

I think the Mets would have continued to battle all year. And it would have been interesting to see if Montreal could have held on to win the division. But we'll never know what would have happened, because the season came to sudden stop on August 11.

• • •

Like most baseball lifers, I'm fiercely protective of the sport.

That made 1994 awful for me. The strike that wiped out the final two months of the season and the entire postseason made me realize how much the game had changed since I started my professional career.

The 1994 strike disturbed me, but it didn't surprise me. With each passing year, baseball became more about money. My tenure as GM of the Cubs from 1982 to 1987 really opened my eyes to the players association's growing clout. But as a former player, I didn't view the union's activities in purely black-and-white terms. The union had done a lot of important work, like fighting to help former players gain money for pensions and medical needs. But it also pushed for changes that hurt the game. As GM of the Cubs, I never minded paying a player what he was worth as long as he helped us win and put asses in seats. The most disappointing outcome of the union's increased power was that teams found themselves paying huge sums to mediocre players and non-performers.

In the face of skyrocketing payrolls, the owners attempted to institute a salary cap. That's what led to the strike.

These issues are more relevant today than ever.

In a world of long-term, guaranteed contracts, it's difficult to cut non-performers loose. The 2012 trade that brought Adrian Gonzalez, Carl Crawford, and Josh Beckett to the Dodgers was an exception. Stuck with underachieving players, the Red Sox were fortunate to find a team willing to take hundreds of millions of dollars in guaranteed contracts off their hands. The same goes for the Marlins, who traded several of their best players to the Blue Jays after the 2012 season.

• • •

We didn't reach my goal of .500 in 1994, but we came pretty damn close, finishing at 55–58. Despite our losing record and third-place finish, I got some Manager of the Year votes.

In mid-September, the remainder of the season was officially canceled.

John Franco, the Mets' player representative, reacted to the news with a well-scripted line in *The New York Times*: "Hitler couldn't stop the World Series, Vietnam couldn't stop the World Series, other disasters—the earthquake [in 1989]—couldn't stop the World Series. But a couple of owners...they got together and they stopped the World Series."

I didn't have Johnny's flair for the dramatic, but I shared his disgust for what transpired. Baseball took a big hit when greed wiped out the end of the '94 season. Both sides could afford to hold the game hostage for a while. "I don't anticipate many of [the players] going out and getting jobs," I said at the time. "A few of them might have to fire their gardeners and chauffeurs." The same could have been said for the owners.

The strike lingered into the off-season. As spring training neared, the owners announced that, if need be, they'd play the 1995 season with substitute players. I didn't like the idea one bit. Nobody in an on-the-field leadership position did. Dressing up subpar players in major league uniforms would make a mockery of the game. But it wasn't in my nature to give anything but my best effort, so I set out to make my replacement team the best in the league.

The replacement Mets probably wished they had never signed up in the first place, or at least wished they had been picked up by another team. When they reported for spring training, I put them through the same regimens and routines as the regular players. That included four-hour workouts with lots of running.

Any major leaguer who wanted to cross the picket line was welcome to join us. That was their choice. I wouldn't have called them scabs. They would have heard plenty of that from the union and its supporters, however.

Hundreds of former major leaguers and a handful of minor leaguers chose to defy the union by signing on as replacements.

Each replacement player got a $5,000 signing bonus and the chance to make up to $275,000 in salary. More importantly, I suppose, they got to chase a dream, even if that meant incurring the scorn of the real major leaguers whose objectives they were helping to undermine.

We used tryout camps and our scouting department to find about half of the 28 fill-in players who reported to Mets camp in Port St. Lucie. Quite a few got contracts based on word of mouth, without anybody in the organization actually having seen them play.

Even when the 1995 season was close to starting with replacement players, I maintained faith that common sense would prevent that from happening.

"I think, if I'm allowed to think, that after six months they've banged it out as hard as they're going to and they've come at last to recognize the resolve of each other," I told the *Daily News*. "Now quit the bullshit and let's get after it…The players, the owners, Congress, they're all getting antsy."

Five bills aimed at ending the strike had been introduced on Capitol Hill. None of them passed.

The bullshit continued for a few more days. We went to Cleveland for the final exhibition game before the games started to count. A loss in the snow against the Indians dropped our spring training record to 7–17. The next day, we were scheduled to play the major league opener against the Marlins in Joe Robbie Stadium. But shortly after we left the field against the Indians, the owners and players union announced they had reached an accord. Our regular players started reporting the next day for an abbreviated spring training.

Baseball would pay a heavy price for canceling the 1994 World Series and coming to the brink of using replacement players for the 1995 regular season. It took the Mets and other teams years to achieve pre-strike attendance levels. I understand the reasoning of the fans who stayed away. Baseball had let everyone down. The whole ordeal confirmed that greed was badly damaging the game.

24

TEAM CHEMISTRY IS A chicken-or-the-egg kind of deal. Does winning create chemistry? Or does chemistry help teams win? Either way, I'd been searching for the right mix of players on my ballclub since I took over the Mets.

The team that took the field for a belated, post-strike season opener on April 26, 1995, looked a lot different than the team I inherited from Jeff Torborg two years earlier. Todd Hundley, Bobby Bonilla, and Jeff Kent were the only players in the Opening Day lineups in 1993 and 1995. Bret Saberhagen was the only pitcher in the starting rotation at the beginning of 1993 who was still in the rotation when we broke camp in 1995. And only two of those players would still be on the team in August.

My goal of surrounding promising up-and-comers with hard-working veterans was impossible to realize without the help of the Mets front office. But as he went about overhauling the roster, general manager Joe McIlvaine only occasionally took my advice. I did manage to convince him to make an offer to free agent center fielder Brett Butler, who had helped teams in Atlanta, Cleveland, San Francisco, and Los Angeles during his 14-year career. Brett's desire to stay on the West Coast made him reluctant to come to New York. But Sabes, John Franco, and I lobbied him. It cost the Mets about $2 million to

300 THE MOUTH THAT ROARED

sign Brett to a one-year deal, but I was convinced his talent and leadership made it a worthwhile investment.

An important step was getting my younger players to buy into my program. It felt like that might be happening. After I criticized the team for its lackadaisical play at the start of the season, outfielder Ryan Thompson said, "I ain't going to argue with the big guy. If he says we need to hustle more, we better do it."

I'm not really sure why we didn't win more games in 1995. For a while, I blamed our slow start on young players not getting to experience a full spring training. But a couple of months into the season, that started to sound like a weak excuse.

Our poor play prompted another round of housecleaning. It started with the release of relief pitcher Josias Manzanillo, whose ineffectiveness cost us several games early in the season. Bonilla groused that Manzanillo, who immediately got picked up by the Yankees, didn't deserve to take the fall for the team.

Unbeknownst to me, Manzanillo may have sought an artificial advantage while with the Mets. His apparent steroid use earned him a mention in the Mitchell Report, a 2007 report commissioned by Major League Baseball about players' use of performance-enhancing drugs.

• • •

By late July, we were 20 games under .500 and stuck in the National League East cellar.

McIlvaine's next moves bypassed the margins of the team and hit right at its core. He traded Bonilla to the Orioles for Damon Buford and Alex Ochoa. A couple of days later, he dealt Saberhagen to the Rockies for Juan Acevedo and Arnold Gooch. Next to go was Brett Butler, who got traded back to the Dodgers for two minor leaguers.

McIlvaine and co-owners Fred Wilpon and Nelson Doubleday didn't share their thought processes with me, but the logic behind the trades was pretty obvious. Between them, Bonilla, Sabes, and Butler earned almost as much money as the rest of the team they left behind. What's the point of paying that kind of money to players if you're still going to end up in last place?

In three short years, the Mets went from having one of the highest payrolls in baseball to one of the lowest.

Our hopes now rested with what the front office hoped was a younger and hungrier bunch. Based on their inexperience, I didn't have a real feel for a lot of my players. If one of the replacement guys from spring training had snuck into the clubhouse and suited up, I might not have noticed.

The Mets needed to be dismantled, no question about it. It's not hard to tear something down. But I questioned whether McIlvaine had a plan for building it back up.

I let it be known that I didn't think a team could be successful without any veterans in the lineup or pitching rotation. "Managers and coaches can't do it all," I told *The New York Times*. "You have to have help in the clubhouse."

But then something unexpected happened after the All-Star break: we played extremely well.

The kids showed they were hungry. Pitchers Jason Isringhausen and Bill Pulsipher and position players Carl Everett, Edgardo Alfonzo, and Rico Brogna, none older than 25, helped carry us to a 44–31 record after the All-Star break.

In the final week of the season, McIlvaine announced that my coaches and I would return for at least one more season.

Our strong finish raised expectations going forward. That put a lot of pressure on young pitchers who, in my mind, still weren't ready for the major league grind. These guys had been pleasant surprises in 1995, but I didn't think they were ready to carry the hopes of the organization on their shoulders. We needed to keep adding to the team.

The front office disagreed. And that led to my downfall.

• • •

McIlvaine publicly acknowledged that my background as a front office guy was an asset to the team.

Too bad he and Mets ownership didn't take that a step further by valuing my input more.

Maybe the timing of my tenure with the Mets was the problem. The relationship between Wilpon and Doubleday had started to deteriorate. Wilpon began asserting himself as the point man for every Mets decision, while Doubleday slowly faded into the background.

Under adverse conditions, my staff and I had accomplished an awful lot. Now we wanted to take the next step. But Wilpon wouldn't allow us to. Not only didn't he add to the team, but he also allowed our public relations team to tout our three young starting pitchers, Isringhausen, Pulsipher, and Paul Wilson, as the next coming of Tom Seaver, Nolan Ryan, and Jerry Koosman. Behind "Generation K," as the trio was called, fans were led to believe it was going to be 1969 all over again.

That's amazing pressure to put on a trio of pitchers who were barely over the legal drinking age.

At least Isringhausen and Pulsipher paid their dues in the minors and showed initial signs of being successful major league pitchers. Both had been knocking around the team's farm system since 1992. Pulsipher, a left-hander, posted four straight winning records in the minors before getting called up in 1995. Isringhausen, a 44th-round draft pick out of Lewis & Clark Community College in Illinois, came out of nowhere to establish himself as one of the top young prospects in the game.

In 14 starts in 1995, Isringhausen went 9–2 with a 2.81 ERA. Pulsipher went 5–7 with a 3.98 ERA.

Wilson, the first overall pick in the 1994 amateur draft out of Florida State, wasn't even a proven minor leaguer yet. Pegged immediately as a future star, poor Paul went out and lost all seven of his decisions his first year in the lower minor leagues. In 1995, he improved by winning 11 games between Double-A Binghamton and Triple-A Norfolk. He had started to figure things out, the operative word being *started*. Who was the real Paul Wilson—the guy who couldn't win a game in A-ball or the guy who showed promise in Binghamton and Norfolk?

In my opinion, Wilson needed at least another year in the minors to answer that question. And Isringhausen and Pulsipher needed time to grow into the roles the organization expected them to fill.

I tried to state my case to McIlvaine that we needed to acquire a pitcher, but I had a helluva time reaching him.

I liked Joe, but he was an absentee general manager at times. Whenever I called or dropped by his office, his secretary would invariably say, "Joe's out of town, Dallas. Can he get back to you?" At first, I didn't think much of it. As a former GM myself, I knew the job demanded a lot of travel. But it seemed odd that his secretary never gave me more information on his whereabouts. Eventually I started asking where Joe was exactly.

"He's traveling," his gal would say.

"Where is he traveling?"

"I'll need to check on that. I just know he's traveling."

I ended up hearing through the grapevine that he might be spending a lot of time on non-baseball activities in Atlantic City.

Joe's disappearing act obviously created communication problems between us. Back in my Phillies days, the manager and general manager had daily discussions about every facet of the team. Maybe Joe and Fred were having those conversations outside my presence, but I don't think so. It's a shame, really. If we had all met regularly to share ideas about the team, we could have helped ourselves a lot.

• • •

I'll start with my positive memories of the 1996 season.

Todd Hundley, who never really distinguished himself offensively or defensively in his first six seasons with the Mets, had an unbelievable year. I credit bullpen coach Steve Swisher, himself a former major league backstop, for helping Todd revitalize his career. Swish would have Todd report two hours before scheduled workouts to run and talk pitching and catching.

Todd's defense improved a lot, and at the plate, he was off the charts. He hit 41 home runs, the single-season record for a catcher at the time. His previous season-high had been 16 homers. I'd like to think Todd's work ethic, rather than anything artificial, led to his breakout year. But the Mitchell Report quoted a former Mets clubhouse employee as saying he sold Todd steroids in 1996. I never knew Kirk Radomski, so I can't say whether he was telling the truth or not.

All I can speak about is what I personally observed that season. A lot of the younger players on the team couldn't wait to get out of the clubhouse after games, but Todd and outfielder Bernard Gilkey, whose 30 home runs and 117 RBIs in '96 were also career highs, hung around as late into the night as I did. Sometimes I'd stop and have a beer with them and yak about the game. I viewed Todd and Bernard as old-school players who genuinely enjoyed being at the ballpark.

I also got tremendous contributions from leadoff hitter Lance Johnson, who batted .333, stole 50 bases, and led the majors in hits and triples.

The production from these veteran players compensated for Brogna, Everett, and Alfonzo coming back to earth in '96. The young guys were still learning what playing every day in the major leagues was all about.

If only our pitching had been as unhittable as advertised.

• • •

Pulsipher didn't have a chance to live up to the hype. He missed the entire 1996 season with an injury to his left pitching elbow and didn't pitch again in the majors until 1998.

His absence put even more pressure on Isringhausen and Wilson, who hardly looked like stars in the making. After his impressive rookie year, Izzy stumbled badly. By mid-August, he was 5–13 with a 4.85 ERA.

At that point in the season, Wilson was 4–9 with a 6.47 ERA.

Almost every team in the majors hit in 1996. What separated the winning teams from the losing ones was pitching.

A game against the Padres in Monterrey, Mexico, on August 16 summed up our season well. By the end of the sixth inning, we trailed Fernando Valenzuela and the Padres 15–0. Robert Person was the primary victim of the San Diego onslaught, but our bullpen took some licks, too. We rallied in the late innings to make the final score 15–10.

All season long, subpar starters were handing the ball to ineffective relievers. That's not a recipe for success.

On a West Coast road trip, I saw my old minor league teammate, Jerry Kettle, behind the dugout before a game at Dodger Stadium. We chatted for a while. He was the pitching coach at the nearby University of La Verne. Before that, he worked for the Pasadena Police Department. It was good to see him. Suddenly, I had an idea.

"Hey, Jerry, how'd you like to be a bench coach for me?"

"That's a good one, Big D," he said, laughing.

All joking aside, I think Jerry knew enough about the Mets to realize that his current job offered more security.

Because of their potential, Izzy and Wilson had the most to lose from our team's woes. And the front office risked hurting their confidence by insisting they continue pitching. As we fell further in the standings, I decided to make my complaint public.

"These guys don't belong in the big leagues," I told reporters during the West Coast road swing. "That might sound harsh and negative. But what have they done to get here?"

My comment about our pitchers didn't sit well with McIlvaine. "I'm not sure how much that builds their confidence when you criticize them like that," he fired back.

Joe should have known that a strong performance and winning are what really build confidence.

In the following days, I told the press that our current roster wasn't good enough to compete.

That's when McIlvaine and Wilpon decided the team wasn't the problem. I was.

With our record at 59–72, I got fired, along with bench coach Bobby Wine and pitching coach Greg Pavlick. After the season, the rest of my coaching staff got pink slips.

"I'm not blaming Dallas," McIlvaine said in announcing my dismissal. "You have to make choices at times and we're making a choice."

In response, Steve Jacobson of *Newsday* wrote, "Casey Stengel used to say, 'I can make a living telling the truth.' Dallas Green was fired for telling it."

That's kind of the way I saw it, too.

Bobby Valentine, who was managing at Triple-A Norfolk, got my job. Bobby's always been a capable baseball man. He also thinks he knows more about the game than anyone else. I don't know whether he lobbied for my job or not, but I wouldn't have put it past him. He's that kind of guy.

What was Bobby's plan for turning the team around?

"We need a stronger foundation for this team to be good," he said. "I don't think it can all be done in-house."

I couldn't have agreed more.

"I think the wrong reasons were given for my being fired," I told *The (Bergen) Record* a few days after returning home. "I came here at a very difficult time. I've gone through hell and back with strikes, firecrackers, bleaches, replacement players, injuries, lack of performance… I'm always irritated that people don't think I can work with young people. I've done that all my life. I raised four children. I raised 150 players [a year] with the Phillies."

Bobby's 12–19 record at the end of the '96 season showed he couldn't win with the group of players the Mets had, either.

• • •

I don't know if Fred Wilpon would have recognized a baseball player if one walked into the room. But as the team's co-owner, he was certainly entitled to give any order he wanted to McIlvaine. I'm convinced Wilpon told him to let me go. To this day, I'm pissed off about that.

I've never worried about getting fired. In all my stops in baseball, I've focused on accomplishing self-imposed goals. Holding onto my job was always secondary. I got kicked out of Chicago, but I left knowing I had helped boost the Cubs organization. With the Yankees, George Steinbrenner pulled the carpet out from under me so quickly that I couldn't really feel much disappointment.

The Mets situation was different. My coaching staff and I worked our asses off to change the culture of a team that had disgraced Wilpon in the early 1990s. He never gave us credit for our efforts. He didn't seem to care that I was managing a different group of players every season.

After my firing, Isringhausen stated the obvious, telling *The New York Times* he had been one of the biggest disappointments of the year. But he took it a step further. "I feel bad for Dallas," he said. "It's really kind of my fault. I wish I could change it all, but there is nothing I can take back now. He took the fall for us. I'll take everything he said about me into consideration and go home and take a long, good look in the mirror."

Generation K never got off the ground. Izzy went on to have a long and successful career as a closer with Oakland and St. Louis. Wilson and Pulsipher battled injuries that kept them from ever reaching their potential.

I told McIlvaine he was going to be the next to go, and that turned out to be the case. In July 1997, Wilpon canned him. He later became an assistant to the general manager with the Twins and Mariners. I guess he didn't always report to the office there, either.

Joe's successor, Steve Phillips, came in and built a team that allowed Bobby Valentine to say he managed in a World Series.

• • •

After my firing, former Met Dwight Gooden, back in baseball with the Yankees, ripped into me in a single-source story in the *Daily News*: "When you did well, he was your best friend. When you struggled, he was against you. He pointed fingers all the time. When we won, it was us. When we lost, it was them guys."

He went on to criticize me for not backing him during his struggles with substance abuse. According to Dwight, I drank to excess, so I should have had more understanding for someone in his predicament.

That was a cheap shot. Anybody who's known me (or read this book) is aware I like my cocktails. But for Dwight to insinuate that I was an alcoholic hit below the belt.

Dwight's legal troubles continued long after he berated me in the *Daily News*. It's a shame. The guy had Hall of Fame talent, but he blew it. I've tried never to hold grudges against people, and I'm sorry Dwight held one against me. He was just another baseball player who wouldn't look in the mirror. He tried to get by on what he once was, not on what he had become. And he expected the rest of us to do the same.

I was never contacted for that newspaper story. Dwight gave them more than enough material to fill a page. It took me a long time to realize it, but I came to understand that the media doesn't always want both sides of the story. Sometimes they just want the most provocative side.

• • •

Through 1996, I had managed eight years in the big leagues. But only one time did I lead a team from the first day of spring training to the last day of a 162-game season. That was in 1980 when the Phillies won the World Series. The other seven seasons featured strikes or a midseason hiring or firing.

I'm one of a handful of people who have managed both the Yankees and Mets; both jobs provided me with a lot of exciting moments. In the Bronx, I got to put on a historic uniform and manage in a legendary stadium. In Queens, I got to lead a club that had briefly supplanted the Yankees as the best team in New York City. Despite how things worked out with both jobs, I loved my time in New York.

There was just one catch, however: in both situations, I came on board at the wrong time. In 1989, the Yankees were retrenching, and George Steinbrenner's pockets were nowhere near as deep as they had been or would later become. The Mets, meanwhile, were in complete disarray and went from being one of the most to one of the least expensive teams in baseball while I managed them.

While both New York jobs had a prestige factor, neither really presented me with a chance to do the only thing I ever cared about: winning.

25

OUT OF THE FISHBOWL, I returned to the open spaces of our farms in Pennsylvania and Maryland.

The time away from the game allowed me to spend time with Sylvia and our four kids. A lot had happened in our children's lives while we were in New York. John had established himself as a major league scout, Doug started flying commercial jets, Dana became a food services manager, and Kim found work in the biotech industry. I couldn't have been more proud of all of them. They all continue to excel in their chosen fields. Kim, the Little League pioneer, left her research job in the early 2000s to become an engineer and paramedic for the Oakland Fire Department. She also played on the women's national rugby team.

Sylvia and I have worked hard to nurture a close-knit family feeling. Our children are always welcome at our home, and we continue to enjoy spending time with them and our grandkids. Dana had a home built on our Conowingo farm, and she and her husband, Mark, manage the property. Doug now flies for an air cargo company.

After leaving the Mets, I decided home was where I wanted to be.

When newly hired Phillies general manager Ed Wade, a first-time GM, offered me a special assistant's job in 1998, I jumped at the chance. "I've had a good ride in the game," I told Eddie. "All I want to do now is help in any way I can."

I grew up in the Philadelphia area rooting for the Phillies, signed with the Phillies out of the University of Delaware, and spent most of my playing career in the organization. Take the 14 years I worked for the team and you can understand why the Phillies were in my blood.

At the age of 63, I was really excited to come back.

The Phillies also had Paul Owens as a special assistant. Lee Elia's promotion from scout to director of minor league instruction made it start to feel a little like 1980 again.

But it wasn't 1980.

In the four years since their last World Series appearance in 1993, the Phillies hadn't come within 20 games of first place.

In the coming years, we'd lose more than just games. One by one, many of my closest friends in the organization passed away.

My first season back in Philadelphia was the first without Richie Ashburn in the broadcast booth. For 35 years, he called Phillies games on radio and television, first with Bill Campbell and Byrum Saam and then with Harry Kalas. Before his broadcasting career, he spent all but three seasons of his Hall of Fame playing career with the Phillies. Unfortunately, I never got to call Whitey a teammate. Richie died of a heart attack in September 1997. I joined his processional in Fairmount Park in Philadelphia. One fan left his transistor radio at a makeshift memorial for Whitey.

• • •

I looked forward to entering a new phase of my career outside the glare of the spotlight.

Leave it to Bobby Valentine to weigh in with his spin on why I took the position with the Phillies. Referencing a scouting job I took with the Mets a couple of years before becoming their manager, he said, "Was that the [same] job he had here when he got Jeff Torborg fired?"

Good for Bobby. It was a nice quip by a guy who specialized in rubbing people the wrong way. Two years later, he actually fooled people into thinking he was a great manager by leading the Mets to the National League pennant. To me, however, Bobby will always be the guy who dressed up in a Groucho Marx disguise and snuck back into the dugout after being ejected from a game in 1999. The guy has always been a phony.

His first year as Red Sox manager in 2012 further exposed the real Bobby V. He couldn't handle the adversity of losing some players to injury. Hell, he couldn't even show up to the ballpark on time, a tardiness habit I understand he developed while blowing smoke as a commentator at ESPN.

Back to his cheap shot: Bobby's insinuation that I had designs on managing the Phillies again had no basis in reality. I knew in my heart that I didn't want to be a general manager or field manager anymore. And I told Eddie and team president David Montgomery as much. I just wanted to work for the Phillies again. At the time I took the job, Terry Francona was in his second season managing the team. I never ended up replacing Francona or any of the other managers who followed him. Ironically, Bobby was the one who years later took Francona's job in Boston. Valentine lasted just one season. After the Red Sox imploded, Bobby also got fired.

• • •

The 1998 season was an unforgettable, and ultimately, infamous one. According to *The New York Times*, eight of the 13 players who hit 40 or more home runs in 1998, including Mark McGwire and Sammy Sosa, are now suspected of having taken performance-enhancing drugs.

That was hard for me to accept. I always trusted baseball players were above doing anything detrimental to their well-being and the integrity of the game.

In my playing days, we had greenies and red juice, the type of energy boosters you can find at gas stations and convenience stores these days. I never thought they had much of an effect on me. Would players of my era have been tempted to take steroids if they had been available? I can't answer that question, but I'd like to think that most of us would have resisted the temptation.

Steroids had clearly become a part of the game before I even recognized it. I can't help but wonder now whether some of the guys I managed injected themselves with drugs.

It wasn't until McGwire and Sosa started bashing home runs at an unrealistically high rate that I really put two and two together. Even then, the whole affair was high on speculation and low on proof. That's because players were adhering to the code of the clubhouse, which says you're not supposed to talk about what teammates do, say, or ingest in private.

As GM of the Cubs, I pushed for drug testing in the early 1980s. At that time, it seemed cocaine was the drug taking over the game. I got so concerned about it that I summoned several players to my office and confronted them about whether they were using the drug. Cocaine had the potential to destroy lives and careers, but it never was going to fundamentally change how the game was played.

I guess I was naïve about steroids and the other stuff. We all were.

• • •

In 2000, we celebrated the 20th anniversary of the 1980 World Series team.

Most of the team reunited for the occasion. In an interview with the *(Allentown) Morning Call*, former catcher Bob Boone pretty well summed up the complicated relationship I had with the team that year. "We hated him," Boone said. "He was driving us. I don't know if it was a unique approach, but it was a relationship that worked. I don't know if *hate* is the right word, but that's irrelevant, because it worked."

Six years later when I earned a spot on the Phillies Wall of Fame, Booney weighed in again. Asked if any players still felt ill will about our clashes in 1980, he said, "It took a lot of time. Probably, he gets a few more Christmas cards now."

As far as I could tell, the only guy on the 1980 team who held a real grudge against me was Ron Reed. Ronnie and I had almost come to blows during a doubleheader in Pittsburgh that season. After that, Ronnie got pissed off at me for not using him out of the bullpen as much as he would have liked. To me, Ronnie showed his true colors by declining to take part in the World Series parade after our Game 6 victory over Kansas City. How could a guy turn down the chance to be with his teammates on such a special day? When I see him, we're cordial to each other. But I know he doesn't think very highly of me.

Most of the other fences have been mended.

My stormy relationship with Greg Luzinski typified the day-in, day-out battles of the 1980 season. I called Bull out for underachieving and not watching his weight and periodically benched him when I thought rookie Lonnie Smith could do a better job for us. I think Bull was hurt by my actions more than he was angry with me.

I had no qualms about highly recommending Bull for a public relations job he started with the Phillies in 2004. Since then, I've spent a lot of time with him in spring training. I admire how cordial he is with sponsors and fans. He's a friendly person who likes to share his experiences in baseball. He's become a huge part of the Phillies family.

Pete Rose, the heart and soul of the '80 team, is notably absent at team-sponsored alumni events. His lifetime ban from baseball prevents him from making official appearances at major league ballparks. I still see Pete from time to time, however. He hasn't changed a bit, and I mean that in the best way possible.

Pete had a lot of challenges off the field. Very few ever became public. Though he led a reckless life, Pete was almost always the first of my players to show up at the ballpark. And when he got there, his mind was on baseball and nothing else; he played with more gusto and grit than anybody I ever saw.

Dating back to the 1919 Black Sox scandal, gambling on the game has been considered the worst possible sin for a player, or in Pete's case, a manager. But he never took steroids or human-growth hormones, and he was the epitome of a guy who played the game the right way.

I respect Pete, but I also respect baseball. I'm torn over the question of whether he should go into the Hall of Fame. I've talked to many former greats who are adamantly opposed to Pete's enshrinement. They feel he committed an unforgiveable sin. I understand that point of view, but if it were up to me, he'd be in the Hall of Fame.

• • •

At the time of the 20th anniversary celebration, the Phillies were stuck in last place, en route to their seventh straight losing season. The following year, Larry Bowa replaced Francona as Phillies manager. Bowa's fiery nature contrasted sharply with Francona's laid-back demeanor.

I sat in on all the interviews of prospective managerial candidates. Everyone in the room knew Bo had tremendous passion for the game. His first managing stint with the Padres in the late 1980s hadn't gone well, but he had since established himself as an outstanding third-base coach and baseball man for several teams, including the Phillies.

Mindful of his idiosyncrasies, which included body language that betrayed his emotions a little too much, I still felt he was an ideal fit for the Phillies. As a player, he wasn't endowed with a lot of natural talent. He willed himself into becoming a ballplayer by outworking everybody else. It served to reason that his work ethic might rub off on his players. Bowa fought me like hell when I first took over the Phillies. Seeing the game through the eyes of a manager, I think he got a much better understanding of what I went through with the '80 team.

In his first year on the job, the Phillies finished in second place, just two games behind the division-winning Braves.

Bowa eventually became his own worst enemy. He often wore a pained expression on his face in the dugout. The TV cameras loved him for that. But after a while, people started wondering about his relationship with his team.

Like me, he clashed with some of his players, most notably third baseman Scott Rolen, whom he took to task for not hitting in the clutch. I decided to chime in when I concluded Rolen lacked the drive to succeed: "Scotty's satisfied with being a so-so player. I think he can be greater, but his personality won't let him."

In the field, I thought Scotty ranked up there with Brooks Robinson and Mike Schmidt defensively. But I felt he wasn't fulfilling his potential as a hitter. I didn't dislike Scotty. I just hoped he could give us more. But instead, he wanted more from us. He complained that management wasn't spending enough money to put a winning team on the field.

My job wasn't to call out the supposed best players on the team, but if asked, I had no problem sharing my opinion. Scotty was never content in Philadelphia. He had productive seasons for us in 2000 and 2001. His two home runs against the Braves in the first game back after the 9/11 terrorist attacks gave fans at the Vet a final positive memory of him. But when it became clear he had no intention of re-signing with Philadelphia after the '02 season, Eddie traded him to the Cardinals. He's been booed in Philadelphia ever since.

• • •

As young baseball executives, Paul Owens and I watched the last game played at Connie Mack Stadium in 1970. That place held a lot of special memories for both of us. I played there as Pope was rising through the ranks of the Phillies front office. But Veterans Stadium, which opened in April 1971, ended up being the ballpark where we enjoyed our greatest successes. To that point, it was the only stadium where the Phillies had won a world championship.

At the end of the 2003 season, Philadelphia geared up for another changing of the guard as the Vet, considered a state-of-the-art facility in the early 1970s, awaited implosion. Citizens Bank Park, a cozy baseball-only stadium, was in line to host Opening Day in 2004.

On September 28, 2003, I drove in from my Maryland farm to watch the last nine innings ever played at the stadium on the corner of Broad and Pattison. After the Sunday afternoon game against the Braves, several dozen former Phillies were scheduled to gather on the field for a farewell ceremony. We all hoped Pope would be out there among us, but we knew that was far from guaranteed. He had been battling a chronic respiratory illness for many months, and it appeared he didn't have much time left.

As the game entered the late innings, Pope's son escorted him into the stadium. Before disease sapped all his strength, Pope was the most hearty and vibrant man I knew. It was difficult to see him in such a weakened state, sitting in a wheelchair. But his presence there that day showed he was a fighter—and a Phillie—to the end.

Longtime Phillies public relations director Larry Shenk did a wonderful job putting together the ceremony, which kicked off with Pope riding onto the field in a golf cart. Ed Wade and I helped him off the cart so he could stand on the field one last time.

Pete Rose wasn't permitted to attend the event because of his permanent ban from official major league events. To honor Pete, I laid his No. 14 jersey over the first-base bag.

"I'm very, very proud of what we accomplished," I told the fans, before reminding them of how special they were to me. "I've been in baseball for 45 years, in Chicago and New York, but nobody, *nobody* will touch the Philadelphia Phillies fans. We love you!"

The ceremony concluded with Tug McGraw reenacting his celebration on the mound after striking out Willie Wilson of the Royals to end the 1980 World Series. Tugger, too, was battling health problems; six months earlier, he had a brain tumor removed. When he threw his arms in the air just as he did that October night in 1980, the fans went wild. Before we left the field, I posed for a picture with Pope and Tugger.

After the ceremony, I sat with Pope in the Vet's executive dining room. I wish I could say it was like old times, but it wasn't. Over the course of our 47-year friendship, we talked a lot of baseball and had a lot of laughs. Now, he was a 79-year-old man using his last reserves of energy to conceal the horrible pain we all knew he was experiencing.

By the time Citizens Bank Park opened in April 2004, Pope and Tugger weren't with us anymore.

• • •

Larry Bowa's hiring before the 2001 season infused life into the team. In his first year on the job, he won the Manager of the Year Award for bringing the Phillies to within a couple games of first place. But despite his best efforts, Bowa couldn't get his teams over the hump. He led the Phillies to winning seasons in three of his four years in the dugout but could never get them above second place or into the playoffs as a wild-card team. With two games left in the 2004 season—which was supposed to be the year a team other than the Braves finally won the National League East—he was fired.

The following spring training I expressed my disappointment with the team's performance. "This team has been together for a good amount of time now," I told the *Philadelphia Inquirer*. "It's time it played up to its capabilities. It's time for them to look in the mirror and recognize that they're the ones who have to perform. It's not the manager that has to perform. They can blame Larry Bowa for last year, but now there's no one to blame. I think they're smart enough to realize that the onus is on them. Quit barking and whining. Stop worrying about the ballpark, the manager, and the pitching coach, and play ball. And win."

Charlie Manuel, who had managed Cleveland to a division title in 2001, took over for Bo. The fans who flocked to the new stadium were starting to get restless. It had been more than a decade since the team made the playoffs and 25 years since we won the championship.

Citizens Bank Park is very much a hitter's park. In our first season in the stadium, we hit the second-most home runs in the National League, paced by Jim Thome's 42 blasts. Thome was one of several players the Phillies had splurged on a couple of years earlier to show the team's commitment to moving in the right direction. It wasn't a hard sell to get a slugger to sign with us. But bringing elite pitchers to Philadelphia was a more difficult task. Who would want to pitch in a park where some routine fly balls left the ballpark? In 2004, our pitchers gave up the second-most homers in the league.

Charlie's first year on the job brought another second-place finish and no playoff appearance. The 2005 Phillies, featuring blossoming stars Ryan Howard, Chase Utley, and Jimmy Rollins, showed a lot of promise, however.

• • •

The mouth could still roar.

During a rough patch for the Phillies in 2006, I offered up a critique of Charlie to Philadelphia radio talk show host Howard Eskin. I said every manager chooses how he wants to run his team and then lives with the results of those choices. I said my predecessor, Danny Ozark, chose to handle his players one way, and I opted to approach the job differently.

It was mild by my standards, innocuous, even. But Charlie, who was getting beat up in the press a lot in those days, viewed my words as a slap against *his* way of doing things. I was on the field before a June game when Charlie confronted me.

"I don't want you on my goddamn field!" he growled at me.

Most people didn't see this side of Charlie, whom the press had painted as a good-natured hillbilly kind of guy. I was taken aback.

"I'll get on the goddamn field anytime I want to, Charlie!" I responded.

It got heated. If a couple of players hadn't wandered over to see what was going on, I'm not sure what would have happened. Charlie was really mad.

The headline of a June 2006 column by Stan Hochman for the *Philadelphia Daily News* threw more fuel on the fire. It asked, "Is it Dallas Green Time Again?" The column, written during a stretch when the Phillies lost 13 of 15 games, itself posed a couple more questions: "Is it time for déjà vu all over again? Is it time for Green and his big mouth and his throwback ideas about how the game should be played to be turned loose on this stumblin' bumblin' fumblin' ballclub?"

I threw cold water on that idea, citing my advanced age and lack of interest in taking someone else's job.

Fortunately, the Phillies played winning baseball down the stretch and salvaged another second-place finish.

General manager Pat Gillick asked me to visit with Charlie during the off-season to smooth things over. At our meeting, I clarified the meaning of what I said and made it clear I wasn't after his job. We shook hands and have been on good terms ever since.

• • •

My first year back in Philadelphia in 1998, we drafted Pat Burrell with the first overall pick of the draft. After reaching the majors in 2000, he played very erratically. Every productive season was seemingly followed by a poor one. It bothered me that a player with such talent wasn't fulfilling his potential. And I told him that when we hung out together in spring training. Then I told the world.

"It's time for Pat to look in the mirror," I told the *Philadelphia Inquirer.* "He's got to become a baseball player and want to be a contributor and want to be the Pat Burrell that we all anticipated he was going to be when we signed him as a kid. He's 30 years old. Damn, time is slipping by here."

I think he took it to heart. Pat never became the superstar we thought he might be, but he and the rest of the team took an important step in 2007.

No longer satisfied with second-place finishes, they went on a memorable run in the final two and a half weeks of the season to catch the Mets and win the National League East. It was 1964 in reverse, with Philadelphia coming out on top this time. The Phillies ran into an even hotter Rockies team in the League Division Series, but simply making the postseason was a major breakthrough. A season after Howard won National League MVP in 2006, Rollins kept the award in the Phillies family.

We all know what happened the next year. Following another late-season comeback to win the division, the Phillies felt like a team that was ready to make a deep postseason run. From my perch, I saw even further growth on the field and in the clubhouse. The team played with a pride and character that I believe is an essential part of winning. Charlie deserves a lot of credit for engineering that. Cole Hamels emerged as an ace who could win in the playoffs. Brad Lidge was perfect as a closer. And our lineup clicked.

After beating the Milwaukee Brewers and Dodgers to get to the World Series, we took out a feisty Tampa Bay Rays team to celebrate our first championship in 28 years. That was a wonderful season, and I was ecstatic to see the organization capture another title. In the years since 1980, a generation of young Phillies fans had grown into adulthood without seeing the team go all the way. To them, the 2008 championship must have felt like a first.

The revenue generated by ticket and merchandise sales in 2008 helped us keep building the team. In a complete reversal of the past, the Phillies started freeing up money to sign top free agents and keep existing players. In another break with the past, stars like Roy Halladay and Cliff Lee, undeterred by the dimensions of Citizens Bank Park, actually wanted to come and play in Philadelphia.

There have been two no-hitters in postseason history—Don Larsen's perfect game for the Yankees in the 1956 World Series and Roy Halladay's no-hitter against the Reds in the 2010 League Division Series. I have to think I'm one of the only people who attended both.

From 2007 to 2011, the Phillies won five straight National League East titles.

Winning does wonders for a guy's reputation.

A few years after my dust-up with Charlie, Hochman wrote, "Yo, I'm here to tell you that Charlie Manuel is the best Phillies manager in the last 50 years. Maybe forever! Been here six years, in the playoffs the last four, in the World Series twice. Won it once."

Stan ranked Gene Mauch, who managed me for five seasons, as the second-best skipper in Phillies history. Of me, he wrote, "Green's way of creating team unity was to get everybody mad at him! That might work, but not for the long haul."

26

ON THE MORNING OF SEPTEMBER 11, 2001, *hijacked airliners slammed into the World Trade Center and the Pentagon, part of a coordinated terrorist attack on the United States that claimed nearly 3,000 lives.*

Several hours earlier, 90 miles northeast of the Pentagon, John and Roxanna Green welcomed their second child into the world, a girl they named Christina-Taylor.

The first photo of Christina-Taylor, snapped in the hospital shortly after her birth, was later featured in a book about children born on that tragic day. She and the other 9/11 babies symbolized the notion that renewal and hope will ultimately triumph over destruction and hate.

Christina-Taylor embodied that spirit.

Her dad, John, a former professional baseball player, worked as a scout for the Baltimore Orioles. Her mom, Roxanna, stayed home to care for her and her older brother, Dallas, who was named after her paternal grandfather, George Dallas Green.

Christina, as she became known to friends, gravitated to baseball. Her father had a strong connection to the game, but so did her grandfather, a lifelong baseball man who managed a World Series–winning team in 1980.

As a nine-year-old, Christina-Taylor was the only girl on her Little League baseball team in Tucson, Arizona, where her family relocated after her father took a scouting job with the Los Angeles Dodgers.

Equally comfortable on the ballfield and in the classroom, she brought home perfect grades and glowing assessments from her teachers. For a child her age, she showed an unusual interest in current affairs and the workings of government. Always seeking to get involved, she sat on her elementary school's student council as a third grader.

On January 8, 2011, Christina-Taylor was offered an opportunity to see democracy in action. An adult neighbor invited her to a Saturday morning meet-and-greet with an Arizona congresswoman who was making the rounds in her home district. They'd make a day of it, the neighbor told Roxanna, with lunch and manicures afterward.

On a crisp and clear Tucson morning, Christina-Taylor joined dozens of other constituents of U.S. Rep. Gabrielle Giffords in the parking lot of a Safeway grocery store. She planned to say hello to Giffords and possibly ask a question if she could think of a good one.

As Christina-Taylor waited in line, a young man approached the group. He had no intention of asking a question, however. He was there to incite terror.

Over the next 16 seconds, he fired 31 shots from a semi-automatic pistol, including one to the head of Giffords, who miraculously survived her injuries.

Six people were killed in the rampage, including Christina-Taylor. The neighbor who brought her to the event was injured trying to shield her from the gunfire.

Born on a day that spurred myriad conversations about the world we live in, killed on a day that revived some of those conversations, Christina-Taylor Green became a tragic symbol of lost life, innocence, and infinite potential.

But for her grandfather, his eyes hidden by dark sunglasses at a press conference a month after the incident, she was and will always be the little girl he called Princess.

• • •

On the morning the planes hit the World Trade Center, Sylvia and I were driving back from Christiana Hospital in Wilmington to our

Maryland farm. We had just come from seeing our beautiful new granddaughter, Christina-Taylor, for the first time. We heard about the terrorist attacks on the car radio. Feeling like we needed to see the unfolding events with our own eyes, I stopped at a nearby shopping center. At a Radio Shack store, we stood in front of a television and watched the news in disbelief.

A little less than 10 years later, Sylvia and I were at our vacation home in Providenciales, an island in the Turks and Caicos, looking forward to a lazy Saturday. We don't normally watch much TV while we're on the island, but we happened to turn the set on that morning. One of the all-news channels was reporting that Arizona congresswoman Gabrielle Giffords and several others had been shot at a public event on the northwest side of Tucson, Arizona. Among the victims was a young girl. The breaking news would have gotten anybody's attention, but because our son, his wife, and their two children lived in Tucson, it definitely grabbed ours.

John and his family lived on the opposite side of Tucson, but we still felt like we should check in with him. Sylvia called his cell phone, but it went to voice mail. We continued watching the coverage and waited to hear back from him. A short time later, John called. The little girl being talked about on the news was our granddaughter Christina-Taylor.

It's hard to describe the emotions I felt at that moment. Just two weeks earlier, John and his family had spent Christmas with us in Providenciales. It was a wonderful time. The images of Christina-Taylor splashing in the Caribbean Sea were still fresh in my mind.

I was numb and screaming mad.

Sylvia and I made preparations to fly to Arizona. The next day, authorities released the names of the victims. Giffords, the target of the shooter, was clinging to life after being shot in the head at point-blank range. Christina-Taylor was the youngest of the six people killed in the massacre. The situation might have been even worse if bystanders hadn't wrestled the gunman to the ground.

In my professional life, I've always enjoyed the challenge of fixing problems on a baseball field. Sometimes I succeeded, and other times I fell short. But I always tried. In the wake of this tragedy, I realized there was nothing I could do to fix what happened. As much as Sylvia and I hurt (and continue to hurt), we realized our son and daughter-in-law were the ones coping with the kind of immeasurable pain that can only come from losing a child. I couldn't fix that. The only thing I could do was be there for my son and his family. In the days following Christina-Taylor's death, that meant sitting and crying with them.

Her obituary read, "Our beloved Christina-Taylor was taken from us on January 8, 2011. There are no words to express how much she will be missed."

And there are still no words to adequately describe my feelings about what happened. Sylvia and I had no idea that such an extremely personal tragedy would affect an entire nation.

Though she and I have different opinions about President Barack Obama, I'll say this about the president: the speech he gave in Tucson the week following the shooting nailed a lot of the emotions I was feeling at the time. His words about Christina-Taylor in particular moved me profoundly.

> *And I believe that, for all our imperfections, we are full of decency and goodness, and that the forces that divide us are not as strong as those that unite us. That's what I believe, in part because that's what a child like Christina-Taylor believed...She saw public service as something exciting and hopeful. She was off to meet her congresswoman, someone she was sure was good and important and might be a role model. She saw all this through the eyes of a child, undimmed by the cynicism or vitriol that we adults all too*

often just take for granted. I want us to live up to her expectations.
I want our democracy to be as good as Christina-Taylor imagined
it. I want America to be as good as she imagined it. All of us, we
should do everything we can to make sure this country lives up to
our children's expectations.

It provided me with some comfort to know that our loss was felt deeply by so many Americans. Sylvia and I got hundreds of cards from friends, many of them from the baseball world.

I spoke to the media when I got to Phillies spring training in Clearwater. I apologized to the reporters for not returning their calls. They knew that wasn't my style. But for the first time in my life, really, I didn't have the words to express what I was feeling.

During the press conference, I addressed the fact that the gunman had been able to purchase a semi-automatic weapon that held 33 bullets. "That doesn't make sense to me," I said. "I guess I didn't think about that until this happened. What other reason is there to have these guns except to kill people?"

I've been around guns my whole life. My father and grandfather took me hunting as a kid, and it remains a favorite pastime of mine. But I don't have a Glock, an assault rifle, or any of the other high-powered firearms frequently used in mass killings. I don't understand why these weapons continue to be sold.

I can't help but think of the Tucson shooting when I hear about other shooting tragedies, like the ones at a Connecticut elementary school and a crowded Colorado movie theater in 2012. We don't seem to be getting any better at preventing that kind of tragedy.

I'm an eye-for-an-eye kind of guy. It angered me that some lawyers tried to say the guy who killed my granddaughter was not competent to stand trial. He was competent when he bought the gun, and he was competent when he squeezed off the rounds that killed my granddaughter and the others.

I've honored my son and daughter-in-law's wishes by not mentioning the gunman by name. His was an attention-seeking act. And we refuse to give him any more attention than he's already received. The seven life sentences he received in 2012 guarantees he'll never see the light of day again.

As hard as it was, I've tried to put aside my anger in favor of celebrating the life of a special child.

Christina-Taylor loved baseball. She had played Little League for two years. Her goal was to become the first female to play in the major leagues.

About a month after his sister's death, Little D returned to his Little League team. It was difficult for him, because he associated baseball with Christina-Taylor. Now, for the first time, he was alone in the back seat of his father's car, an 11-year-old kid still trying to understand what happened to his sister.

John called me to tell me all about Little D's first game back, played on a field that has since been dedicated to Christina-Taylor's memory. Little D missed the first ground ball hit his way. It took a bad hop and smacked him right in the face. Anyone who's ever taken a ball to the kisser knows how much that can sting. But he shook it off and prepared himself for the next play. "He fielded the next four balls cleanly and threw them to first," John told me. "I was proud of him, Dad."

Life can have some pretty bad hops, too. Terrible ones, in fact. But I guess you find a way to endure the sting and soldier on. Following an injury in 1959, my arm never fully healed, but I kept on pitching. After losing my granddaughter, my heart will never fully heal, but I'll go on.

It helped me to get back to work in the Phillies front office. As I said at the time, "You sink yourself into the work and you don't see a little girl with a hole in her chest as much."

On our next trip to Providenciales the following winter, I took time to compile some of my most cherished memories of Christina-Taylor in one place. The photos, poems, and newspaper clippings in the resulting scrapbook help remind me what a special little girl she was.

A year after the shooting, Roxanna came out with a book titled *As Good As She Imagined*, the words the president used in his speech when talking about Christina-Taylor. Putting their thoughts into words helped her and my son with the grieving process.

On September 11, 2012, John and Roxanna were honored at the new 9/11 memorial in New York City. Roxanna has been active in running a foundation named after Christina-Taylor. John has found solace in his work as a scout for the Dodgers.

As my daughter-in-law told the *Arizona Republic*, "Losing a child really is the worst thing that could ever happen to you. People say that all the time, but when it happens, it really is the worst thing that could happen to you."

No mother and father should have to go through what they did.

As I said when I addressed the media a month after her passing, "We just miss the hell out of her. I'm supposed to be a tough sucker, but I'm not very tough when it comes to this."

I still tear up sometimes when I think of her or see something that reminds me of her. During the 2012 Little League World Series in Williamsport, she was honored in the game program along with a young fireman who lost his life on 9/11. Over in the Little League Museum, I saw a display showing Christina-Taylor in her baseball uniform.

I can only hope our little Princess inspired other little girls to pick up a baseball mitt, run for student council, or simply dream big.

27

WITHIN THESE PAGES, I'VE SHARED a lot of reflections on my six decades in baseball. At the age of 78, most of my career is behind me now. But I still enjoy working with the Phillies front office to help make the organization a winning one. My love of competition and camaraderie of the game fuel me. In my work for the team, I share thoughts on draft prospects, farmhands, and current major leaguers. But away from the executive offices, I think about the game in general.

Obviously, baseball has changed a lot since I signed a professional contract in 1955. In cities like Philadelphia, where the Phillies have established themselves as a consistent winner, I'd say it's changed for the better. In smaller markets like Pittsburgh, where the once-proud Pirates have fallen on hard times, I'd say it's changed for the worse. There are exceptions to every rule, but I think it's well-documented that winning puts rear ends in seats and generates excitement, not to mention revenue. It's fun for fans to watch winning baseball and feel pride in their team. The Phillies have sold out Citizens Bank Park almost every game for the past three seasons, but if the team hadn't re-signed Cole Hamels in 2012 or were to part with other stars, there'd be so much uproar we wouldn't be able to open the gates in 2013. The more the fans support you, the easier it is to continue to put a quality product on the field.

By far my biggest complaint about the game is the oversized role of player agents. They, more than anybody, run the sport now. Every year, we see certain players sign contracts that defy logic. Thanks to the late Marvin Miller and his efforts on behalf of the players association, it's become commonplace for .250 hitters and 10-game winners to secure guaranteed long-term contracts that make them millionaires many times over. They are not necessarily paid for their performance, but rather for their years of major league service.

The rise of the agents has even affected how the game is played. There's no financial incentive for players to master game-situation baseball. Making an out to advance a runner doesn't help a player's personal statistics. When negotiating a contract, it's home runs and RBIs and OPS that count. What's worse is when a draft pick becomes a multimillionaire before even playing a day in the minors, much less the big leagues.

As I said earlier, in my playing days, the pendulum was totally on ownership's side. But over the years, it's swung completely in the other direction. I partly fault former Major League Baseball commissioner Bowie Kuhn for allowing that to happen. I liked Bowie, but he and his lawyers weren't tough enough to stand up to the union in the late 1970s and early 1980s. And baseball kept shooting itself in the foot by agreeing to rules that hampered teams' ability to improve themselves.

The worst job in baseball these days is general manager. He has no autonomy. Any GM who wants to make a deal has to knock on his owner's door and ask for the money. The smaller-market teams don't have the money, which forces them to get creative. Every now and again, an Oakland or a Tampa Bay will defy the odds by winning without high-priced players. But that's based at least partly on these teams acquiring top prospects for high-priced veterans. Some of those prospects eventually become too expensive for these teams to retain. Then the cycle begins again.

Marvin always maintained that teams couldn't spend money they didn't have. He squeezed us, and we squeezed back. We tried the collusion business in the 1980s, but it didn't work. The union kept getting stronger, and we kept making concessions that hampered teams' abilities to improve themselves. Now, we're where we are today. I'd hate to see Marvin go into the Hall of Fame, as some people suggest he might, but I'll be the first to admit he had a major impact on the game.

Somehow we have to bring this situation under control. Otherwise, agents are going to put teams out of business. If I were commissioner, I'd try to get agents to agree to legal and reasonable controls that would lead to the betterment of the game. I realize the idea of a salary cap is farfetched, however. You never hear agents talk about what's best for the game. They only care about what's best for their clients, and unfortunately, owners and general managers fall into the trap of making free agent signings they know hurt the game.

Paul Owens and I always looked back nostalgically on baseball in the 1970s. We considered it the best era in the game's history. The union had enough clout to prevent players from being treated like dirt, but it had yet to become all-powerful. And from a management standpoint, there were fewer complications. Team owners were more apt to rubber stamp decisions made by general managers. As a result, teams like the Reds, the Dodgers, and the Phillies remained intact for long periods of time. That created an ideal situation for fans who got to watch winning baseball *and* players they'd gotten to know over the span of many years.

There's plenty of blame to go around, but I hold the players union most responsible for the performance-enhancing drug crisis that consumed baseball in the 1990s. For years, players had taken pills to keep their motors running during a long season. When I came to the Cubs in 1981, I had an inkling we might soon have a more significant problem on our hands. Some Olympic athletes were starting to inject themselves with steroids or growth hormones. The last thing we needed was baseball players with souped-up engines. For the sake of the integrity of the game, I felt in the early 1980s that Major League Baseball should institute drug testing. The union didn't want to discuss the issue, however. Every time we'd bring it up, they'd shut us down. A couple of decades and a tainted era later, the union got called on the carpet. Congress subpoenaed several players to testify about their use of steroids. And the Mitchell Report concluded that baseball owners shared responsibility for the problem by turning a blind eye to what was happening. But I'd argue it was the union that prevented baseball from attacking the problem earlier.

Now that we hopefully have that problem under control, I think there are measures we can take to improve the game. I'd start with the quality of the umpiring. Incorrect calls have always been a part of the game, because umpires are human beings, and human beings aren't perfect. But it seems umps these days are blowing more calls than ever before. There needs to be more accountability. If that means expanding replay review of questionable calls in the postseason, when every play has immense importance, then I'm all for it. I also would strongly support a grading system for umpires. Those who don't get passing grades should be demoted to the minors. That's what happens to players, after all. I have a lot of respect for most umpires and have enjoyed friendships with some, but it's clear we need to hold them more accountable. I'm proud of the umpires who have had the courage to admit making mistakes in crucial situations.

At its core, baseball remains a great sport. And I still see a lot of guys who play the game with every ounce of their being. To me, Chase Utley, Cole Hamels, Jimmy Rollins, and Roy Halladay epitomize what it means to be a "gamer."

I've seen players with vast talent fail to become successful major leaguers, because they don't have the right work ethic. Bryce Harper of the Washington Nationals reminds me of Pete Rose when Pete first broke into the majors. Like Pete, Harper runs to first base on ball four and oozes a certain confidence through his body language. My manager, Gene Mauch, hated Pete and called him every name in the book during games. But Pete didn't care. He had an inner strength you can't teach. Bryce might be one of those guys, too. We'll see, I guess.

Some things don't change. High schools and colleges still don't train guys to be major league players; the minor leagues do. The tendency these days is to rush touted prospects up to the majors. The reason for that is obvious: organizations spend millions of dollars just to sign their top draft picks, and they want to see an immediate return on their investments. That can be the worst thing for a player. For every Harper, Mike Trout, and Stephen Strasburg, there are dozens of other players who need more time to grow into major leaguers. If you train a guy right and watch him progress steadily, you're going to have a better player over the long haul.

• • •

My name was brought up a lot when the Cubs hired former Red Sox general manager Theo Epstein as team president before the 2012 season. I guess my motto, "Building a New Tradition," applied to what Theo is hoping to accomplish.

We'll see what happens now. Some of the young turks who populate team offices may not be as schooled in the game of baseball as the executives of my era. We had scouting and playing backgrounds and knew how to evaluate talent out in the field. Many general managers today only know how to evaluate talent in front of a computer.

I always liked to conduct my trading business face to face. I felt it was a lot easier for someone to say "no" to you over the phone. When you're looking someone in the eye, you get a better read on their thoughts and interest level, or lack thereof. The young GMs go to meetings and sit across a table from each other, staring into their phones. Instead of going outside the room and talking it out, they negotiate deals by text message.

They don't say much in public, either, which is ironic considering there are a lot more media outlets to spout off to these days. Part of that is because general managers don't want to get into pissing matches with their players. They stay tight-lipped out of deference to team owners and the fear of being fired. The players, in turn, are reluctant to make waves when they're pocketing $20 million a year. That leaves the fans in a different position, too. In the '80s, they could turn on their radio and hear Larry Bowa blasting me for being such a mean guy, or they could read the papers and hear my beefs. Nowadays, if a fan wants to hear an opinion, he has to get it from a talk show host who is far removed from what's really going on in the clubhouse.

There are hardly any mouths that roar.

• • •

I'm gearing up for my 55th spring training, my 42nd in Clearwater, Florida. I have a lot of good memories of time spent at Phillies camp. I've seen a lot of baseball and forged a lot of friendships there.

As I focus on the present, I also think about the past.

It's where I learned Lee Elia was a damn good cook. At the Island House, our spring training hangout in Clearwater, the owner would chase all the other customers off around midnight and let our gang stick around a while longer. With the doors shut and the blinds drawn, we'd play liar's poker into the wee hours of the morning. On one particular night in the late 1970s, the session broke up at about 4:00 AM. As minor league director, I was due to report to work in a few hours. Paul Owens had a less strenuous day planned, but he wanted to be at least somewhat sober when he got to the spring training complex.

"Let's go to Elia's house and get dinner," I suggested.

We went to his house and banged on the door. The lights in the house switched on, and Lee came to the door in a robe. After muttering a few choice words, he went into the kitchen and cooked spaghetti and meatballs for us. Lee and I went directly from the house to our minor league facility. We played hard and we worked hard.

• • •

I feel fortunate to still be involved in helping the Phillies.

I'll be proud to see Ryne Sandberg in the third-base coaching box for the Phillies in 2013. I'm proud of Ryno for paying his dues as a minor league manager. Not many Hall of Famers do that. Ryno and I go way back. He is the greatest player I can take credit for drafting and developing.

And that's the part of the game I still love most.

When I first joined the team's front office in 1969, Pope gave me wide-ranging freedom to implement a program for scouting and developing players. The reason the Phillies hired me back in 1998 was to bring my experience to bear on a new generation of players. I've worked for three general managers in my current tenure with the team—Ed Wade, Pat Gillick, and Ruben Amaro Jr. Ruben's father was a teammate of mine and coached for me. I've always said the Phillies are like family.

I'm no longer in charge of running any programs, but my role with the team isn't ceremonial, either. I go to draft meetings, visit our minor league sites, and stay in close contact with our scouting supervisors. I emphasize the importance of putting developing players in situations where they can be challenged but also successful. This game is all about adversity, so why not experience it in the minor leagues first? I also think it's important to create a winning atmosphere at the minor league level. Get the players their at-bats and innings pitched, but also try to win ballgames.

Every organization has its share of ups and downs. I know that from experience.

The Philadelphia teams I played on in the early 1960s included cellar dwellers and near-pennant winners.

The Phillies couldn't buy a win in the late 1960s and early 1970s, but by the end of the '70s, they were a perennial playoff team. I am honored to have been able to bring the team its first world championship in 1980. There was a purpose behind all my yelling and screaming that season. It was to motivate a group of players I wasn't going to allow to fail after three near-misses.

I became the general manager in Chicago at a time when the Cubs had sunk to one of the lowest points in franchise history. A few years later, we were celebrating a division title. But then there was another downturn.

The Yankees team I managed for a few months in 1989 was a patchwork of aging veterans and underwhelming prospects. Several years after my firing, the Yankees were still struggling to regain their reputation as winners. Then they became a dynasty again.

The Mets, maybe the best team of the second half of the 1980s, were the major league's worst team the year I took the helm in 1993. It took until the end of the decade for the team to get back on top.

Every ballclub that's experienced a period of success has to regroup and recalibrate at some point. And every team that's been mired in failure has to look at what it could be doing differently.

What makes the game special is all the small stuff that happens on the road to success or failure, the adversity, the peaks and valleys of a season, and the hard work and good times that combine to create wonderful memories.

I put my players through hell at times. I have always believed that athletes should perform to the best of their God-given abilities. All players, especially those who are being paid good money to play a game, occasionally need a reminder of this simple idea. And it was my job to do the reminding.

ACKNOWLEDGMENTS

I WOULD FIRST AND FOREMOST like to thank my wife, Sylvia, who stood by my side and endured all the trials and tribulations of the game with me. While I was off doing my thing, she took the lead in raising our children, Dana, John, Kim, and Doug, all of whom grew up in baseball and rooted like the devil for their dad's teams.

When I reflect on my six decades in the game, I realize how much of it was made possible by the players, coaches, and friends who stayed loyal to me, despite my occasional mistakes and frequent screaming and yelling sessions.

I'd also like to acknowledge our good friends on Providenciales, an island where we've spent winters for nearly three decades. It's a great place to unwind after a long baseball season.

I had resisted writing a baseball book for quite some time, but Sylvia and my co-author, Alan Maimon, convinced me it was time to put my experiences down in print. This book is a memento for my family, especially my grandkids, Holly, Hunter, Benjamin, Finn, and Dallas Jordan. It is also for Christina-Taylor Green, who was nine years old when she was shot and killed on January 8, 2011. She loved her Pop Pop and baseball, and I'm sure she's playing baseball with the guys in heaven.

—Dallas Green

THE STORY OF MY INVOLVEMENT in this book dates back to a summer day in 1986, when my 13-year-old self first met Dallas Green. I had written him prior to a family trip to Chicago to let him know that I had ambitions of one day becoming a general manager. In his reply, he invited my parents, my sister, and me up to his executive suite at Wrigley Field to say hello. On the day of our visit, a tall and imposing man with a firm handshake greeted me and said with a smile, "So, you're the guy who wants to take my job!" I didn't end up working in a baseball front office, but 25 years after that initial encounter with Dallas, I had the opportunity to sit down with him and document his long and illustrious career in the game.

I would like to thank my wife and kids for their love and support during the writing of this book. Thanks especially to my youngest daughter, Annabelle, who kept me company as I spent summer evenings banging away at the keyboard.

As he did with my previous books, Chuck Myron provided terrific advice and skillful and thorough editing. Adam Motin at Triumph Books took the completed manuscript and turned it into what you see here.

Thanks also to Adele MacDonald of the Phillies for her help in facilitating interviews with Dallas and others.

Dallas and I would both like to thank Ruben Amaro Jr., Pat Corrales, Lee Elia, Jerry Kettle, Gary Matthews, Keith Moreland, Dickie Noles, Larry Shenk, Jayson Stark, Steve Swisher, Ed Wade, and Bobby Wine for sharing their memories of key moments and fun times in Dallas' baseball career.

—Alan Maimon